The Psilocybin Strain Bible

By
Jon Allen Stamets

Published Dec 2024
ISBN# 9798305010152

Introduction

The planet is home to an enormous variety of psychedelic mushroom strains. A wide variety of hallucinogenic mushroom strains, sometimes referred to as magic mushrooms, are covered in this book, although not all of them are. There are numerous ways in which magic mushrooms can affect the human body.

This guide aims to educate readers on the different varieties of magic mushrooms and assist them in comprehending the effects of each strain, their origins, and some that are used in religious rites. Magic mushrooms have the potential to induce hallucinations, which qualify as "visual distortions."

Visual distortions refer to alterations in perception that affect how we see the world around us. These distortions can occur under the influence of various substances, including psychedelics like magic mushrooms. Here are some common visual distortions associated with psychedelic experiences:

Tracers and Afterimages:

When you move your hand or an object in front of you, you may notice a lingering trail or "tracer" behind it. This effect occurs because the brain processes visual information differently, leading to a delay in how we perceive movement.

Afterimages are similar to tracers but occur after staring at a bright object and then when you look away, you might see a ghostly image of that object superimposed on your surroundings.

Breathing and Flowing Surfaces:

Under the influence of psychedelics, surfaces may appear to breathe, ripple, or flow. Walls, floors, and even natural landscapes can seem like they're alive and pulsating. This effect is especially pronounced when looking at patterns, such as carpets, wallpaper, or tree bark. The patterns may shift and undulate, creating a mesmerizing visual experience.

Enhanced Colors and Patterns:

Magic mushrooms can intensify colors, making them appear more vibrant and saturated. You might notice that everyday objects suddenly seem more vivid and alive. Geometric patterns, fractals, and intricate designs become more pronounced. Some users describe seeing intricate mandalas or kaleidoscope type visuals.

Size Distortions:

Objects may appear larger or smaller than they actually are. This effect can be disorienting but also fascinating. For example, a simple chair might seem like a massive throne, or a small plant could appear like a towering tree.

Morphing and Transformations:

Visual distortions can lead to objects changing shape or transforming into something else entirely. Walls might melt, faces might shift, and ordinary items can take on surreal qualities. This effect is often described as "shapeshifting."

Depth Perception Alterations:

The perception of depth and distance can be altered. Objects may seem closer or farther away than they are. Some users report feeling like they can see "layers" of reality, as if they're peeling back the surface of the world.

Closed-Eye Visuals (CEVs):

When you close your eyes, magic mushrooms can induce a vivid array of colors, shapes, and scenes. These CEVs can be intricate and dreamlike.

Some users intentionally explore CEVs during their trips, as they can be highly immersive and introspective. It is important to remember that individual experiences vary, and not everyone will encounter all these visual distortions. The intensity and type of visuals depend on factors like dosage, mindset, setting, and personal sensitivity to psychedelics. Always approach these substances with care and in a safe environment and with a trusted, sober companion.

Thank You

Thanks to all the sources across the internet and the information provided for me to glean in order to compile this informational guide to magic mushrooms! Undoubtedly, there are more strains to learn about and some will not be listed here. Those strains will be added in later editions/revisions of the book.

Disclaimer

This book is written purely for entertainment and educational purposes only. The information in this book is not to be used as a substitute for medical advice, diagnosis or the treatment of any health condition or problem. The Author does not endorse or condone the use of any drugs and strongly advises against the use of drugs or intoxicating substances. You are advised to never eat any mushroom that an expert in mycology hasn't identified for you. Some mushrooms have the potential to be poisonous. Never consume a mushroom that you, the reader, can't positively or accurately identify. This book is not to be used for mushroom identification. Do not touch and/or pick any unknown mushrooms.

The author makes no guarantee nor expressed or implied representations whatsoever regarding the accuracy, completeness, timeliness, comparative or controversial nature, or usefulness of any information contained or referenced in this book. The author does not assume any risk whatsoever for your use of the information contained herein. Information changes frequently and therefore information contained in this book could become outdated, incomplete, or incorrect. The author is not affiliated with any of the websites mentioned in this book, or the product(s) they may sell.

Again, **do not eat magic mushrooms.** Remember it's your body so be careful with what you put into it.

Table Of Contents

A+ Strain

A+ Strain (AKA the A-strain) is a popular Psilocybe cubensis mushroom favored for its **above-average potency**. It is a cultivated strain of the well-known psychoactive mushroom species, Psilocybe cubensis. Here are some key points about the A+ strain:

Appearance: The A+ strain is typically cream-colored to white, sometimes with a bluish tint.
When damaged, it bruises blue very obviously.
The spores are purple-black, and once they mature, they will cover the stem-ring and make it appear black.
Because these mushrooms have reduced pigmentation, not none at all, they are technically "leucistic," not albinos.

Parentage and Similarity:
There is also a more typically-pigmented strain called A+. The two are very similar and undoubtedly closely related.
Curiously, sources differ as to which is the parent strain, but logic suggests that the non-albino version came first. Either way, AA+ is the more popular of the two.
There is persistent speculation that albino A+ is actually part-Panaeolus, since its high is reportedly reminiscent of the effects of some of the more potent Panaeolus species.
Actually, such hybridization between different genera is likely impossible, but there may be some coincidental biochemical similarity.

Effects: Eating Psilocybe cubensis results in changes in mood and thought-pattern and, at higher doses, hallucination.
Nausea is also common.
The high usually begins about half an hour after ingestion and lasts six to eight hours, though longer trips are possible.
Some users report that albino A+ starts fast, is often funny, and causes hallucinations that make the world appear gelatinous.
Curiously, albino A+ is also known for having a particularly strong flavor that some users don't like.

Potency: Albino A+ is one of the **more potent** Psilocybe cubensis strains.
Growing Albino A+:
Albino A+ can be grown by any method generally used for Psilocybe cubensis.
It's not a picky strain and is considered easy to grow.
Many growers report that it is a slow strain, though, with a very long colonization time and very slow fruiting.
However, the reliability of the strain's growth, the generosity of its flushes, and the plentiful production of spores by its mature specimens make albino A+ a favorite among magic mushroom growers despite its sometimes slow progress123.

Resources:
1. https://tripsitter.com/magic-mushrooms/strains/a-strain/
2. https://magic-mycology.com/the-ultimate-guide-to-psilocybin-mushroom-strains-varieties-origins-and-effects/
3. https://magic-mycology.com/top-magic-mushroom-strains-the-ultimate-list-of-varieties-effects-2023/

Acadian Coast

The Acadian Coast strain is a lesser-known Psilocybe cubensis mushroom variety. Here are some key points about this intriguing strain:
Appearance and Origin:
The Acadian Coast mushrooms were believed to have been collected around the subtropical wetlands of Louisiana along the Mississippi River.
Their caps are typically a light caramel color when young, becoming a lighter, nearly golden hue as they mature[1,2].
The name "Acadian" likely refers to the historical migration of the Acadians (later known as "Cajuns") from the Vendée region of Western France to Canada and eventually to Louisiana[2].

Cultivation and Characteristics:
Acadian Coast mushrooms are abundant fruiters with rizomorphic mycelium.
They produce a prolific pinset, resulting in medium to large fruits.
Optimal colonization temperatures are 84–86°F, while fruiting temperatures range from 74–78°F[3].

Potency: **Average**
The specific psychedelic potency of Acadian Coast shrooms is not widely documented due to their rarity.
Most sources suggest that their potency fluctuates between 0.25% – 0.75% psilocybin and about 0.00% – 0.30% psilocin (0.25–1.05% combined).
For comparison, the average potency of Psilocybe cubensis species is around 0.8% psilocybin and psilocin combined (total tryptamines)[1].

Effects:
Acadian Coast mushrooms are known to produce mild visuals and a more intense body-centered trip.
Their effects are similar to other popular strains like Golden Teachers, Cambodians, and the Argentinian strain[1].
In summary, the Acadian Coast strain remains mysterious in terms of its origins, but its unique appearance and potential effects make it an interesting addition to the world of magic mushrooms[1,2].

Resources:
1. https://tripsitter.com/magic-mushrooms/species/acadian-coast/
2. https://www.magicmushroomaps.com/strains/acadian-coast
3. https://completemyco.com/blogs/complete-university/strain-highlight-acadian-coast
4. https://microzoomers.co/strains/acadian-coast-cubensis/
5. https://doubleblindmag.com/acadian-coast-mushrooms/

The Ajax Strain

Ajax strain of magic mushrooms is an intriguing variety within the world of Psilocybe cubensis. Although it might not be as widely recognized as some other strains, it has gained popularity among cultivators and enthusiasts. Let's explore the key details about the Ajax strain:

Origins and Characteristics:
The Ajax strain was originally collected from farmland near Jacksonville, Florida.
It is known for its aggressive mycelial growth and impressive potency.
The mushrooms exhibit unique traits that make them stand out among
other cubensis varieties[1].

Growing Experience:
Cultivators have reported remarkable results with the Ajax strain:
Fast Growth: It grows rapidly, often reaching maturity within 3 weeks from spore inoculation to harvest.

Impressive Yield: Some growers have obtained substantial yields, including mushrooms weighing over 30 grams.
Multiple Flushes: The strain is known for producing multiple flushes, allowing cultivators to harvest several times from the same substrate.
Fuzzy Feet: Interestingly, Ajax mushrooms tend to develop "fuzzy feet" more than other strains, regardless of environmental conditions[1].

Visual Appearance:
The appearance of Ajax mushrooms is similar to other cubensis strains, with a few

distinguishing features:
The caps are dome-shaped, sometimes described as "nipply."
Despite their potency, they maintain a visually appealing appearance.
The veil remnants on the stem contribute to their overall look[1].

Spore Syringes and Distribution:
The original specimens of Ajax were printed and distributed to a small group of mycologists across the United States.

In **summary**, the Ajax strain offers a blend of rapid growth, impressive potency, and intriguing visual characteristics. Whether you're a seasoned cultivator or a curious mycophile, encountering Ajax mushrooms can lead to exciting and transformative experiences. Information purposes only.

Resources:
1.   https://www.reddit.com/r/shrooms/comments/stbz56/ajax/
2.   https://pnwspore.com/product/ajax/
3.   https://www.shroomery.org/forums/showflat.php/Number/24610747
4.   https://tripsitter.com/magic-mushrooms/strains/

Alamo Strain

 Alamo (Albino Amazonian):
The Alamo strain is an albino iso originally credited to James Block and Jason Redman. It offers a captivating and otherworldly adventure for both experienced psychonauts and curious beginners.
With its distinctive appearance and potent effects, the Alamo strain stands out in the realm of psilocybin mushrooms.
Unfortunately, detailed information about the Alamo strain remains somewhat elusive, adding to its mystique.
Users who venture into the Alamo experience may find themselves unlocking hidden treasures and exploring new dimensions of consciousness1.
Remember that each psilocybin mushroom strain has its unique characteristics, and the Alamo strain is no exception. (I will update this in a later edition when I get more information)

Resources:
1. https://magic-mycology.com/the-ultimate-guide-to-psilocybin-mushroom-strains-varieties-origins-and-effects/
2. https://tripsitter.com/magic-mushrooms/strains/
3. https://www.psychedelicpassage.com/psychedelic-mushroom-strains-by-potency-30-popular-varieties/

Albino A+

The **Albino A+ strain** is a fascinating variety of Psilocybe cubensis mushrooms. Let's delve into the details of this unique strain:

Appearance and Characteristics:
The Albino A+ strain is characterized by its lack of pigmentation, resulting in a white to cream-colored appearance.
When damaged, these mushrooms bruise blue, a common trait among Psilocybe cubensis varieties.
The spores of Albino A+ are purple-black, which contrasts with the white color of the mushrooms.
Due to their reduced pigmentation, they are technically considered "leucistic", not true albinos.

Potency and Effects: **Above Average**
Albino A+ is known for its above-average potency compared to other Psilocybe cubensis strains.
When consumed, these mushrooms induce changes in mood, thought patterns, and, at higher doses, hallucinations.
The trip typically begins about 30 minutes after ingestion and can last six to eight hours or longer.
Some users report that Albino A+ produces a fast onset, often accompanied by a sense of humor, and causes hallucinations that make the world appear gelatinous.
Growing Albino A+:

Cultivating Albino A+ follows similar methods used for other Psilocybe cubensis strains.
It is considered easy to grow, making it a favorite among magic mushroom cultivators.
Although it may be slow to colonize and fruit, the reliability of its growth, generous flushes, and abundant spore production make it a popular choice.
Parentage and Speculation:
Albino A+ is closely related to the more typically pigmented A+ strain.
There is speculation that Albino A+ might have some genetic similarity
to Panaeolus species, although hybridization between different genera is unlikely.

In **summary**, the Albino A+ strain stands out for its lack of pigmentation, potent effects, and popularity among growers. Whether you're a seasoned psychonaut or a curious beginner, exploring this unique strain can lead to intriguing experiences in the world of magic mushrooms . This is for information purposes only.

Resources:

1. https://tripsitter.com/magic-mushrooms/strains/albino-a-plus/
2. https://tripsitter.com/magic-mushrooms/strains/true-albino-teacher/
3. https://healing-mushrooms.net/albino-a

Albino Burma

The **Albino Burma** strain is a unique variant of the classic Burma strain of Psilocybe cubensis mushrooms. Let's explore the fascinating characteristics of this strain:

Appearance and Origins:
Albino Burma is not a true albino (as it still produces some pigment), but it exhibits ghostly white caps throughout its development.
The original Burma sample was collected from just outside of Yangon, Myanmar (formerly known as Burma), which explains its name1.
These mushrooms tend to be medium to large in size, with a robust stem and a broad, bell-shaped cap2.

Potency and Effects: Above Average
While specific potency data for Albino Burma is not widely documented, the Burma strain itself is known for its high potency.
When consumed, Albino Burma mushrooms induce changes in mood, thought patterns, and, at higher doses, hallucinations.
The trip typically begins approximately 30 minutes after ingestion and can last six to eight hours or longer.

Cultivation:
Albino Burma is a leucistic variant of the Burma strain, making it a popular choice among indoor growers.
Despite its name, it still produces some pigment, but its caps are generally a beautiful pale white color3.

In **summary**, Albino Burma mushrooms offer a unique appearance and potential effects, making them an intriguing addition to the world of magic mushrooms. 4521. This is for information purposes only.

Resources:

1. https://tripsitter.com/magic-mushrooms/strains/albino-burma/
2. https://completemyco.com/blogs/complete-university/strain-highlight-albino-burma
3. https://www.bing.com/search?q=albino+burma+strain&FORM=bngcht&toWww=1&redig=B 0162F6E2BE04D8CA1D1AF203B137574
4. https://tripsitter.com/magic-mushrooms/strains/

Albino Chodewave

The **Albino Chodewave** strain is a remarkable variant of the original Chodewave strain of Psilocybe cubensis mushrooms. Let's explore the intriguing features of this unique strain:

Genetics and Origins:
Albino Chodewave is an albino variant of the original Chodewave strain.
The exact origins of the Chodewave strain remain somewhat mysterious, but it likely emerged from a mutation of the original Chodewave.
The strain's genetics are a blend of two other well-known strains: Penis Envy and Tidal Wave.

Appearance and Potency: Above Average
Albino Chodewave mushrooms produce pure white fruits, lacking any pigmentation in the cap, stem, or spores.
Despite their albino status, they are very potent due to their lineage.
In the Spring 2022 Psilocybin Cup, a sample of Albino Chodewave grown by the cultivator "Purple Mystic Myco" won the title of "Therapeutic Champion" with an impressive overall tryptamine content of 1.47%.
The strain's potency is rated as "above average", making it a sought-after choice for psychonauts.

Cultivation:
Albino Chodewave mushrooms are relatively easy to cultivate.
They exhibit characteristics similar to both Penis Envy and Tidal Wave strains.
These mushrooms are fairly resistant to contamination and are not prone to aborting during growth.
Cultivators can use substrates such as rye grain or BRF (Brown Rice Flour & Vermiculite) for successful cultivation.

In summary, the Albino Chodewave strain combines mystery, potency, and unique appearance, making it a standout contender in the world of magic mushrooms123.

Resources:

1. https://tripsitter.com/magic-mushrooms/strains/albino-chodewave/
2. https://magic-mycology.com/the-ultimate-guide-to-psilocybin-mushroom-strains-varieties-origins-and-effects/
3. https://tripsitter.com/magic-mushrooms/strains/chodewave/

Albino Golden Teacher

Albino Golden Teacher strain is a fascinating variation of the well-known Golden Teacher (Psilocybe cubensis) mushroom. Let's delve into the characteristics and effects of this unique strain:

Golden Teacher:
The original Golden Teacher strain is widely recognized for its spiritual and introspective effects.
It has a distinctive appearance with golden-yellow caps and thick white stems.
Golden Teachers are known for their teaching properties, often providing users with insights, wisdom, and personal growth during their psychedelic experiences.

Albino Golden Teacher:
The Albino Golden Teacher is a leucistic variation of the Golden Teacher strain.
Unlike true albinos, which have colorless spores, Albino Golden Teachers still exhibit some pigmentation.
Their caps are typically cream-colored to white, sometimes with a bluish tint when bruised.
The spores of Albino Golden Teachers are purple-black, and once mature, they cover the stem-ring, giving it a black appearance.
This strain is popular among growers due to its high potency and generous flushes.

Potency: High potency

Effects:
Eating Psilocybe cubensis mushrooms, including the Albino Golden Teacher, results in changes in mood and thought patterns.
At higher doses, users may experience hallucinations.
Unfortunately, nausea is also common.
Dangerous side effects are rare but possible, especially in children.
The high usually begins about 30 minutes after ingestion and lasts six to eight hours, although longer trips are possible.
Some users report that Albino Golden Teachers have a particularly strong flavor.

Growing Albino Golden Teacher:
Albino Golden Teachers can be grown using methods generally used for Psilocybe cubensis.
While they may be slow to colonize and fruit, they are reliable in terms of growth and produce impressive flushes.
Their plentiful spore production makes them a favorite among magic mushroom growers.

In **summary**, the Albino Golden Teacher strain offers a unique twist on the classic Golden Teacher experience, combining potency, introspection, and wisdom.

Resources:
1. https://healing-mushrooms.net/albino-a
2. https://mushboyz.com/product/albino-riptide/
3. https://thehigh.guide/mushroom-strain-albino/
4. https://doubleblindmag.com/albino-a-mushrooms/

Albino Jedi Mind F*** (JMF)

Albino JMF mushroom strain is a fascinating variation of the well-known Jedi Mind Fu** (Psilocybe cubensis) strain. Let's explore the characteristics and effects of this **unique strain:**

Origins and Potency: The Albino JMF strain is inspired by the original Jedi Mind F*** (JMF) mushrooms, which are Psilocybe cubensis mushrooms known for their powerful effects on the mind. While the name "Jedi Mind F***" suggests intense effects, **the actual potency of JMF doesn't match the exaggerated claims**. Analytical data places JMF within the standard range **considered average** for Psilocybe cubensis mushrooms[1]. Some people link the unique name of this strain with its powerful hallucinations and profound reflective nature, which can feel so intense that the mushrooms seem to temporarily take over one's mind and emotions.

Effects: At lower doses, users may experience enhanced mood, increased creativity, and heightened sensory perception. At higher doses, these effects can escalate to include: **Visual hallucinations**: Users may see vivid and colorful patterns, shapes, and distortions. **Profound introspection**: JMF can lead to deep self-reflection and insights. **Mystical experiences:** Some users report feeling connected to a higher consciousness or experiencing a sense of unity with the universe[2].

Cultivation: The Albino JMF strain is a bit more challenging to cultivate than beginner-friendly strains.It is not as resistant to contamination, and it tends to be slower to fruit. **Cultivation difficulty**: Intermediate. **Recommended substrate**: Rye Grain.

History and Origins:
Like many Psilocybe cubensis strains, there's a lot of mystery around the origins of Albino JMF. Some conversations suggest that JMF might be a genetic offshoot from the Z-Strain, another mushroom strain with a questionable origin story.
Other stories mention a mycologist named "Agar Joe" or "Myco Joe," who allegedly found this mushroom growing in the wild in Georgia. He isolated the mushroom to obtain stable spores that were as contamination-resistant as possible.
Albino JMF is a newer strain that emerged in the early 2000s and hasn't been around as long as other well-established strains like Golden Teacher or Koh Samui[1].
In **summary**, the Albino JMF strain offers a unique twist on the classic Jedi Mind F*** experience, combining potency, introspection, and mind-altering effects. If you decide to explore this strain, approach it with care, respect, and mindfulness, especially considering its potential intensity[12].

Resources:

1. https://tripsitter.com/magic-mushrooms/strains/jedi-mind-fuck/
2. https://www.nxtpsychedelics.com/news/articles/psychedelics/jedi-mind-fuck-mushroom-guide/
3. https://www.seattlemet.com/discover/magic-mushrooms/jedi-mind-fuck-mushroom/
4. https://healing-mushrooms.net/jedi-mind-fuck
5. https://www.nxtlifescience.com/psychedelics/jedi-mind-fuck-mushroom-guide/
6. https://www.themagicdispensary.com/jedi-mind-fuck-mushrooms-what-is-all-the-hype-about/

Albino Makilla Gorilla

Albino Makilla Gorilla strain is a relatively new cultivated variety of Psilocybe cubensis. It was developed by crossbreeding two other strains: Albino Penis Envy (APE) and Melmac. Both APE and Melmac were themselves derived from the famous Penis Envy strain, known for its potency and distinctive appearance (which, as the name suggests, resembles a penis due to its very narrow cap). However, unlike its parent strains, Makilla Gorilla didn't inherit the phallic look, and its cap is somewhat narrow without albinism1. Here are some key details about the Albino Makilla Gorilla strain:

Appearance:
The mushrooms produced by this strain are large, with a thick, meaty stem and a moderately-sized cap.
The stem is white or often bruised blue, while the cap is a pale caramel color.
The flesh of these mushrooms is unusually dense, so it's essential to use a scale rather than eyeballing doses to determine how much you're consuming.

Effects:
Visual: The strain is reputed to be very visual, although this reputation may be due to people accidentally taking higher doses than intended because of its potency and density.

General Effects: Like most Psilocybe cubensis strains, it alters mood, fosters different thought patterns, and causes hallucinations (especially at higher doses). There's usually some degree of "body high" as well.

Variation: Most variation in psilocybin experiences comes from dose size, mindset, setting, and personal biochemistry.

Potency and Dosage: High Potency
The prospect of a giant mushroom that is also unusually potent can be exciting or intimidating.
Any degree of intensity, from micro to heroic, is possible with any psilocybin mushroom, provided the dose is right.
With high-potency strains like Makilla Gorilla, it's crucial to be careful not to take too much. Accidentally taking an unexpectedly high dose can lead to dangerous side effects.
It's better to take less than you want than to risk taking too much, especially with a high-potency mushroom.

In summary, the Albino Makilla Gorilla strain offers a fascinating combination of potency, unique appearance, and potential for intense psychedelic experiences. Whether you're seeking visual distortions, heightened senses, or profound self-insights, this strain is worth exploring123.

Resources:
1.   https://healing-mushrooms.net/makilla-gorilla
2.   https://thinkmushrooms.ca/makilla-gorilla-mushroom-review/
3.   https://edendirect.com/products/copy-of-eden-albino-penis-envy-ape-magic-mushrooms

Albino Melmac

The **Albino Melmac** strain is a fascinating variant of the Psilocybe cubensis mushroom family. Let's explore the intriguing features of this unique strain:

Origins and History:
The Albino Melmac mushrooms are a product of human invention, resulting from generations of selective breeding in a lab.
They are believed to be variants of the famed Penis Envy mushrooms, which gained popularity in the psychedelic community.
Some sources even suggest that Albino Melmacs are closer to the original Penis Envy, introduced to mycologists around the world in the 1970s, although this claim remains subject to debate1.

Distinctive Appearance:
Albino Melmac mushrooms exhibit a unique appearance:
Their stems are contorted and tangled, giving them a gnarly and otherworldly look.
The caps have wavy patterns, adding to their distinctiveness.
When touched, they bruise blue, a common trait among Psilocybe cubensis varieties.
The strain's name likely draws inspiration from the fictional home planet of Alf, the main character from the popular 80s sitcom1.

Potency and Effects: Above average
Albino Melmac mushrooms produce psilocybin, the primary psychoactive compound found in magic mushrooms.
When ingested, psilocybin is metabolized into psilocin by the human body, leading to altered perception, mood changes, and hallucinations.
Despite their unusual appearance, Albino Melmacs offer all the benefits expected from any Psilocybe cubensis mushroom.

Revival and Popularity:
Like many "OG" strains of mushrooms, Albino Melmacs are regaining popularity amidst the current psychedelic revolution.
Their rich history, unique appearance, and potency make them a favorite among mycologists and consumers alike1

History and Popularity:
Terrence McKenna: The story traces back to activist and writer Terrence McKenna, who collected spore samples from an interesting psilocybe in the Amazon Rainforest. These spores were later cultivated and propagated by other mycologists.
Richard Guitierrez (Rich Gee): Richard Guitierrez is credited with creating the modern Penis Envy strain, which has been a favorite among psychedelic enthusiasts worldwide.

Homestead's Variant: In the 1980s, Homestead experimented with the original Penis Envy genetics, leading to the creation of the unique variant—Melmac.
Resurgence: Like many "OG" strains, Melmacs are regaining popularity during the current psychedelic revolution.
Effects and Characteristics:
Psychoactive Compounds: Melmac mushrooms produce psilocybin, the primary psychoactive compound in magic mushrooms. When ingested, psilocybin is metabolized into psilocin by the human body.

Similar Benefits: Despite their unusual appearance, Melmac mushrooms offer the same benefits as any other Psilocybe cubensis variety.
In summary, Albino Melmac combines a rich history, distinctive appearance, and potent effects, making it a sought-after strain among mushroom enthusiasts12.

In **summary**, Albino Melmac mushrooms stand out for their twisted stems, wavy caps, and potent effects. Whether you're a seasoned psychonaut or a curious explorer, these otherworldly mushrooms offer a fascinating journey into altered states of consciousness.1.

Resources:
1. https://doubleblindmag.com/melmac-mushroom-strain/
2. https://tripsitter.com/magic-mushrooms/strains/melmac/
3. https://healing-mushrooms.net/melmac-mushroom

Albino Penis Envy

Albino Penis Envy (APE), or simply APE, is a cultivated variety of Psilocybe cubensis, one of the best-known and popular "magic" mushrooms. Let's explore the fascinating aspects of this unique strain:

Appearance:
As the name implies, the fruiting bodies of APE do look rather penile, but this characteristic can be found in many mushroom species.
APE is characterized by its pale-capped sub-variety of the original Penis Envy (PE) strain. The caps of APE are almost white, setting them apart from the typical brownish caps of wild-type P. cubensis.

Origins and Parent Strain:
APE still belongs to the species P. cubensis, much like how white tigers bred for circuses and zoos are still tigers.
The original PE strain is reputedly one of the most powerful varieties of P. cubensis.
APE is rumored to have been discovered in South America by the well-known author and ethnobotanist, Terence McKenna.

Cultivation and Rarity:
APE can be difficult to grow, which contributes to its rarity.
Despite the challenges, it remains popular among entheogen users who can obtain it through cultivation or purchase.

Effects and Risks:
P. cubensis, including APE, is mind-altering and can cause a range of effects, such as hallucinations, mood changes, new beliefs or ideas, and anxiety.
The results of taking APE can vary dramatically, depending on individual chemistry, mental state, and surroundings.
While not risk-free, reasonable caution can minimize potential risks associated with mushroom use.

Potency: Very potent

In summary, Albino Penis Envy mushrooms offer a unique appearance, potency, and a wide range of effects, making them a sought-after strain among psychedelic enthusiasts12.

Resources:
1. https://healing-mushrooms.net/albino-penis-envy-ape
2. https://www.seattlemet.com/discover/magic-mushrooms/albino-penis-envy-mushroom/
3. https://bluestemspores.com/albino-penis-envy-ape-mushrooms-myths-vs-reality/
4. https://www.happiemushrooms.com/blog/albino-penis-envy-an-unusual-variant-of-the-original-penis-envy
5. https://tripsitter.com/magic-mushrooms/strains/albino-penis-envy/

Albino Penis Envy Revert

APE Revert is a strain of Psilocybe cubensis that stems from the popular and potent Albino Penis Envy (APE) strain. Let's dive into the intriguing details:

Origins and Name:
Albino Penis Envy (APE): Developed by "Workman" at Sporeworks, APE is identical to the original Penis Envy (PE) strain, except it produces completely white fruits. APE retains the same phallic-shaped mushrooms as PE but stands out due to its unique appearance.

APE Revert: The "Revert" part of the name refers to a strain that has been "reverted" to an older phenotype. Essentially, APE Revert is an off-shoot of the original APE strain, created by reverting it to a phenotype closer to that of PE. This reversion is believed to improve potency and yield, although it affects other features of the mushrooms.

Appearance:
APE Revert mushrooms aren't as phallic-shaped as Penis Envy or as white as APE. Most APE Revert specimens are much lighter in color than regular mushrooms but still retain some pigmentation.
The caps of APE Revert are wider and more convex compared to the original APE.

Potency and Yield: Very Potent
APE Revert shares the same other-worldly potency as APE. It's just as powerful and mind-altering.
Interestingly, APE Revert has the potential to produce some monstrous mushrooms. An anonymous grower reported harvesting 6.26 grams (dry) from a single APE Revert mushroom.

Guaranteed Albino Fruits:
If you're specifically looking for guaranteed albino fruits, APE Revert might not be the strain for you. However, if you want big yields of large, mostly-white, highly potent shrooms, APE Revert is worth exploring.

Availability and Cultivation:
APE Revert spores are available from various vendors across the globe.
Cultivating APE Revert involves using substrates like rye grain or BRF (brown rice flour & vermiculite).

In summary, APE Revert offers a fascinating twist on the already enigmatic Albino Penis Envy strain, combining potency, unique appearance, and the potential for impressive yields123.

Resources:
1. https://tripsitter.com/magic-mushrooms/strains/ape-revert/
2. https://planetspores.ca/product/albino-penis-envy-mushroom-spores/
3. https://pnwspore.com/product/albino-penis-envy-revert/

Albino Roller Coaster

(**ARC**) magic mushroom strain is a fascinating variety that combines the genetics of two other potent strains: Tidalwave and Albino A+. Let's explore its unique features:

Origins and Genetics:
The Albino Roller Coaster strain is a sister strain to Tidalwave.
It was created from the same original 2017 PE/B+ fusion project by Magic Myco, a Canadian mycology group. The strain emerged years later due to chance genetic expression, resulting in a mutation known as Leucism. Leucism causes a lack of pigmentation, leading to gorgeous snow-white fruits1.

Appearance:
Albino Roller Coaster mushrooms have a unique and ghostly white appearance.
Their caps and stems exhibit this striking coloration. Despite being called "albino," they can still produce some pigments if exposed to light2.

Psychedelic Effects:
Users can expect a potent and transformative experience:
Colorful Visuals: Intense visual distortions and hallucinations.
Deep Introspection: A journey within the self.
Euphoria: Feelings of joy and interconnectedness.
The name "Roller Coaster" hints at the unpredictable and dynamic nature of the trip1.

Dosage Recommendations:
For beginners, it's essential to start low and go slow.
Recommended dosages: Microdose: 125mg Low Dose: 0.5-1.5g Medium Dose: 2-3.5g Full Dose: 3.5g+
Experienced users may find around 2 grams to be a good starting point1.

Potency: Above Average

Lab Grade Quality:
These mushrooms are considered "Lab Grade" due to their exceptional quality.
They were grown by professional mycologists in a purpose-built facility.
The facility maintains high sterility using HEPA filtration systems, ensuring top-quality fruits.

In **summary**, the Albino Roller Coaster strain offers a blend of potency, introspection, and stunning visuals. Whether you are a beginner or an experienced user, these snow-white mushrooms promise an intriguing and transformative journey1.

Resources:
1. https://microcybin.io/product/albino-roller-coaster-mushrooms/
2. https://fungimaps.com/dried-mushrooms/albino-roller-coaster/
3. https://www.magicmushroomsdispensary.ca/product/albino-roller-coaster-magic-mushrooms/
4. https://fungimaps.com/dried-mushrooms/albino-rollercoaster-magic-mushrooms/

Albino Riptide

Albino Riptide mushroom strain is a hybrid of two popular psilocybe cubensis spores: the True Albino Teacher (TAT) and the Tidal Wave spores. Let me break down the characteristics of this unique strain:

True Albino Teacher (TAT):
TAT is a carefully cultivated, non-standard strain with caps and stems of ghostly white appearance. It is grown in agar, moved to a sterilized grain, and fruited in a sanitized laboratory environment. TAT is highly potent and best suited for experienced enthusiasts of psychedelic mushroom spores.
Tidal Wave:
Tidal Wave spores are fast-growing, easy fruiting mushrooms with considerable contamination resistance. They have brain-like structures and can grow quite large. Tidal Wave spores are rare and highly potent, so any mushroom strains developed from them inherit these qualities.

Albino Riptide Characteristics:
Pale yellow caps and thick stems. Can grow up to three or four times the size of regular mushrooms. High level of contamination resistance and easy fruiting.
Above-average potency.
Ideal for intermediate enthusiasts due to its challenging cultivation requirements.
The combination of TAT and Tidal Wave makes Albino Riptide a rare and exciting strain to explore.
As for the effects of Albino Riptide mushrooms, here's what you can expect:
General Effects:
Eating Psilocybe cubensis mushrooms results in changes in mood and thought patterns. At higher doses, hallucinations may occur.
Unfortunately, nausea is also common.
Dangerous side effects are rare but possible, especially in children.
The high usually begins about half an hour after ingestion and lasts six to eight hours, although longer trips are possible.

Potency: Above average
Albino Riptide is one of the more potent Psilocybe cubensis strains.

Growing Albino Riptide:
Albino Riptide can be grown using methods generally used for Psilocybe cubensis. While it may be slow to colonize and fruit, it is reliable in terms of growth and produces generous flushes. This is for information only.

Resources:

1. https://healing-mushrooms.net/albino-a
2. https://mushboyz.com/product/albino-riptide/
3. https://doubleblindmag.com/albino-a-mushrooms/

Albino Treasure Coast

Albino Treasure Coast is a fascinating magic mushroom strain that has captured the interest of growers and users alike. Let's explore the key details about this unique variety:

Origins and Development:
Albino Treasure Coast (often abbreviated as ATC) is closely related to its parent strain, Treasure Coast (TC).
The albino version of TC was developed using a technique called tissue isolation. Genetic samples were isolated in a petri dish until the albino genetics were identified.
Through several generations of cultivation, the strain's genetic lineage was strengthened, maintaining the albino traits from one generation to the next.

Appearance:
Despite the name, Albino Treasure Coast mushrooms aren't true albinos (which would exhibit a complete lack of pigmentation).
Instead, they are leucistic, meaning they have a reduction in pigmentation rather than a total absence of pigment.
The fruiting bodies of ATC are fluffy-white and visually appealing.

Cultivation and Resistance:
Growers appreciate ATC for its resistance to disease and its ability to produce aesthetically pleasing mushrooms.
These mushrooms range from light brown to completely white, with varying stem thickness.
They tend to grow in tight, thick groups, often with pieces still stuck together at their base.

Potency and Trip Experience: below average
Estimating potency is challenging due to natural variations in growing conditions.
Users describe the trip experience as average, with a nicely balanced effect.
The average potency of ATC is estimated to be between 0.50% and 1.00% of total tryptamines.
While one sample tested weaker (around 0.33% total tryptamines), previous experience suggests ATC is still roughly average in potency.

In summary, Albino Treasure Coast offers a unique blend of aesthetics, resistance, and a balanced trip experience, making it a favorite among mushroom enthusiasts123. This is for information only.

Resources:
1.   https://tripsitter.com/magic-mushrooms/strains/albino-treasure-coast/
2.   https://healing-mushrooms.net/treasure-coast
3.   https://bcbudsupply.com/shop/shrooms/dried-shrooms/albino-treasure-coast/
4.   https://tripsitter.com/magic-mushrooms/strains/treasure-coast/

Alacabenzi

Alacabenzi, also known as Alcabenzi or Alacabenzi Psilocybe cubensis, is a fascinating magic mushroom strain that emerged in 2001 as a result of a genetic union
between Psilocybe Mexicana and a Psilocybe cubensis from Alabama1. Let's delve into the intriguing details of this strain:

Parent Strains:
Psilocybe Mexicana: Known for its historical use by indigenous cultures in Mexico, Psilocybe Mexicana contributes to the genetic makeup of Alacabenzi.
Psilocybe cubensis (Alabama): The Alabama strain of Psilocybe cubensis is the other parent. This hybridization process resulted in Alacabenzi.
Inherited Traits: As with many hybrid magic mushrooms, Alacabenzi inherits traits from both its parents.

Appearance:
Alacabenzi mushrooms exhibit a distinct appearance:

Caps: They have sizable, robust caps in a reddish-brown hue.

Stems: The stems are thick and white.
While not true albinos, Alacabenzi mushrooms are considered leucistic, meaning they have a reduction in pigmentation rather than complete absence2.

Potency; Average

Popularity and Usage:
Alacabenzi first appeared in the late 90s and gained popularity during the early 2000s as one of the most commonly used psychedelic mushrooms3.
Users describe the Alacabenzi experience as mild, euphoric, and insightful.
In summary, Alacabenzi is a unique strain with a rich genetic history, intriguing appearance, and a reputation for providing a balanced and transformative psychedelic experience23. For information only.

Resources:
1.   https://microzoomers.co/strains/alcabenzi/
2.   https://www.psychedelicpassage.com/psychedelic-mushroom-strains-by-potency-30-popular-varieties/
3.   https://tripsitter.com/magic-mushrooms/strains/alacabenzi/
4.   https://frshminds.com/psilocybin-mushroom-species-guide/psilocybe-cubensis/alacabenzi-magic-mushrooms/

Alice Strain

Alice Strain of magic mushrooms, also known as **AA+ Iso**, is renowned for its unique effects, which can vary from person to person. The Alice strain of magic mushrooms, also known as AA+ Iso, offers a unique twist to the psychedelic journey. Derived from the AA+ strain (Albino A+), Alice is revered for its potent visuals, introspection, and deepening of the psychedelic experience1. Users often describe an enhanced sense of wonder and connection with their surroundings when exploring the whimsical landscapes of their minds.

Visual Distortions:
Alice mushrooms are known for their vivid and intricate visual hallucinations.
Users often report seeing patterns, colors, and shapes that appear to dance, shift, or breathe.
The visual experience can be both awe-inspiring and surreal, resembling a dreamlike state.

Enhanced Perception:
Alice tends to heighten sensory perception.
Colors may appear more vibrant, and sounds may become more pronounced and detailed.
Users often feel a deeper connection to their surroundings and an increased appreciation for the beauty of the natural world.
Introspection and Emotional Insights:
The Alice strain encourages introspection and self-reflection.
Users may experience profound insights into their thoughts, emotions, and life experiences.
It can lead to a better understanding of oneself and one's place in the universe.

Euphoria and Joy:
Many users describe feelings of euphoria, happiness, and childlike wonder.
The name "Alice" is often associated with Lewis Carroll's "Alice's Adventures in Wonderland," and the strain aims to evoke a similar sense of curiosity and delight.

Potency: Average

Mindset and Setting:
As with any psychedelic substance, the effects of Alice mushrooms are influenced by mindset and setting.
A positive and open mindset, along with a comfortable and safe environment, can enhance the overall experience.
Remember that individual reactions to psychedelics can vary significantly, and it's essential to approach them with respect and mindfulness. If you choose to explore the Alice strain, consider starting with a low dose and gradually increasing to find your optimal experience.

Resources:
1. https://magic-mycology.com/the-ultimate-guide-to-psilocybin-mushroom-strains-varieties-origins-and-effects/
2. https://mushroom-growing.com/alice-in-wonderland-mushroom/
3. https://tripsitter.com/magic-mushrooms/strains/a-strain/

Allen Strain

The **Allen strain** is a cultivated variety of Psilocybe cubensis, known for its unique characteristics and fascinating history. Let's explore the intriguing aspects of this strain:

Origins and Discovery:
The Allen strain is believed to be an offshoot of the famous Thai strain.
It was first collected in a sample of elephant dung several decades ago.
Named after "Mushroom" John Allen, an ethnomycologist, who discovered several popular shroom strains worldwide, including Ban Hua Thanon, Burma, Cambodian, Corumba, Hanoi, Kathmandu, Malaysian, Thai, and others.
Mushroom John collected various samples during his excursions through Southeast Asia in the 1990s, primarily in Thailand.
The concept of individual "strains" of magic mushrooms wasn't prevalent at the time, but John Allen named the samples after the regions where he collected them, and these names have persisted.

Rapid Colonization: The Allen strain is revered for its rapid colonization times during cultivation.

Potency: Average

Bulbous Caps: The fruiting bodies of Allen mushrooms have bulbous caps that flatten out quickly as they mature, providing a visual cue for harvest readiness.
Creative Experience: Most users find that taking Allen shrooms leads to a highly creative experience, making it a popular choice for microdosing to tap into new creative avenues.

Cultivation and Availability:
Cultivation: Allen mushrooms can be grown by beginner growers and experts alike.
Substrate Recommendation: They thrive on substrates like rye grain or a mixture of brown rice flour and vermiculite.

In summary, the Allen strain combines rapid colonization, creative effects, and a connection to the legendary Mushroom John Allen, making it a sought-after strain among mushroom enthusiasts12.

Resources:

1. https://tripsitter.com/magic-mushrooms/strains/allen/
2. https://www.bing.com/search?q=Allen+strain+mushroom&FORM=bngcht&toWww=1&redig=BB546045C8A0443B92608B14F38B1148
3. https://frshminds.com/psilocybin-mushroom-species-guide/psilocybe-cubensis/allen/
4. https://tripsitter.com/magic-mushrooms/strains/peruvian/

Amanita Muscaria

Commonly known as the **fly agaric** or **fly amanita**, is a distinctive and colorful mushroom belonging to the genus Amanita. Here are the key details about this intriguing fungus:

Appearance and Characteristics:
Distinctive Appearance: Amanita muscaria stands out due to its large, white-gilled, white-spotted, and usually red cap. The cap often resembles a bottle cap or a convex shape when fully matured.

Color Variations: Despite its easily distinguishable features, Amanita muscaria exhibits several known variations or subspecies, resulting in different color patterns and sizes[1].

Psychoactive Compounds:
Amanita muscaria contains muscimol, a psychoactive compound responsible for its effects.

Less Hallucinatory: Unlike other entheogenic mushrooms containing psilocybin and psilocin, muscimol tends to elicit less hallucinatory effects. Instead, it has a calming and anesthetic-like quality. Some users compare its effects to ketamine, with mild sedation and relaxation at lower doses and potential stupor or drowsiness at higher doses[2].

Traditional Use and Modern Retail:
Indigenous peoples in regions like Siberia and Scandinavia have embraced Amanita muscaria for centuries.
To avoid its toxic effects, they fed the mushroom to reindeer and then drank their psychoactive—and detoxified—urine to experience its effects.
Modern retailers now sell Amanita muscaria products in various forms, such as extracts, powders, capsules, or edibles.
Retailers typically offer microdose products, inducing mild, soothing effects rather than full-on psychoactive trips.

Safety and Legal Considerations:
Amanita muscaria is not illegal in most places, making it an attractive alternative for those seeking a legal mind-altering experience.
As with any psychoactive substance, responsible use and awareness of legal regulations are essential.

In **summary**, Amanita muscaria offers a unique and distinct journey, different from psilocybin-containing mushrooms. Remember to approach these mushrooms with respect and mindfulness[2][1]. Remember this is for information purposes only.

Resources:
1. https://en.m.wikipedia.org/wiki/Amanita_muscaria
2. https://www.leafly.com/news/strains-products/i-tried-amanita-muscaria-the-delta-8-of-mushrooms-heres-how-it-went
3. https://psychedelicspotlight.com/a-beginners-guide-to-amanita-muscaria-mushrooms/

Amazon

The **Amazon** Mushroom Strain, also known as PES Amazonians (PES standing for Pacifica Exotica Spora), is a remarkable variety of Psilocybe cubensis. Originating in South America, this genetically isolated strain is believed to maintain similar traits to mushrooms found in certain parts of the Amazon rainforest. Let's explore the fascinating aspects of the Amazon strain:

Appearance and Potency: Very Potent
The Amazon strain produces some of the largest mushrooms you'll ever see.
The fruiting bodies have pale-capped sub-varieties compared to the typical brownish caps of wild-type P. cubensis.
Despite their size, these mushrooms are exceptionally potent.
The average psilocybin and psilocin levels in the Amazon strain are reported as 1.12% and 0.20%, respectively, resulting in a total tryptamine concentration of 1.36%[1].

History and Indigenous Use:
The Amazon strain has a long history of use by indigenous people in Central and South America.
These mushrooms were part of spiritual ceremonies throughout the Amazon region long before Europeans arrived.
Over time, the strain entered the public consciousness and was sold commercially in various places.

Mislabeling and Public Perception:
Sporeworks, a reliable spore vendor, accidentally mislabeled the Amazon strain as B+, a different strain.
Despite the error, some people still interchangeably use B+ and Amazon to refer to this strain, even though they are fundamentally different.

Effects and Duration:
The Amazon strain induces moderate hallucinations but provides a notably strong body high.
Users report decently long hallucinogenic experiences without feeling overwhelmed.
The high can last for almost 8 hours, making it a unique and worthwhile experience[1].

In summary, the Amazon Mushroom Strain combines impressive size, potency, and a rich history, making it a sought-after choice for both experienced and inexperienced users alike[1].

Resources:
1. https://tripsitter.com/magic-mushrooms/strains/amazon/
2. https://www.themagicdispensary.com/shroomers-guide-to-the-amazon-mushroom-strain/
3. https://www.magic-mushrooms-shop.com/en/blog/pes-amazonian-strain-month-august
4. https://microzoomers.co/strains/amazon/
5. https://www.shroomhub.io/amazonian-mushrooms-101-a-full-guide/

Arenal Volcano

The **Arenal Volcano** mushroom strain, also known as Costa Rican Cubensis, is a fascinating variety of Psilocybe cubensis. Let's explore the key details about this unique strain:

Origins and Discovery:
The Arenal Volcano strain was discovered in, you guessed it, Costa Rica.
More specifically, it was found in the foothills of the famous Arenal Volcano—an active andesitic stratovolcano located outside the town of La Fortuna.
Supposedly, the infamous mycologist and frequent Shroomery user named "Rhino" found the strain, domesticated it, and introduced the spores to the market.

Appearance and Characteristics:
The fruiting bodies of the Arenal Volcano strain are about as "normal" as they could be.
They're medium to large, with the cap ranging between 20 and 70 millimeters and the stem around 150 to 200 millimeters in length.
The stems are light yellow, and the caps are golden, turning brown through maturity.

Potency and Effects: Below Average
Although the Arenal Volcano strain isn't particularly potent, it has a nice euphoric and entactogenic effect.
Waves of warm energy flow over the body, and light visual hallucinations can be noted.

Cultivation:
The Arenal Volcano strain can be cultivated by intermediate growers looking for an interesting wild strain to grow.
It's relatively easy to get high yields of healthy mushrooms over the course of several flushes.
Keep in mind that this strain favors colder temperatures, even though it was discovered in a tropical country.

In **summary**, the Arenal Volcano mushroom strain offers both an intriguing history and a unique psychedelic experience. Remember to approach these mushrooms with respect and mindfulness1.

Resources:

1. https://tripsitter.com/magic-mushrooms/strains/costa-rican/
2. https://mushroomgenie.com/product/arenal-volcano-mushrooms/
3. https://www.mushrooms.com/arenal-volcano-cosata-rica-psilocybe-cubensis-mushroom-spore-syringe

Argentina

The **Argentina** Mushroom Strain, also known as PES Amazonians (PES), is a remarkable variety of Psilocybe cubensis. Originating in South America, this genetically isolated strain is believed to maintain similar traits to mushrooms found in certain parts of the Amazon rainforest. Here are the key details about the **Argentina strain**:

Characteristics:
Productivity: The Argentina strain is known for being a prolific flusher, often exceeding 10+ flushes from a single cake during cultivation.
Ease of Cultivation: It is easy to grow and thrives in indoor conditions with consistent humidity and temperature controls.
Long-Lasting Harvest Cycles: Many growers report harvesting flushes reaching into the double digits—these shrooms just keep going!
Appearance: The Argentina strain produces average potency mushrooms with relatively mild visuals but a much deeper body trip compared to other strains.

Origins and History:
Collection: The original sample of Argentina mushrooms was collected in the mountainous rainforests around Tafi del Valle in Northern Argentina.
Age: This strain is one of the oldest on the market today, with the original sample thought to have been collected in the late 1950s or early 1960s.
Climate Preference: Argentina shrooms thrive in particularly moist, warm climates during the summer months.

Potency and Psilocybin Content: Average
Rough Estimate: The potency of Argentina shrooms varies, with estimates ranging between 0.25% and 0.75% psilocybin by weight.
Higher Estimates: Some sources suggest that the combined potency of psilocybin and psilocin could reach up to 2%.

Psilocin and Psilocybin: Like other strains of Psilocybe cubensis, Argentina shrooms contain both psilocin and psilocybin, responsible for their psychedelic effects.

Availability and Cultivation:
Substrate Recommendation: Argentina shrooms thrive on substrates like rye grain or a mixture of brown rice flour and vermiculite.

In summary, the Argentina Mushroom Strain combines ease of cultivation, long-lasting harvests, and a rich history, making it a sought-after choice for mushroom growers and enthusiasts alike1.

Resources:
1.   https://tripsitter.com/magic-mushrooms/strains/argentina/
2.   https://microzoomers.co/strains/argentina-strain-cubensis/
3.   https://magic-mycology.com/the-ultimate-guide-to-psilocybin-mushroom-strains-varieties-origins-and-effects/

ATL #7 Large Sclerotia –

ATL #7, also known as **Psilocybe galindoi**, is a fascinating strain of magic mushrooms that produces both sclerotia (commonly called "truffles" or "stones") and traditional mushroom fruiting bodies. Let's explore the intriguing aspects of this unique strain:

Taxonomic Confusion:
ATL #7 has been sold under different species names, leading to confusion.
Some sources claim it is a strain of Psilocybe galindoi, which is sometimes considered a subspecies of Psilocybe mexicana. Others treat it as a full species in its own right. There are also claims that "P. galindoi" isn't a valid name at all and that it is simply P. mexicana. DNA analysis suggests that ATL #7 isn't P. mexicana or P. galindoi.

Potential Species:
Psilocybe mexicana: A psychoactive mushroom capable of producing "truffles." It has an ancient history of spiritual use by the Mazatec peoples.

Psilocybe atlantis: Described as a close relative of P. mexicana native to Georgia, USA. Some reports suggest it is the same as P. tampanensis.
Psilocybe tampanensis: Another truffle-forming psychoactive mushroom discovered near Tampa, Florida. It appears to be native to the subtropical band of eastern North America.

Psychoactive Properties:
ATL #7 contains psilocybin and psilocin, resulting in effects similar to other psilocybin-containing mushrooms.
These effects include mood variation, altered perception, and sometimes nausea and balance issues.

In summary, ATL #7 is a mysterious and potent strain that produces both truffles and mushrooms, adding to its allure among psychedelic enthusiasts1.

Resources:
1. https://healing-mushrooms.net/atl-7
2. https://www.shroomery.org/forums/showflat.php/Number/15929923
3. https://sporeswaps.com/shop/actives-spores/lc/atl-7-sclerotia-philosophers-stones-p-tampanensis-liquid-culture-lc-research-syringe/
4. https://files.shroomery.org/attachments/19436940-Truffle%20Tek%20by%20Violet.pdf
5. https://www.lilshopofspores.com/cgi/display.cgi?item_num=7035&title=-Psilocybe-galindoi-ATL%237-Spores
6. https://sporeworks.com/Psilocybe-tampanensis-ATL-7-Large-Sclerotia-TM-Spore-Syringe-Microscopy-Kit.html
7. https://www.reddit.com/r/shrooms/comments/a0ig0d/115g_fresh_sclerotia_of_psilocybe_galindoi_atl_7/?rdt=54997
8. https://en.m.wikipedia.org/wiki/Psilocybe_tampanensis
9. https://psillow.com/species/psilocybe-galindoi/
10. https://www.bing.com/search?q=ATL+%237+strain&FORM=bngcht&toWww=1&redig=E56AE38604F1498590AF46BEA86C9284
11. https://www.en.psilosophy.info/species/psilocybe_galindoi.htm
12. https://basidiumequilibrium.com/product/atl7-tampenensis/

Australian

Australian magic mushrooms, sometimes called "Aussie" or "Gold Tops," are a strain of Psilocybe cubensis mushrooms that grow in Australia and New Zealand. These mushrooms are distinct from Psilocybe subaeruginosa, which is an entirely different species of psychedelic shroom that also grows natively in Australia and is also known as "Aussie shrooms"1. Here are some key details about the Australian strain:

Appearance:
Australian magic mushrooms have rounded golden tops, which contribute to their nickname "Gold Tops."
The appearance of these mushrooms is similar to other Psilocybe cubensis strains, with pale-capped sub-varieties compared to the typical brownish caps of wild-type P. cubensis.

Potency: Average
The strength of the effects depends on various factors, including growing conditions, genetics, and harvest methods.
While there isn't enough quantitative data for precise potency averages, most people who have taken Aussie Gold Tops consider them to be about average in terms of potency. Even average-potency mushrooms can deliver life-changing spiritual experiences, depending on the dose, set, and setting.

Cultivation:
Aussie Gold Tops grow relatively easily, like most Psilocybe cubensis shrooms, and produce bountiful flushes that are sure to impress.
Recommended Substrate:
When cultivating Australian magic mushrooms, consider using substrates such as dung, rye grain, or a mixture of brown rice flour and vermiculite.

In **summary**, Australian magic mushrooms offer a unique appearance, average potency, and the potential for transformative experiences, making them a sought-after strain among psychedelic enthusiasts1. Information purposes only.

Sources:
1.   https://tripsitter.com/magic-mushrooms/strains/australian/
2.   https://www.bing.com/search?q=australian+mushroom+strain&FORM=bngcht&FORM=bngcht&toWww=1&redig=89CEFAF1E71940868F950AC22BA4EBEE
3.   https://tripsitter.com/magic-mushrooms/strains/wollongong/
4.   https://tripsitter.com/magic-mushrooms/strains/tasmanian/

Avery's Albino

Avery's Albino is a rare strain of Psilocybe cubensis, relatively new to the market. It's believed to be an albino mutation of the Cambodian strain. Unlike many other strains with the "albino" name tag, Avery's Albino is a true albino. Its fruiting bodies lack any pigment, giving it excellent bag appeal. But appearance isn't the only thing going for this strain. Avery's Albino is known for its mellow and highly creative high. In terms of potency, it's about average for what you can expect from other cubensis mushrooms. Cultivation-wise, it's fairly easy to grow with a bit of experience. While not the best beginner strain, it's manageable for intermediate growers with a few harvests under their belt1.

History:

Avery's Albino is somewhat mysterious. Some sources claim it's a true albino variety of the A-Strain, while others suggest it's an albino isolation of the Cambodian strain. Allegedly created by Shroomery user "Albinous White," who cloned a Cambodian albino mutation over multiple generations until the new genetics stabilized, the strain was named after his daughter, Avery. Avery's Albino shares qualities with both the A-Strain and the Cambodian strain, making it hard to definitively pinpoint its origin. However, its growth characteristics and appearance lean more toward the Cambodian strain, making that theory more likely1.

Potency: Average

Avery's Albino provides a mellow yet intense and highly creative experience. The body high is strong, and both closed- and open-eye visuals can be good with higher doses. Psilocybin and psilocin content in samples of Avery's Albino averaged 0.58% and 0.04%, respectively, resulting in a total average tryptamine concentration of 0.64%1. Overall, Avery's Albino stands out not only for its stunning appearance but also for its unique effects, making it a sought-after strain among mushroom enthusiasts.

This is for information purposes only.

Sources:

1.   https://tripsitter.com/magic-mushrooms/strains/averys-albino/
2.   https://mushroom.cat/avery-albino-mushrooms/
3.   https://mmjdirect.co/product/albino-avery/

Aztec God

Aztec God is a fascinating strain of Psilocybe cubensis, known for its potent effects and intriguing history. Let's dive into the details:

History and Origins:

The name "Aztec God" is fitting due to the notable hallucinogenic profile of this strain. While ancient civilizations in Central America did consume magic mushrooms for religious and spiritual purposes, it's unlikely that the strain sold as Aztec God today is directly related to those ancient shrooms.

The strain we have today earned its epic name from wild shrooms growing in Central America, specifically in Paso de Cortes in Mexico, near the Popocatepetl mountains. French mycologist Roger Heim discovered and isolated this strain in 1956.

Ancient references, cave paintings, and statues suggest that magic mushrooms were an important part of Central American culture for hundreds, if not thousands, of years. However, the specific species consumed by these civilizations likely belonged to different species, such as Psilocybe aztecorum or Psilocybe caerulescens.

Despite the historical ambiguity, today's Aztec God strain remains a favorite among shroom users seeking a deeply introspective and spiritual experience1.

Potency: Average

Appearance and Effects:

True Aztec God Shrooms are a potent strain of Psilocybe Cubensis.

They produce a mind-bending experience, characterized by intense visual and auditory hallucinations.

Users often report a sense of spiritual growth during their trips.

The strain contains high concentrations of psilocybin and lower concentrations of psilocin, which are the active compounds responsible for the psychedelic effects.

While we can't promise encounters with ancient Aztec entities, the name and effects of Aztec God shrooms certainly evoke a mystical vibe2.

Cultivation and Availability:

Aztec God shrooms are cultivated from Psilocybe cubensis spores.

They thrive on substrates like manure or coconut coir.

The strain is considered intermediate in terms of cultivation difficulty.

In **summary**, Aztec God shrooms offer a journey into the mystical and introspective realms, making them a sought-after choice for those seeking profound experiences.

Sources:

1. https://tripsitter.com/magic-mushrooms/strains/aztec-god/
2. https://www.mindmend.co/product/aztec-god-mushrooms/
3. https://www.thebluntness.com/posts/aztec-god-mushroom
4. https://microdosemushroomsusa.com/product/aztec-god-mushroom/

B+ Strain

B+ is a popular strain of Psilocybe cubensis, known for its potency, ease of cultivation, and pleasant effects. Here are the key details about the B+ mushroom strain:

Origins and Cultivation:
The B+ strain is an excellent starting point for new users looking to explore psychedelics. It provides all the characteristic effects of magic mushrooms while offering a pleasantly mellow, level-headed experience.
The strain's origins are somewhat mysterious. It was allegedly created by Mr. G, a legend in the mushroom cultivation space. Mr. G is also credited with creating other strains like the A+ Strain and Albino Treasure Coast.
Some sources claim that B+ is a hybrid between P. cubensis and P. azurescens, but this remains widely contested and unproven. Nevertheless, the strain exhibits growth characteristics reminiscent of both alleged parent strains.
B+ mushrooms are known for their large size, often producing absolute monsters under optimal growing conditions.

Potency: Average
The potency of B+ mushrooms varies, but analysis from the Psilocybin Cup reveals the following average content:
Psilocybin: 0.59%
Psilocin: 0.11%
Total tryptamines: 0.73%
The strongest sample submitted hit a peak of 1.38% psilocybin.
While some mushrooms can contain over 1% psilocybin and psilocin, most B+ mushrooms fall within the average range of 0.50% to 0.90%[1].

Characteristics:
B+ mushrooms are easy to work with and accept a wide range of growing conditions and substrates.
They produce large, thick caps and are not the fastest growers but certainly not the slowest either.
Overall, B+ mushrooms offer a balanced experience, making them a favorite among both beginners and experienced users.

In **summary**, B+ mushrooms are gentle giants—potent enough to provide a magical experience yet approachable for those new to psychedelics[1234].

Sources:
1. https://tripsitter.com/magic-mushrooms/strains/b-plus/
2. https://mushly.com/psychedelic-mushrooms/b-plus-mushrooms
3. https://www.themagicdispensary.com/understanding-b-cubensis-potency/
4. https://healing-mushrooms.net/b-plus-mushrooms

B+ XL

B+ XL strain of magic mushrooms is an excellent choice for new users looking to explore psychedelics. Here are some key details about this strain:
Overview:
The **B+ strain** belongs to the species Psilocybe cubensis and is renowned for its pleasant and mellow effects.
It provides all the characteristic effects of magic mushrooms without being overly intense, making it suitable for beginners.
The strain is often recommended as a starting point for those curious about psychedelic experiences1.

Origins and Cultivation:

The B+ strain was allegedly created by a legendary mushroom cultivator known as Mr. G. While its exact genetic origins are contested, it is said to be a hybrid between P. cubensis and P. azurescens (although this has not been scientifically proven).
B+ mushrooms are known for their large size when grown under optimal conditions, often producing impressive specimens1.

Potency: Average

The potency of B+ mushrooms varies, but they typically fall within the average range for Psilocybe cubensis strains.
Analysis from samples submitted to the Psilocybin Cup revealed an average potency of approximately 0.59% psilocybin and 0.11% psilocin.
The total tryptamine content averaged around 0.73%, with the strongest sample reaching 1.38%1.

Cultivation and Availability:

B+ mushrooms are relatively easy to cultivate, making them accessible for home growers.

In **summary**, the B+ XL strain offers a gentle introduction to the world of magic mushrooms, combining approachability with a touch of psychedelic wonder. Whether you're a curious beginner or an experienced explorer, the B+ strain invites you to embark on a mellow journey of self-discovery and altered perception.

Sources:
1. https://tripsitter.com/magic-mushrooms/strains/b-plus/
2. https://www.themagicdispensary.com/understanding-b-cubensis-potency/
3. https://www.seattlemet.com/discover/magic-mushrooms/b-plus-mushroom/

Ban Hua Thanon

Ban Hua Thanon is an intriguing strain of Psilocybe cubensis that has captured the interest of growers and psychonauts alike. John Allen, a renowned mycologist, found Ban Hua Thanon (BHT) growing on the island of Koh Samui in Thailand. This location is close to where he collected the more famous "Koh Samui strain" during his travels in the 90s. Some sources mistakenly claim that Ban Hua Thanon was discovered on a Vietnamese island called "Ban Hua Thanon." However, this information is incorrect.
Despite not achieving the same popularity as other Southeast Asian strains, Ban Hua Thanon has carved out a niche following among growers in the United States.

Characteristics:
Contamination Resistance: Ban Hua Thanon is highly regarded for its excellent resistance to contamination. This trait makes it a fantastic choice for beginner cultivators who may encounter challenges during the growing process.
Heat Tolerance: The strain can withstand higher temperatures, making it adaptable to various environmental conditions.

Aggressive Colonizer: Ban Hua Thanon exhibits rapid colonization habits, allowing it to thrive even in unoptimized growing environments.

Yield Potential: While its potency is comparable to other Southeast Asian strains (such as Ban Phang Ka and Lipa Yai), Ban Hua Thanon compensates with good yields over several dense flushes.

Appearance: The mushrooms resemble Golden Teachers, featuring long white stems of moderate thickness and rounded golden caps. A darker brown circle often appears at the center of the caps, occasionally accompanied by a small nipple.

Potency and Effects: Average
Ban Hua Thanon's potency is average among Psilocybe cubensis strains. Its psilocybin levels are relatively typical, but the strain's effects are highly regarded by those who have tried it.
The high from Ban Hua Thanon is often described as spiritual, with the possibility of good open-eye visuals when consuming two or more grams of dried mushrooms.
While precise psilocybin content data is lacking, anecdotal reports suggest that Ban Hua Thanon may be more potent than described by spore vendors. It could be comparable to its close relative, Koh Samui, which can produce over 1% psilocybin (dry weight) under optimal conditions12.

In summary, Ban Hua Thanon may not stand out for its appearance or psilocybin levels, but its resilience, colonization vigor, and decent yields make it a well-rounded choice for cultivators seeking a forgiving yet rewarding strain13.
Sources:
1.   https://tripsitter.com/magic-mushrooms/strains/ban-hua-thanon/
2.   https://www.myco.ca/ban-hua-thanon-cubensis-mushrooms-the-origin
3.   https://tripsitter.com/magic-mushrooms/strains/cambodian/

Ban Nathon

Ban Nathon is a fascinating strain of Psilocybe cubensis that shares similarities with its Southeast Asian counterparts. Let's delve into the details:

Discovery and Origins:
John "Mushroom" Allen, the renowned mycologist, discovered Ban Nathon during his extensive travels in Southeast Asia.
Ban Nathon is closely related to Ban Hua Thanon, another Thai strain found on the island of Koh Samui.
While Ban Nathon may not have achieved the same popularity as other Southeast Asian strains, it has carved out a niche following among some growers in the United States.

Characteristics and Cultivation:
Contamination Resistance: Ban Nathon is highly regarded for its excellent contamination resistance. This trait makes it an excellent choice for beginner cultivators who may encounter challenges during the growing process.
Heat Tolerance: The strain can withstand higher temperatures, making it adaptable to various environmental conditions.

Appearance:
Ban Nathon mushrooms resemble the classic cubensis appearance. They have rounded golden caps and long white stems of moderate thickness.
Yield Potential: While its potency is comparable to other Southeast Asian strains, Ban Nathon compensates with good yields over several dense flushes.

Potency and Effects: Average to above average
Ban Nathon's potency is average among Psilocybe cubensis strains.
The high from Ban Nathon is often described as spiritual, with the possibility of good open-eye visuals when consuming two or more grams of dried mushrooms.
While precise psilocybin content data is lacking, anecdotal reports suggest that Ban Nathon may be more potent than described by spore vendors. Perhaps its potency is more comparable to its close relative, Koh Samui, which can produce over 1% psilocybin (dry weight) under optimal conditions12.

In summary, Ban Nathon may not be the most visually striking strain, but its resilience, colonization vigor, and decent yields make it a solid choice for cultivators seeking a forgiving yet rewarding strain1.

Sources:
1.   https://tripsitter.com/magic-mushrooms/strains/ban-hua-thanon/
2.   https://goldenteacherspores.org/magic-mushroom-strain-info/ban-nathon-magic-mushroom-psilocybe-cubensis/
3.   https://frshminds.com/psilocybin-mushroom-species-guide/psilocybe-cubensis/ban-hua-thanon/

Ban Phang Ka

Ban Phang Ka is a lesser-known Psilocybe cubensis strain that hails from the island of Koh Samui in Thailand. Discovered by the legendary mycologist John "Mushroom" Allen during his extensive travels in the 1990s, this strain has several unique characteristics that make it appealing to both beginners and experienced cultivators[1]. Here are the key details about the Ban Phang Ka strain:

Contamination Resistance and Adaptability:
Like most Southeast Asian strains, Ban Phang Ka is highly contamination-resistant. It can thrive even in unoptimized growing environments.
The rhizomorphic mycelium of Ban Phang Ka is extremely aggressive, allowing it to colonize the substrate quickly.
Mushrooms develop rapidly and grow in dense clusters flush after flush.
While the strain typically produces medium-sized fruits, it's known to throw up one or two bigger mushrooms in the second or third flush.
The caps of Ban Phang Ka are golden brown, bulbous, and speckled with white spots. As they mature, the caps flatten out and become more saucer-shaped.
The stems (stipes) are white and relatively thick, developing blue hues when bruised[1].

Potency: **Above average**
Ban Phang Ka's potency is average among Psilocybe cubensis strains.
While precise psilocybin content data is limited, anecdotal reports suggest that it may be more potent than described by spore vendors.
Its effects are characterized by spiritual insights and the possibility of good open-eye visuals when consuming two or more grams of dried mushrooms[1].

Cultivation and Availability:
Ban Phang Ka is a good choice for beginners due to its resistant traits.
It's also suitable for commercial growers or those aiming to produce a large quantity of mushrooms quickly.

In **summary**, Ban Phang Ka may not be as well-known as some other strains, but its resilience, colonization vigor, and decent yields make it a solid choice for cultivators seeking a forgiving yet rewarding strain[1].

Sources:
1.   https://tripsitter.com/magic-mushrooms/strains/ban-phang-ka/
2.   https://tripsitter.com/magic-mushrooms/strains/cambodian/
3.   https://tripsitter.com/magic-mushrooms/strains/thai/

Ban Thurian

Ban Thurian is a lesser-known Southeast Asian Psilocybe cubensis variant that offers a well-rounded experience for both beginners and seasoned cultivators. Let's explore the key details about this intriguing strain:

Discovery and Origins:
The Ban Thurian strain was discovered by the legendary mycologist John "Mushroom" Allen during his travels through Southeast Asia in the 1990s.
Allen found the first sample growing directly from a patch of water buffalo dung close to Ban Thurian on the island of Koh Samui, Thailand.
Ban Thurian is one of the many variants within the Psilocybe cubensis species that were first discovered in Southeast Asia1.

Characteristics and Cultivation:
Contamination Resistance: Ban Thurian is an excellent choice for beginner cultivators due to its resistance to contamination.
Fast Colonization: It exhibits rapid colonization speeds, making it easy to work with during the growing process.

Environmental Adaptability: Ban Thurian can thrive in a variety of environmental conditions, making it forgiving for growers.

Appearance: These mushrooms have bulbous golden caps and white stems, resembling the classic cubensis appearance.

Moderate Size: While not the largest strain, Ban Thurian produces decent-sized mushrooms.

Potency: The strain has **average potency**, containing around 0.80% psilocybin.
Effects: In higher doses, Ban Thurian provides a rapid onset of effects and vivid visuals1.

Availability and Cultivation:
Spore samples of Ban Thurian are available from various vendors in the United States, Canada, and most of Europe.
You can find Ban Thurian spores as prints, swabs, or sterile spore syringes.
Cultivating Ban Thurian mushrooms is relatively straightforward, especially for those new to growing magic mushrooms1.

In **summary**, Ban Thurian may not be as famous as some other strains, but its ease of cultivation, moderate potency, and forgiving nature make it a solid choice for both beginners and experienced cultivators1.

Sources:

1.   https://tripsitter.com/magic-mushrooms/strains/ban-thurian/
2.   https://tripsitter.com/magic-mushrooms/strains/tak-mountain/
3.   https://tripsitter.com/magic-mushrooms/strains/thai/

Big Mex

Big Mex (also known as **Psilocybe Cubensis Mexicana** or Mexican Magic Mushrooms) is a strain that offers a consistent and mild psychedelic experience. Here are the key details about this strain:

Origins and Discovery:
Big Mex mushrooms are commonly referred to as Mexican Magic Mushrooms.
The first sample was collected in Northern Mexico, around the area where the Aztecs once lived.
The Aztecs and other ancient Central and South American groups referred to psilocybin-containing mushrooms as "god's flesh" or "the flesh of the gods".
While this name sounds romantic, it may be another mistranslation of Nahuatl, the region's native language, for the word "teonanacatl", which simply means "sacred mushroom" describing the fleshy mushroom fruit1.

Characteristics and Effects:
Big Mex is known for a good balance of visual effects as well as spiritual exploration.
Its potency is about average for what you can expect from the Psilocybe cubensis species, making it an excellent starting point for beginners.
While experiences can vary, some people find Big Mex to be just as powerful as any strain in high doses. However, if you're looking for a smoother, less intense trip, Big Mex is a dependable option.
The overall effect of Big Mex is typically happy and energetic, making it suitable for social gatherings or creative endeavors.
It produces mild visual hallucinations, along with a sense of euphoria and enhanced creativity1.

Potency: Average

Cultivation and Availability:
Big Mex spores are relatively easy to grow and deliver a great trip.

In summary, Big Mex mushrooms provide a manageable and uplifting experience, making them worth checking out for those seeking a standard yet enjoyable journey123. Information only.

Sources:

1. https://tripsitter.com/magic-mushrooms/strains/bixmex/
2. https://simplyshrooms.co/product/big-mex/
3. https://psychews.com/product/big-mex-magic-mushrooms/

Blue Magnolia

Blue Magnolia mushrooms are a fascinating strain of Psilocybe cubensis, a type of psilocybin mushroom. Let's explore the key details about this visually stunning and potent strain:

Origin and Discovery:
The Blue Magnolia strain was first discovered in 2015 in the United States.
It originated from a wild strain of cubensis found in the Gulf Coast region in Mississippi.
Tissue samples from the original mushroom were shared among hobbyists on an internet mushroom forum, leading to its cultivation and popularity1.

Appearance and Identification:
Blue Magnolia magic mushrooms have distinct features:
Cap: The cap is light-colored, ranging from golden orange to yellow.
Stem: The stem is light yellow or white.
Size: These mushrooms are typically medium to large, with thick, fleshy stems.
Veil Remnant: As the mushroom matures, the veil breaks, leaving a dark-colored veil remnant behind the stem. This dark coloration consists of spores, as Blue Magnolia is an excellent spore producer.
Bruising: When injured or cut, Blue Magnolia mushrooms bruise a dark blue, contributing to their name1.

Potency and Dosage: **Very potent**
Blue Magnolia is known to be one of the most potent strains of Psilocybe cubensis.
Dosages can vary based on individual sensitivity and growing conditions:
Mild Effects: A single dose can range from 0.25 to 1.5 grams.
Moderate Effects: 1 to 2.5 grams.
Strong Effects: 2 to 3.5 grams.
Users should start with a low dose and gradually increase to become familiar with the effects1.

Psychedelic Experience:
Blue Magnolia induces intense physical euphoria accompanied by vivid visuals.
Its potency makes it a sought-after choice for those seeking profound psychedelic journeys.
Effects can vary from person to person, emphasizing the importance of responsible dosing and set and setting1.

In **summary**, Blue Magnolia mushrooms combine visual beauty with potent effects, inviting explorers to venture into the realms of consciousness and self-discovery1.

Sources:
1. https://thickspores.com/mushrooms/blue-magnolia/
2. https://groups.google.com/g/magic-mushroom-group/c/0Pye4uJeMXs
3. https://magic-mycology.com/blue-magnolia-rust/
4. https://www.mushmellow.com/strains/blue-magnolia

Blue Meanies - Psilocybe Cubensis

Blue Meanies is a name applied to at least two different mushrooms, but here we'll focus on the Psilocybe cubensis strain known as Blue Meanie1. Let's explore the details:

Origins and Characteristics:
Blue Meanie is a cultivated strain of Psilocybe cubensis that has been collected from Australia.
Its fruiting bodies typically have medium-sized, light-brown caps and a webby partial veil that tears just before spore release.
The strain is called "Blue Meanie" because it bruises bluish when handled, although it's not particularly "mean" or aggressive.
Psilocybe cubensis, including Blue Meanie, is one of the most popular hallucinogenic mushroom species worldwide. It grows wild in various regions and feeds on mammal dung, although it can also be cultivated on other substrates.

Potency and Effects: Above Average
Blue Meanie is considered among the most potent P. cubensis strains.
Its effects are visual, physical, euphoric, energetic, and introspective.
The trip usually begins 45 minutes to an hour after ingestion, but effects can intensify over time.
Users are advised not to take more until they understand the full impact of their initial dose.
Responsible use includes having a sober friend present to assist with practical matters or any unexpected issues during the trip.
It's essential to note that psilocybin-containing mushrooms, including Psilocybe cubensis, are illegal in most jurisdictions1.

Safety and Precautions:
Psilocybe mushrooms are relatively safe, but they are not risk-free.
Users may experience nausea, and more significant side effects are possible.
Responsible users pay attention to safety, increase dosage cautiously, and have a sober friend present during the trip.

In **summary**, Blue Meanie is a potent strain of Psilocybe cubensis, offering a unique and intense psychedelic experience. However, always prioritize safety and adhere to legal regulations regarding magic mushrooms1.

Sources:

1. https://healing-mushrooms.net/blue-meanie-cubensis
2. https://mushly.com/psychedelic-mushrooms/blue-meanie-mushrooms
3. https://fungimaps.com/learn/blue-meanie/
4. https://thinkmushrooms.ca/blue-meanies-information-and-review/

Blue Meanie – Panaeolus Cyanescens

Others names for this include – **Huasteca, Jamaican, Australia, Rainbow eucalyptus, Alabama Magic, Brooksville Florida, Estero, Mezala, TTBVI, Thai mystery**. Blue Meanies (Panaeolus cyanescens) are a potent species of psilocybin-containing mushrooms. Let's explore the key details about this fascinating strain:
Blue Meanies (also known as Panaeolus cyanescens) are relatively small mushrooms that often go unnoticed by foragers.
Despite their unassuming appearance, they pack a punch in terms of potency.
Panaeolus cyanescens is the strongest member of the Panaeolus genus, delivering comparable potency to the average Psilocybe cubensis mushroom.
These mushrooms are known for turning dark blue when picked, which contributes to their name.

Characteristics: Blue Meanies have light gray-colored caps and are generally very small.

Growing Environment: They thrive in grasslands, heathlands, and open pastures.
Psilocybin Content: Panaeolus cyanescens contains around 0.7% psilocybin and 0.1% psilocin. Psilocybin is metabolized into the active form, psilocin, once inside the body.

Origin: Unlike other psychedelic mushroom genera, Panaeolus species don't normally produce psilocybin or psilocin. It's believed that Panaeolus cyanescens acquired these tryptamines through bacterial gene transfer from nearby Psilocybe mushrooms.

Panaeolus cyanescens is a coprophilous (dung-inhabiting) species which grows in tropical and neotropical areas in both hemispheres. It has been found[2] in Việt Nam, Africa (including South Africa, Madagascar and Democratic Republic of the Congo), Australia, Bali, Belize, Brasil, Borneo, the Caribbean (Bermuda, Grenada, (Barbados, granyte) Jamaica, Trinidad), Puerto Rico, Costa Rica, India, Malaysia, Indonesia (including Sumatra), Sri Lanka, Cambodia, Thailand, Japan, Mexico, Oceania (including Fiji and Samoa), the Philippines, SouthAmerica (including Bolivia, Brazil, Paraguay, Colombia, Venezuela, Ecuador), South Korea, Tasmania, and the United States (California, Hawaii, Louisiana, Mississippi, Alabama, Florida, Tennessee, Texas, Kentucky, Virginia and North Carolina).
https://en.wikipedia.org/wiki/Panaeolus_cyanescens

Cultivation and Availability:
Blue Meanies are found in various regions around the world, thriving in tropical and subtropical climates.
They grow in specific environments such as fertilized grasslands and decomposing organic matter like dung.
While not as popular with home growers as Psilocybe cubensis due to lower yields, they remain a sought-after strain for their potency.

Legalities:
It's essential to be aware of the legal status of psilocybin-containing mushrooms in your jurisdiction.

Responsible use and safety precautions are crucial when consuming any psychedelic substance.

In summary, Blue Meanies (Panaeolus cyanescens) may be small in size, but their potency and unique characteristics make them a fascinating addition to the world of magic mushrooms123.

Sources:
1.   https://tripsitter.com/magic-mushrooms/species/panaeolus-cyanescens/
2.   https://doubleblindmag.com/blue-meanies-mushrooms-panaeolus-cyanescens/
3.   https://psychedelicspotlight.com/the-blue-meanies-mushroom-ulitmate-guide/

Blue Ringer

Blue Ringer mushrooms (scientifically known as Psilocybe stuntzii) are a captivating species of psilocybin-containing fungi. Named after the revered mycologist Dr. Daniel Stuntz of the University of Washington, these mushrooms pay homage to his significant contributions to mycology12.

Appearance and Unique Feature:
Blue Ringers have medium-sized caps measuring 1.5 to 5 cm across and stems standing 2 to 8 cm tall.
Their colloquial name, "Blue Ringer," alludes to a remarkable feature – when touched or damaged, they reveal a distinctive blue bruising.
This unique trait, shared by many psilocybin mushrooms, occurs due to the oxidation of psilocin, a potent psychoactive compound found in these fungi.

Psychedelic Nature:
Blue Ringer mushrooms are psychedelic wonders. Their psychoactivity arises from the presence of psilocybin and psilocin, powerful compounds known to induce profound shifts in consciousness.
Once ingested, psilocybin converts into psilocin, interacting with the brain's serotonin receptors, leading to a wide range of effects, from altered thoughts to vibrant visual hallucinations.
It is essential to approach these mushrooms with respect and caution, as their psychedelic nature demands careful consideration of set and setting.

Preferred Growing Environments:
Blue Ringer mushrooms thrive in the cool, moist climate of the Pacific Northwest in the United States.
They are particularly abundant in Washington and Oregon, often found in lawns, pastures, and grassy areas.
These fungi have a fondness for human-disturbed locations, frequently appearing around landscaping mulches, woody debris, and decaying wood chips.
Their peak fruiting season is during the fall, but they can be found from August to December, especially after heavy rainfall.

Morphological Characteristics:
Recognizing Blue Ringer mushrooms in the wild requires a keen eye for their specific features.
Their distinctive blue bruising upon handling is a reliable identifying trait.
Proper identification is crucial to avoid mistaking them for other species.

In **summary**, Blue Ringer mushrooms are both captivating and potent, making them a cherished specimen among mycologists and psychonauts alike1.

Sources:
1. https://gwellamushrooms.com/blogs/magazine/blue-ringer-mushrooms
2. https://realitysandwich.com/blue-ringer-mushrooms-guide/
3. https://doubleblindmag.com/mushrooms/types/psilocybe-cubensis-magic-mushrooms/

Bluey Vuitton

Also known as the **Bluey Vuitton** shrooms, is a remarkable strain within the Psilocybe cubensis family.

Potency: **Very Potent**
The Bluey Vuitton magic mushroom stands out due to its high concentration of psilocybin and psilocin, the primary psychedelic compounds found in these mushrooms. Users praise its potency, which contributes to its powerful psychoactive effects. These effects can vary based on factors such as the user's body chemistry, tolerance, and the mushroom's growing conditions1.

Psychoactive Experience:
The Bluey Vuitton shrooms offer an experience described as intense and transformative.

Key features include:
Cerebral High: Users often experience a strong cerebral high.
Visual Hallucinations: Intense visual distortions and hallucinations.
Creativity and Introspection: Heightened creativity and deep introspection.
Spiritual seekers and psychonauts appreciate the profound experiences associated with this strain1.

Caution and Dosage:
Due to its potency, users should approach Bluey Vuitton mushrooms with caution.
Effects can be overwhelming, especially for those new to psychedelics.
Starting with smaller doses and gradually increasing can help users acclimate to the experience1.

Uniqueness and Aesthetics:
The Bluey Vuitton mushroom strain is known not only for its potency but also for its distinctive blue hue. This aesthetic characteristic, combined with its high potency, makes it an intriguing specimen in the magic mushroom family.
Researchers are also interested in its therapeutic potential1.

Origins:
The Bluey Vuitton strain is believed to be a cross between the Panama and MVP (Most Valuable Producer) strains. It was originally created and cultivated by a mushroom enthusiast named Silly Cybin around 20142.

In **summary**, the Bluey Vuitton magic mushroom offers a unique and intense psychedelic journey. Its potency, distinctive appearance, and transformative effects make it a favorite among psychonauts and researchers alike.
Sources:
1.   https://medium.com/@mystickybuds/the-potency-of-the-bluey-vuitton-magic-mushroom-an-in-depth-analysis-87040d44a213
2.   https://liquid-cultures.com/product/bluey-vuitton/
3.   https://www.bing.com/search?q=bluey+vuitton+mushroom+strain&FORM=bngcht&toWww=1&redig=A7DD2F5EC420470AABDAEED1DDFB8023
4.   https://hexacart.org/product/bluey-vuitton-mushroom-3-5-grams/

Bottle Cap

Psilocybe Baeocystis, commonly known as the 'Bottle Cap', is a wild species of psilocybin-producing fungi found in North America, particularly in areas like British Columbia1. Let's delve into the details:

Physical Characteristics:
The name "Bottle Cap" refers to the distinctive appearance of its cap, which can resemble a bottle cap or a convex shape when fully matured.
The cap's color ranges from brown to purplish-brown, giving it a unique and captivating appearance. Psilocybe Baeocystis mushrooms are distinguished by their bladder-like structure, characteristic of the genus Psilocybe.

Growing Environment:
Psilocybe Baeocystis primarily grows in the Pacific Northwest region of the United States and Canada, specifically in areas such as Oregon, Washington, and British Columbia. These mushrooms are typically found growing in woodchips, garden beds, or wooded areas, especially in forests with damp conditions.
Their geographic distribution extends beyond these regions, but they are most commonly documented in the Pacific Northwest due to the temperate climate and damp soil.

Potency and Effects: Above Average
While not particularly potent compared to other psilocybin-containing mushrooms, Psilocybe Baeocystis may be stronger than Psilocybe azurescens, another common variety.
The main psychoactive compounds found in Psilocybe Baeocystis are psilocybin and psilocin.
Consuming these mushrooms can result in altered perception of time, hallucinations, intense emotions, increased creativity, and enhanced empathy.

Safety and Responsible Use:
As with any psychedelic substance, responsible use is crucial.
Always prioritize safety and adhere to legal regulations regarding magic mushrooms.

In summary, Psilocybe Baeocystis, or the Bottle Cap mushroom, offers a unique and potentially transformative experience for those who explore its effects1. If you decide to explore these mushrooms, remember to approach them with respect and mindfulness.

Sources:
1. https://thinkmushrooms.ca/psilocybe-baeocystis-information-potency-effects-and-dosage/
2. https://www.psychedelicpassage.com/psychedelic-mushroom-strains-by-potency-30-popular-varieties/
3. https://tripsitter.com/magic-mushrooms/strains/

Brazilian

The **Brazilian** strain of Psilocybe cubensis is a fascinating magic mushroom strain with unique characteristics. Let's explore the details:

Origins and Cultivation:
The Brazilian strain is one of those fantastic magic mushroom strains that lends itself perfectly to home growers.
It boasts vigorous growth and disease resistance, making it a popular choice for cultivators.
The strain was first collected somewhere in the Brazilian highlands and then cultured in a lab to produce this genetically-stable strain.

Cultivation: It's relatively beginner-friendly and can be grown on substrates like dung or grains.
Physical Characteristics:
The Brazilian strain stands out due to its large veil, which connects the cap to the stem.
Its caps can reach up to an impressive 18 cm in diameter.
The mushrooms have a brown to purplish-brown color, adding to their allure.

Potency and Effects:
The Brazilian strain is known for its **above-average potency**.
Effects include intense spiritual experiences, heightened sensations of color, and satisfying euphoria.
The high sets in quickly, with effects felt within about 30 minutes of consumption.
While specific psilocybin content data is limited, it's estimated to contain between 1.1% and 1.5% total tryptamine concentrations.
Users also report a uniquely potent "euphoric" effect associated with this strain.

In summary, the Brazilian strain offers both impressive growth and a powerful psychedelic experience, making it a sought-after choice among magic mushroom enthusiasts1.

Sources:

1.   https://www.magicmushrooms101.com/brazilian-shrooms-basics/
2.   https://tripsitter.com/magic-mushrooms/strains/corumba/
3.   https://mushly.com/brazil-mushrooms
4.   https://tripsitter.com/magic-mushrooms/strains/brazilian/

Burmese Yagoon

The **Burmese Psilocybe cubensi**s, also known as Burma cubensis or Burmese Yangon, is a very potent magic mushroom strain indigenous to the Southeast Asian country of Burma (also known as Myanmar). Located between Thailand and Bangladesh, Burma is rich in natural resources and has a tropical monsoon climate with intense rainfall from May to October, creating an ideal environment for mushroom growth1.

Origins and Discovery:
The original specimen of the Burmese Psilocybe cubensis was reportedly found growing in water buffalo dung near the city of Rangoon (also called Yangon).
Rangoon is the largest city in Myanmar, situated at the convergence of the Bago and Yangon rivers. This region's rich intertidal flat ecosystem, abundant in nutrients, provides an ideal environment for spore spreading through various means (birds, animals, algae, etc.)1.

Cultivation and Spread:
Rumors suggest that the original Burmese Psilocybe cubensis specimen was brought to John Allen by one of his students in Burma.
The first flush cultivated from this strain is believed to be the one from which the species proliferated worldwide.
The Burmese strain has a mycelium that spreads aggressively, making it suitable for prolific production and rewarding spore prints.
Consumers report that the Burmese Psilocybe cubensis offers a multi-layered experience with effects including intense euphoria, pigmented visuals, smooth body highs, and light cerebral buzzes.
Overall, it is considered a good candidate for micro-dosing to enhance mood, focus, creativity, or energy levels1.

Potency: Below Average

Historical Significance:
Myanmar (Burma) has a rich history, with evidence of Homo sapiens dating back to 25,000 BP based on stone tool discoveries.
The Burmese people were among the first to turn copper into bronze, grow rice, and domesticate poultry and pigs during the Bronze Age (circa 1400 BCE).
The prolific presence of the Burmese Psilocybe cubensis in the wild may evoke thoughts of McKenna's Stoned Ape theory, which proposed that natural mind-altering substances played a role in human evolution1.

In **summary**, the Burmese Psilocybe cubensis is a sought-after magic mushroom strain due to its high potency and aggressive growth. Its unique characteristics and historical context make it a valuable addition to the world of psychedelic fungi!12

Sources:

1. https://microzoomers.co/strains/burmese-psilocybe-cubensis/
2. https://tripsitter.com/magic-mushrooms/strains/burma/
3. https://healing-mushrooms.net/burma

Burma

Burma mushrooms, scientifically known as Psilocybe cubensis Burma, are a fascinating strain of magic mushrooms. Let's explore the key details about this strain:

Origins and Characteristics:
The name "Burma" reflects the fact that this strain was originally collected in the country of Burma (now known as Myanmar).

Aggressive Growth: Burma mushrooms are known for their fast and aggressive growth. They thrive in various environments, making them a popular choice among cultivators.

Distinctive Appearance: These mushrooms have medium-sized caps that can resemble a bottle cap or a convex shape when fully matured. Their color ranges from brown to purplish-brown.

Variable Species: Psilocybe cubensis is a variable species, and many strains are simply wild variations that have been selectively bred for consistent performance.

Potency and Effects: Average
Burma mushrooms are potent compared to other Psilocybe cubensis strains.
The main psychoactive compounds in these mushrooms are psilocybin and psilocin.
Effects include changes in mood, altered thought patterns, and, at higher doses, hallucinations.
Users often experience a sense of euphoria, connectedness, and sometimes anxiety.
Proper mental preparation and a safe, enjoyable setting are crucial for a positive experience.

Safety and Legal Considerations:
Psilocybin-containing mushrooms are not risk-free. Users should follow safety guidelines to maximize the chance of a positive experience.
It's essential to be aware of the legal status of psilocybin in your jurisdiction.

In **summary**, Burma mushrooms offer both impressive growth and a powerful psychedelic experience, making them a sought-after choice among magic mushroom enthusiasts12. Remember to approach them with respect and mindfulness.

Sources:
1. https://healing-mushrooms.net/burma
2. https://healing-mushrooms.net/psilocybe-cubensis-strains
3. https://tripsitter.com/magic-mushrooms/strains/burma/

Cambodian

Cambodian Cubensis, also known as Cambodian cubes or cubensis, is a potent and easy-to-cultivate strain of magic mushrooms. Discovered by renowned mycologist "Mushroom John" (John Allen), this strain is known for its high potency and ease of cultivation1.
Here are the key details about the Cambodian strain:

Origins and Characteristics:
The Cambodian strain was found growing wild near the famous Angkor Wat temple in Cambodia.
It has been cultivated and developed into a stable strain for home growers.
Cambodian mushrooms have a rapid colonization and growth rate, making them a favorite among cultivators.
Their appearance includes brown caps with pale spots, and they are often described as having a bottle cap shape when fully matured.

Potency and Effects: Average
Cambodian Cubensis is often spoken of as a **very potent strain**.
Its high is relatively mellow, with only slight visuals and not much body buzz.
However, it provides a lot of energy and an energetic, creative high.
The effects can last a very long time, making it important for users to plan accordingly.

Dosage:
Calculating a rough estimate for P. cubensis dosage involves considering the user's weight, the condition of the mushroom (fresh or dried), and the desired experience (intense, mild, microdose, etc.).
Since Cambodian is reported to be on the more potent side, its doses would be slightly smaller than the calculated estimate.
However, individual sensitivity to psilocybin varies, so some trial and error may be necessary.

Safety and Legal Considerations:
Psilocybe mushrooms are relatively safe but not entirely risk-free. Common side effects include nausea and anxiety.
Users should be aware of the legal status of psilocybin in their area.

In summary, Cambodian Cubensis offers both impressive growth and a powerful psychedelic experience, making it a sought-after choice among magic mushroom enthusiasts1. Remember to approach them with respect and mindfulness.

Sources:
1. https://1upmaps.com/cambodian-cubensis-strain-guide/
2. https://healing-mushrooms.net/cambodian-cubensis
3. https://microzoomers.co/strains/cambodian-cubensis/
4. https://healing-mushrooms.net/psilocybe-cubensis-strains

Campinas

The **Campinas strain** of Psilocybe cubensis is a rare and intriguing magic mushroom strain. Let's explore the key details about this unique variety:

Origins and Discovery:
The Campinas strain was initially discovered in Campinas, São Paulo, Brazil, in 2009 by a mycologist associated with Ralphsters Spores.
It took Ralphsters around a year to cultivate and stabilize the strain before preparing spore prints for commercial sale.
The strain was genetically stabilized through several generations of inbreeding to ensure its consistency and viability.

Cultivation and Characteristics:
Challenging Cultivation: The Campinas strain is not recommended for beginner growers. It can be challenging to cultivate due to its instability.
However, with sterile practices and a controlled method, medium to large-sized mushrooms of **above-average potency** are possible.
The fruiting bodies produced by Campinas spores have relatively boring appearances, with flat brown caps and light stems, similar to the Golden Teacher strain.
Despite their unremarkable appearance, these mushrooms are known for their strong closed-eye visuals (CEVs) and pleasant waves of euphoria.

Potency and Psilocybin Content:
The Campinas strain is said to have **above-average potency**.
While specific psilocybin content data is limited, anecdotal reports suggest that it has relatively high levels of psilocybin.
Unfortunately, formal testing through the Oakland Hyphae Psilocybin Cup has not yet been conducted for this strain.

Availability:
Due to its rarity, the Campinas strain remains an exclusive find for those seeking a unique psychedelic experience.

In **summary**, the Campinas strain offers both a challenging cultivation process and a potentially rewarding journey into altered states of consciousness. Remember to approach these mushrooms with respect and mindfulness1.

Sources:
1. https://tripsitter.com/magic-mushrooms/strains/campinas/
2. https://tripsitter.com/magic-mushrooms/strains/corumba/
3. https://goldenteacherspores.org/magic-mushroom-strain-info/campinas-magic-mushroom-psilocybe-cubensis/
4. https://tripsitter.com/magic-mushrooms/strains/

Casper

The **Casper mushroom** strain is a fascinating variety of magic mushrooms. Here are the key details about this unique strain:

Origins and Characteristics:
The Casper strain is relatively rare and not as widely known as some other varieties.
It is sometimes referred to as "Casper's Ghost" due to its appearance.

Appearance: Casper mushrooms have pure white stems and small, fleshy caps. The caps are often described as flat and ghostly white.
The strain is believed to be a mutation or a unique genetic variation of other Psilocybe cubensis strains.

Potency and Effects: Very Potent
While specific potency data for Casper mushrooms is limited, anecdotal reports suggest that they are above average in terms of psilocybin content.
Users describe the effects as euphoric, introspective, and sometimes accompanied by mild visual hallucinations.
As with any magic mushrooms, individual experiences can vary based on factors like dosage, set, and setting.

Cultivation and Availability:
Cultivating Casper mushrooms can be challenging due to their unique characteristics.
The strain is not as commonly available as some other Psilocybe cubensis varieties.
If you're interested in growing Casper mushrooms, it's essential to follow proper cultivation techniques and maintain sterile conditions.

In summary, the Casper mushroom strain offers a distinctive appearance and potentially potent effects, making it an intriguing choice for those seeking a unique psychedelic experience1. Remember to approach these mushrooms with respect and mindfulness.

Sources:
1. https://fullsendorganicks.com/product/caspers-ghost-makshakape/
2. https://www.psychedelicpassage.com/psychedelic-mushroom-strains-by-potency-30-popular-varieties/
3. https://tripsitter.com/psilocybin-cup/

Chilean

The **Chilean strain** of Psilocybe cubensis is a rare and underrated magic mushroom strain. Here are the key details about this unique variety:

Origins and Characteristics:
The Chilean strain was discovered in Chile, a country known for its diverse landscapes, ranging from tropical shorelines to harsh alpine regions.

Appearance: Chilean mushrooms are large Psilocybe cubensis mushrooms that are light tan in color. Their appearance resembles the Amazonian cubensis strain, although the fruiting bodies don't tend to reach the same impressive proportions.
When dried, they take on a powerful blue hue and have a potency comparable to Golden Teachers and other average-potency strains.

Cultivation and Beginner-Friendly:
The Chilean strain is one of the most straightforward strains for beginner growers.
It can handle a wide range of growing conditions and easily holds contamination at bay.
The impressive yields of large fruiting bodies make up for any average potency.

History and Availability:
The history of the Chilean strain is somewhat hazy. It was supposedly first collected somewhere in the Chilean mountains.
The strain has always been elusive, occasionally disappearing from typical spore vendors. Currently, only a few select vendors carry this strain, making it somewhat rare.
Specs:

Potency: **Average**

Cultivation: Easy

Species: Psilocybe cubensis

Substrate Recommendation: Rye Grain

In **summary**, the Chilean strain offers a fantastic beginner-friendly experience with excellent contamination resistance, decent potency, and good yields of giant mushrooms. Despite its rarity, it's a mystery why this strain isn't as popular as others1. Remember to approach these mushrooms with respect and mindfulness.

Sources:
1. https://tripsitter.com/magic-mushrooms/strains/chilean/
2. https://goldenteacherspores.org/magic-mushroom-strain-info/chilean-magic-mushroom-psilocybe-cubensis-c/
3. https://tripsitter.com/magic-mushrooms/species/psilocybe-cubensis/

Chitwan (Nepal)

The **Chitwan strain** of Psilocybe cubensis is a mystical and potent variety of magic mushrooms. Let's explore the key details about this unique strain:

Origins and Discovery:
The Chitwan strain was originally collected by the famous mycologist John Allen during his trip through Asia in the 1990s.
It was supposedly discovered growing in a patch of what looked like rhino or elephant dung up in the mountain region of Chitwan in Nepal.
Unfortunately, apart from this minute piece of information, we don't know much more about the origins of Chitwan.
The mushroom is quite common in Nepal and grows in a variety of different areas in the mountainous regions.

Potency and Effects:
The Chitwan mushroom is **above average** in terms of potency.
Some users compare this shroom to other high-altitude strains, such as Kathmandu, Ecuador, and the Chilean strain.
While specific psilocybin or psilocin levels of the Chitwan strain have not been published, user reports suggest it falls somewhere in the range of 0.60% to 1.00% tryptamines.

Cultivation and Availability:
Chitwan genetics are available in the form of prints and spore syringes from various vendors.
Overall, this is a well-balanced strain with medium-sized mushrooms of above-average potency, the possibility of multiple dense flushes, and reasonable contamination resistance.
While not the best option for beginners, it's ideal for someone with a few grows under their belt who wants to try something different.

In summary, the Chitwan strain offers both impressive potency and a unique psychedelic experience, making it a sought-after choice among magic mushroom enthusiasts.
Remember to approach these mushrooms with respect and mindfulness.12.

Sources:

1. https://tripsitter.com/magic-mushrooms/strains/chitwan/
2. https://completemyco.com/blogs/complete-university/strain-highlight-nepal-chitwin
3. https://mushly.com/psychedelic-mushrooms/nepal-chitwan-mushrooms
4. https://mushly.com/nepal-chitwan-mushrooms/versus/z-strain-mushrooms

Chodewave

The **Chodewave** strain is a mysterious and intriguing variety of Psilocybe cubensis. Let's explore the key details about this unique strain:

Origins and Genetic Lineage:
The Chodewave strain is believed to be a hybridization of two other potent strains: Albino Penis Envy (APE) and Tidal Wave.
Both APE and Tidal Wave are renowned for their impressively high levels of psilocybin and psilocin.
Chodewave mushrooms have thick, white stems and golden-brown, domed caps.

Potency and Tryptamine Content: below average
Despite its impressive genetic lineage, Chodewave mushrooms exhibit an average total tryptamine level of only 0.41%.
This data puts the Chodewave strain in the "weak" potency category, which is surprising given its parent strains' potency.
However, there is potential for higher potency under ideal growing conditions.

Cultivation:
Chodewave is relatively easy to cultivate, even for beginners.

In **summary**, the Chodewave strain remains mysterious due to its unclear history, variable potency, and elusive spore samples. Despite this, it continues to intrigue mycologists and magic mushroom enthusiasts alike. Remember to approach these mushrooms with respect and mindfulness. 1.

Sources:

1. https://tripsitter.com/magic-mushrooms/strains/chodewave/
2. https://www.bing.com/search?q=chodewave+strain+Psilocybe+cubensis&FORM=bngcht&toWww=1&redig=A56122A961AF448C86B86002A75E2139
3. https://sonoranspores.com/product/chodewave-swabs/
4. https://tripsitter.com/magic-mushrooms/strains/albino-chodewave/

Choda Cubensis

Choda mushroom strain (a variety of Psilocybe cubensis).

Strain Characteristics: The Choda strain belongs to the Psilocybe cubensis species, which is one of the most common magic mushroom species worldwide.
Within the Psilocybe cubensis species, there are hundreds of unique strains, each with slight differences in appearance and effects1.
Some key differences that make strains unique include:

Mushroom size: Some strains produce larger mushrooms, while others yield smaller, stubby ones.
Cap color: Mushroom caps can range from white (albinos) to tan, dark brown, or black.
Gill production: Certain strains may barely produce exposed gills.
Flush vitality: Some strains continue to produce mushrooms for multiple flushes1.

Active Ingredients:
All magic mushroom strains, including Choda, contain three active compounds: psilocybin, psilocin, and baeocystin.
These compounds are responsible for the psychedelic effects of magic mushrooms.
The qualitative effects of different strains are virtually identical, and they are active at roughly the same dose1.

Potency: is Said to be high

Qualitative Effects: While specific qualitative effects may be associated with certain strains, it's essential to recognize that all strains within the Psilocybe cubensis species share similar effects. Users commonly report the following effects:
Visuals: Enhanced colors, patterns, and distortions.
Euphoria: Feelings of joy and interconnectedness.
Introspection: Deep self-reflection and insights.
Creativity: Heightened creativity and novel thought patterns.
Mood elevation: Positive emotional states.
Connection with nature: A sense of unity with the natural world1.

Dosage and Experience:
Dosage varies based on individual sensitivity, but a typical starting dose is around 1 to 2 grams of dried mushrooms.
As with any psychedelic substance, set and setting play a crucial role in shaping the experience.

Remember that individual experiences can vary, and it's essential to approach any psychedelic journey with care and intention. This is for information only.

Sources:
1. https://tripsitter.com/magic-mushrooms/strains/
2. https://healing-mushrooms.net/melmac-mushroom
3. https://magic-mycology.com/the-ultimate-guide-to-psilocybin-mushroom-strains-varieties-origins-and-effects/

Colombian Strain

Colombian strain of magic mushrooms is an interesting and somewhat underrated tropical strain. Here are some key points about this strain:

Aggressive Colonizer: The Colombian strain is known for its aggressive colonization rate. It grows a mix of rhizomorphic and cottony mycelium, which contributes to its rapid growth and ability to colonize substrates efficiently.

Unique Variant: One of the distinguishing features of the Colombian strain is the presence of a unique variant with rust-colored spores, aptly named Colombian Rust Spore. This variant sporulates rust brown spores, unlike the dark purplish-black spores found in the original Colombian strain12.

Appearance: Colombian mushrooms have rounded yellowish-white caps and slender white stems. The original sample of this strain was allegedly collected in pasture land just outside the small village of Villa de Leiva, Colombia1.

Potency and Effects: **Above Average**
Potency: While there's no scientific data on exact psilocybin levels, the Colombian strain is generally considered to be above average in potency. Total tryptamine levels are likely somewhere in the range of 0.9%–1.8%.

Social and Empathetic: It's regarded as a "low-anxiety" shroom, making it ideal for socializing and group trips with friends. It can amplify connections and lead to hours of conversation. The feelings are rather "floaty," with intense energy rushes. Closed-eye visuals are often more intense and insightful than open-eye visuals1.

Cultivation Recommendations:
Substrate: The Colombian strain can be cultivated on substrates such as rye grain, bird seed, BRF (brown rice flour), coco coir, and vermiculite.

In **summary**, the Colombian strain offers an interesting combination of growth characteristics, unique spore variants, and a pleasant tripping experience. If you're looking for a social and visually stimulating magic mushroom, the Colombian strain might be worth exploring! This is for information purposes only

Sources:

1. https://tripsitter.com/magic-mushrooms/strains/colombian/
2. https://mushly.com/psychedelic-mushrooms/columbian-rust
3. https://www.magic-mushrooms-shop.com/en/blog/all-about-the-colombian-magic-mushroom

Colombian Rust Spore

The **Colombian Rust Spore** (CRS), also known as Psilocybe cubensis Colombian Rust, is a mutated strain originating from Colombia. This strain is known for its unique characteristic of having orange to reddish-brown spores, which is different from the typical dark purple to black spore color of most Psilocybe cubensis strains1. Here are the key details about the Colombian Rust Spore:

Appearance and Characteristics:
The Colombian Rust strain produces mushrooms with caramel-colored caps when mature. The stems are medium to large in size and bruise green-blue when touched.
The spore color of Colombian Rust is clay brown to red-brown, which sets it apart from other strains.
The spore prints are described as being 25-75 mm in diameter, making them good spore depositors.
The shape of the spores is noted as sub ellipsoid, referring to their slightly elongated shape.
The Colombian Rust strain is reported to have 4-spored basidia.

Potency and Effects: Very potent
Colombian Rust mushrooms are triply as potent as other strains.
Users describe the effects as volcano hell, with walls bending, glowing red heat, and intense visual experiences.
The slightly longer grow time for a proportionally more heavy experience is considered good value for money.

Cultivation:
The Colombian Rust strain can be cultivated using various substrates, including PF Tek and BRF, rye grain, straw, and dung.
While not recommended for beginners, it's a sought-after strain due to its distinct spore color and powerful effects.

In **summary**, the Colombian Rust Spore offers both impressive potency and a unique psychedelic experience, making it a favorite among cultivators and enthusiasts. Remember to approach these mushrooms with respect and mindfulness1.

Sources:

1. https://mushly.com/columbian-rust
2. https://www.mushlovegenetics.com/mushroom-spores/colombian-rust-spore-mushroom-spores/
3. https://tripsitter.com/magic-mushrooms/strains/colombian/

Colorado

The **Colorado mushroom** strain is appreciated for its surprisingly large and vibrantly colored caps and **above-average potency**. Despite the name of this mushroom, it's unclear exactly where the original sample of this mushroom was collected. The problem is that Colorado's below-freezing temperatures aren't conducive to a healthy Psilocybe cubensis. Some people claim to have found these mushrooms growing here in the summer, but without anybody stepping up to take responsibility for isolating this unique strain, the truth remains a mystery1.

Here are the specifications for the Colorado strain:
Potency: **Average**
Cultivation: Beginner-friendly
Species: Psilocybe cubensis
Substrate Recommendations: Rye Grain or Manure

Summary:
The Colorado strain is known for being average in terms of potency. The psilocybin and psilocin levels average at about 0.56% and 0.02%, respectively, resulting in an average tryptamine concentration of around 0.64%. For reference, the average range for Psilocybe cubensis strains falls somewhere between 0.5% and 0.9% total tryptamines1.

If you're interested in growing the Colorado strain, it's relatively straightforward, especially for beginners. However, due to its unique characteristics, it remains somewhat elusive in the world of magic mushrooms1. This is for information purposes only.

Sources:

1. https://tripsitter.com/magic-mushrooms/strains/colorado/
2. https://tripsitter.com/magic-mushrooms/strains/
3. https://magic-mycology.com/the-ultimate-guide-to-psilocybin-mushroom-strains-varieties-origins-and-effects/

Conifer Psilocybe

Psilocybe pelliculosa, commonly known as the Conifer Psilocybe, is a species of fungus found in the Pacific Northwest region of the United States and Canada. Let's explore the key details about this unique mushroom:

Appearance and Characteristics:
Cap: The cap of Psilocybe pelliculosa is obtusely conic, becoming conic-campanulate with age. It typically measures 0.5 to 3 cm in diameter.
Color: When moist, the cap is chestnut brown, then it darkens to dark dingy yellow or pale yellow as it dries. It often has a pallid band along the margin and may be tinged with olive green patches.
Stem: The stem is 60-80 mm long and 1-2.5 mm thick, equal above and slightly enlarged at the base. It is covered with grayish fibrils and becomes blue-green when bruised or with age.
Partial Veil: The partial veil is thin to obscure to absent.

Spore Characteristics:
The spores of Psilocybe pelliculosa are purplish-brown in deposit.
They are subellipsoid to subovoid, measuring 9-13 by 5-7 microns.

Habitat and Distribution:
Psilocybe pelliculosa is commonly found in coniferous woods in the Pacific Northwest.
It grows on the ground in groups or clusters along trails or forest roads.
A single collection has also been reported from Finland and Norway.

Effects and Potency: Below Average
While not as potent as some other Psilocybe cubensis strains, Psilocybe pelliculosa still contains psilocybin and baeocystin at relatively low concentrations.
Users describe the effects as euphoric and sometimes accompanied by mild visual hallucinations.

In **summary**, the Conifer Psilocybe (Psilocybe pelliculosa) offers a unique appearance and a moderate psychedelic experience. Remember to approach these mushrooms with respect and mindfulness.1

Sources:

1. https://ultimate-mushroom.com/edible/813-psilocybe-pelliculosa.html
2. https://en.m.wikipedia.org/wiki/Psilocybe_pelliculosa
3. https://entheonation.com/blog/psilocybin-mushrooms-identification/

Corumba

The **Corumba strain** is a Psilocybe cubensis mushroom strain from Brazil. Although there are hundreds of different magic mushroom species, Psilocybe cubensis is the most popular—primarily because the species is easy to cultivate in an artificial environment.

Origin:
The original Corumba sample was collected from the Brazilian city of Corumbá sometime in the early 2000s.

Appearance:
This strain has relatively large fruiting bodies that grow quickly. The caps are golden brown and bulbous in young mushrooms, flattening out as the mushroom matures. The stems are off-white, thick, and heavy.

Potency: Average
 The Corumba strain can be compared to Golden Teacher in terms of looks and potency. This strain has average potency—producing somewhere in the range of 0.50% to 0.90% psilocybin. The effects of the Corumba strain are deeply introspective, with visual distortions, bodily sensations, and euphoria present throughout the experience.

Summary:
Corumba mushrooms share several similarities with the Brazilian strain, but the fruiting bodies don't reach the same enormous sizes.
 Like most South American strains, Corumba is resistant to contamination, has aggressive colonization traits, and fruits quickly—making it a good choice for beginner cultivators1. Remember this is for information purposes only.

Sources:

1. https://tripsitter.com/magic-mushrooms/strains/corumba/
2. https://magic-mycology.com/the-ultimate-guide-to-psilocybin-mushroom-strains-varieties-origins-and-effects/
3. https://tripsitter.com/magic-mushrooms/strains/

Copelandia

Copelandia cyanescens, commonly known as Copelandia mushrooms or **Blue Meanies**, is a potent and well-known psychedelic mushroom species. Let's explore the key details about this unique strain:

Origins and Characteristics:
Genus: Copelandia cyanescens belongs to the Panaeolus genus, which contains over 100 species of psychedelic mushrooms.
Discovery: The Copelandia genus was created by Italian mycologist Abbé Giacomo Bresadola in the late 1800s as a subgroup of Panaeolus mushrooms.
Spore Color: The specific name "cyanescens" comes from the New Latin word for "bluing," referring to the blue coloration that can often be seen on the caps of these mushrooms.

Appearance: Copelandia mushrooms are small and delicate, with thin, long stems and small caps. They typically grow in clusters on dung, moss, or rotting wood.

Distribution and Habitat:
Tropical Regions: Copelandia mushrooms are found throughout tropical regions of the world.

Religious Use: These mushrooms have a long history of use in religious ceremonies, as they are said to provide users with a direct connection to the divine.

Effects and Potency: Average
The effects of Copelandia cyanescens mushrooms are typically felt within 30 minutes of ingestion and can last for up to six hours.
Common effects include visual and auditory hallucinations, feelings of euphoria, and a sense of well-being.
Some users may experience nausea and vomiting, so it's essential to start with a small dose if trying them for the first time.

Cultivation:
Copelandia mushrooms can be grown at home with minimal effort.
The cultivation of this magic mushroom has been perfected in Hawaii, which is why it's often referred to as the Hawaiian mushroom.

Summary:
Copelandia cyanescens is one of the most potent and well-known psychedelics in the world. Whether found growing wild or cultivated, these mushrooms offer a unique and powerful psychedelic experience. Remember that this is for information purposes only1.

Sources:
1. https://mushroom.cat/copelandia/
2. https://www.zamnesia.com/content/215-what-is-copelandia-cyanescens
3. https://doubleblindmag.com/mushrooms/types/psilocybe-cubensis-magic-mushrooms/

Costa Rican / Arenal Volcano

Costa Rican Cubensis is a naturally-occurring variant of Psilocybe cubensis that is now being cultivated. Although Costa Rica is a tropical country, this variant was found at high elevation and is more used to cooler temperatures, a fact growers should keep in mind. Although spores for the strain are widely available, it is difficult to find information on it from non-commercial sources. Here are the key details about the Costa Rican strain:

Appearance and Characteristics:
The Costa Rican strain produces mushrooms with brown caps and is notable for the thick secondary veil that tends to rip away from the stem at maturity, leaving veil remnants on the cap rather than on the stem.
The stems are medium to large in size, and the overall appearance is similar to the Golden Teacher strain.

Effects and Potency: Below Average
Most users describe the Costa Rican strain as low-potency, making it a good option for beginners or for micro-dosers.
However, there are users who report more powerful effects, as sensitivity to psilocybin can vary significantly from person to person.
Note that it is possible to get an intense experience from any psilocybin mushroom; it just requires taking more to achieve that level.

Cultivation:
The Costa Rican strain can be difficult to grow, partly because it prefers relatively low temperatures.
Colonization times are long, as are fruiting times, and any problems with growing conditions can slow down colonization even further.
For those growers who manage to make the strain happy, it can become a real favorite.

Remember that the use or possession of this mushroom is illegal in most jurisdictions, so please be aware of the legal implications. Always prioritize safety and adhere to local regulations when it comes to magic mushrooms.1.This is for information purposes only.

Sources:

https://healing-mushrooms.net/costa-rican-cubensis
https://tripsitter.com/magic-mushrooms/strains/costa-rican/
https://tripsitter.com/magic-mushrooms/strains/

Cream Lex Luther

Also known as **Lex Luther**, is a variation of the Psilocybe Cubensis mushroom strain. Although its exact origin remains unclear, it is most likely named after the character Lex Luthor from the Superman comic book franchise1. Here are some key details about this intriguing strain:

Appearance:
The mature caps of Cream Lex Luther measure 50-75 mm in diameter.
Initially, the caps are reddish cinnamon-brown in color, but they transition to a golden brown shade as they mature.
The cap shape changes from convex to plane, featuring an obtuse umbo at its center1.

Stems and Gills:
The stems of Cream Lex Luther tend to grow upwards of 200 mm in length and have a pale yellow color.
When bruised, both the stems and the flesh of the mushroom turn a shade of blue-green.
The attachment of the gills in this strain is adnate to adnexed, and the gills transition from a greyish color in initial fruiting to an almost black color in maturity1.

Potency: Average

Habitat and Cultivation:
Like other mushroom spore strains, Cream Lex Luther prefers subtropical climates.
It grows well in either enriched soils or soils heavy in bovine or equine dung.
The spores of Cream Lex Luther are dark purple and ellipsoid in shape1.

In **summary**, Cream Lex Luther is a unique strain with distinctive features, making it a captivating subject for those interested in the world of magic mushrooms! Remember this is for information purposes only.12

Sources:

1. https://hiddenforestsporestore.com/product/lex-luther-mushroom-spores/
2. https://www.shamanmushroomspores.com/product/lex-luther-mushroom-spores/
3. https://www.spores101.co/cream-lex-luthor-petri-plate-spore-print.html
4. https://mycological.co/product/cream-lex-luthor-research-spore-prints/

Creepers

The **Creepers strain** of Psilocybe cubensis is a mysterious and debated variety of magic mushrooms. Let's explore the key details about this enigmatic strain:

Origins and Controversy:
The Creepers strain was first sold by the Shroomery user known as "The Keeper."
There's ongoing debate about whether Creepers truly deserves the title of a unique strain or not.
The Keeper faced criticism for allegedly rebranding existing mushroom strains and inflating prices.
Some speculate that Creepers might be a rebranded Cambodian strain or a copy of the Hawaiian or Tasmanian strain.

Appearance and Characteristics:
Creepers mushrooms typically have a conical or bell-shaped cap ranging from reddish-brown to yellowish-brown.
The cap may also have dark spots or a dark ring around the edge.
The stem is usually thin and can be white or pale yellow.

Potency and Effects: Average
Creepers are considered slightly above average in potency.
Users describe the trip as unlike anything else they've experienced, with a tendency to "creep up on you."
Some trip reports suggest the experience is a bit "darker" than other strains.

Cultivation:
Creepers are suitable for beginner cultivation.
They thrive on substrates like rye grain or brown rice flour.

Remember to approach these mushrooms with respect and mindfulness. This is for information purposes only12.

Sources:

1. https://tripsitter.com/magic-mushrooms/strains/creepers/
2. https://www.magicmushrooms101.com/creeper-shroom/
3. https://frshminds.com/psilocybin-mushroom-species-guide/psilocybe-cubensis/keepers-creeper-magic-mushrooms/
4. https://lordofspore.com/product/psilocybe-cubensis/creeper/
5. https://mushroom-growing.com/creeper-mushroom/

Cuban

The **Cuban strain** of magic mushrooms, also known as Cuban Cubensis, holds a special place in the world of psychedelic fungi. Here's a synopsis of this fascinating strain:

Origins and Discovery:
The Cuban strain was the first Psilocybe cubensis ever discovered. It was found in Cuba by botanist F.S. Earle during a trip to the island in the early 1900s.
Earle named the entire species of magic mushrooms after the location of its discovery — cubensis.
Although magic mushrooms exist in various regions, the Cuban strain is significant because it was the one that Earle categorized and documented first[1,2].

Appearance and Characteristics:
The current Cuban strain available today doesn't directly come from the original samples collected by Earle. Instead, it was obtained from a separate sample about 40 years after his discovery.
The Cuban Cubensis strain has an orange-tinted brown cap and distinctively long, thin stems. It is slightly smaller than most other strains of Psilocybe cubensis.
As expected from the essential origin of Psilocybe cubensis mushrooms, the Cuban strain has an average potency level compared to other strains[1].

Potency and Effects:
While there is surprisingly little specific information on the psilocybin content of this strain, most reports suggest that it is **average** in terms of potency.
However, there are also reports of these mushrooms being extremely powerful, so caution is advised when trying the Cuban strain for the first time.
Each batch of mushrooms can vary in potency, even within the same strain[1].

Historical Significance:
The Cuban strain is not just another regional variety; it's the one that started it all for Psilocybe cubensis.
Packed with psilocybin and bathed in history, this shroom strain is perfect for those looking for intense effects and wanting to experience a part of magic mushroom history[1].
In summary, the Cuban Cubensis strain remains a true OG mushroom, embodying both historical significance and psychedelic potency[1]. Remember that this is for information purposes only.

Sources:
1. https://tripsitter.com/magic-mushrooms/strains/cuban/
2. https://mushly.com/cuba-mushrooms/versus/columbian-rust
3. https://microdosemushrooms.com/shop/cuban-cubensis/

Dancing Tiger - AKA China 29/ EK4

The **Dancing Tiger** mushroom strain, scientifically known as Psilocybe cubensis, is a fascinating and unique variety that originates from Southern China.

Appearance and Characteristics:
The Dancing Tiger strain produces thick flushes of medium-sized mushrooms with domed caps that range in color from chestnut to golden-brown.
As the mushrooms mature, their caps flatten out, often displaying distinct "oatmeal-like" warts on the surface.
The stems of Dancing Tiger mushrooms are white with a yellowish hue and may exhibit slight waviness1.

Effects and Experience:
Dancing Tiger mushrooms are not particularly visual unless consumed in high doses (around 3.5 grams or more, dried weight).
However, their true magic lies in their ability to induce fits of laughter when used socially.
They are often referred to as "laughing shrooms" due to their propensity for hilarity.
The high from Dancing Tiger mushrooms is exceptionally euphoric and energetic, making them a great choice for those seeking a light-hearted and fun experience1.

Cultivation and Availability:
Like most Asian strains, Dancing Tiger mushrooms are easy to grow. They have aggressive mycelium and quickly colonize substrate.
Beginner cultivators will find this strain manageable, and it's also an excellent choice for first-time psychonauts.
The Dancing Tiger strain became popular after its introduction to the Western spore market around 2007. It was originally collected from the foothills of Southern China by a Chinese mycology student who described them as "laughing-dancing mushrooms." Since then, Dancing Tiger mushrooms have been widely distributed and are available online and across Canada through various magic mushroom shops12.

Potency and Tryptamine Content:
The Dancing Tiger strain is rated as "**Average**" in terms of potency.
It contains approximately 0.50% to 0.90% total tryptamines (including psilocybin, psilocin, and baeocystin).
While not intensely visual, these mushrooms provide strong sensations of euphoria and energy, creating a delightful experience for users1.

In **summary**, the Dancing Tiger strain offers a unique blend of laughter, euphoria, and energy, making it a delightful addition to the world of magic mushrooms. Remember this is for information purposes only.

Sources:

1. https://tripsitter.com/magic-mushrooms/strains/dancing-tiger/
2. https://psychedelic-today.com/product/dancing-tiger-mushroom/
3. https://www.shroomery.org/forums/showflat.php/Number/24568270

Dixieland

The **Dixieland** magic mushroom strain, scientifically known as Psilocybe cubensis, is a well-rounded variety that holds appeal for both beginners and commercial growers.
The Dixieland strain was discovered somewhere along the Mississippi River in the United States.
Its name is derived from the term "Dixieland," which is a nickname for the Southern United States.
An amateur mycologist with the online handle "Dial8" found this strain after searching local cow pastures for over two years. It was the first wild Psilocybe cubensis he had encountered during his quest.
The exact location of its discovery remains undisclosed1.

Appearance and Characteristics:
Dixieland mushrooms have bulbous, average-sized caps that range in color from cream to tan.
The stems are white, wavy, and slender, typical of Psilocybe cubensis mushrooms.
In terms of appearance and potency, Dixieland falls within the **average** range for this species1.

Cultivation and Resistance:
The strain appears to be highly resistant to contamination, making it suitable for beginner cultivators.
Decent yields of average-sized, average-potency mushrooms can be obtained over several flushes before the mycelium eventually succumbs to mold.
Commercial growers and amateur cultivators alike find the Dixieland strain to be a predictable choice for cultivation1.

History and Availability:
The Dixieland strain entered the market sometime after 2005.
After discovering these mushrooms, Dial8 cultivated the wild spores and shared his results on the "Mycotopia" forum.

Potency and Effects:
The Dixieland strain is rated as having "average potency" based on trip reports and data from similar strains. It contains approximately 0.50% to 0.90% total tryptamines, including psilocybin and psilocin. Effects include light visual stimulation, intense euphoria, and a sense of calm. Visual hallucinations and the "body high" become more pronounced with doses exceeding three grams1.

In summary, the Dixieland strain offers a reliable and balanced experience, making it a valuable addition to the world of magic mushrooms1.

Sources:

1. https://tripsitter.com/magic-mushrooms/strains/dixieland/
2. https://tripsitter.com/magic-mushrooms/strains/treasure-coast/
3. https://tripsitter.com/magic-mushrooms/strains/

Ecuador

The **Ecuadorian** cubensis, also known as the Ecuador strain, is a fascinating variety of magic mushrooms. Let's explore its characteristics and effects:

Origins and Appearance:
The Ecuador strain is believed to have originated in the Andean region of Ecuador.
It is known for its distinctive appearance:
Short and stubby stem: Unlike some other strains, the Ecuadorian cubensis has a compact stem.
Broad, bell-shaped cap: The cap is wide and often resembles a bell.
Golden color: The cap color ranges from chestnut to golden brown.
Bluing reaction: Like other psilocybin-containing mushrooms, the Ecuador strain exhibits a bluing reaction when damaged or bruised.
These features make it easily recognizable and set it apart from other varieties12.

Potency and Effects:
The Ecuador strain is considered a "classic" strain of psilocybin mushrooms.
It is highly sought after by those looking for a potent psychedelic experience.
While the exact psilocybin and psilocin content is not specified, it is known to be one of the strongest hallucinogenic psilocybin-containing mushrooms.
Users can expect effects such as euphoria, altered perception, and potential visual stimulation. **Potency is above average**.
As with any psychedelic substance, caution and responsible use are essential13.

Cultivation:
The Ecuadorian cubensis strain shares the hallucinogenicity and ease of cultivation of its ancestor, Psilocybe cubensis.
It is a robust mushroom, making it suitable for growing in various climates.
Cultivators appreciate its predictability and reliability during the cultivation process2.

In summary, the Ecuador strain offers a classic psychedelic experience with its unique appearance and potent effects. Whether you're a seasoned psychonaut or a curious explorer, the Ecuadorian cubensis is worth exploring1. Remember this is for information purposes only.

Sources:

1. https://thehigh.guide/voice-memo-trip-report-ecuador/
2. https://microzoomers.co/strains/ecuador-strain/
3. https://thehigh.guide/mushroom-strain-ecuador/
4. https://healing-mushrooms.net/ecuador-cubensis

Elephant Dung Thai

The **Thai Elephant Dung** strain, also known as TED, Thai cubensis, or simply the "Elephant Strain", is an exotic Psilocybe cubensis found emerging naturally from Thailand's elephant excrements.

Origins and Mystery:
The stories surrounding the origins of the Thai Elephant Dung mushroom strain vary. One theory suggests that it could be related to Psilocybe Samuiensis, also known as the Allen Strain. This strain was named in honor of the ethno-mycologist John Allen, who discovered it growing in water buffalo dung on the island of Koh Samui in 1991. Another possibility is that it is related to other dung-loving psychoactive species commonly found in Thailand, such as P. antillarum, Panaeolus Cyanescens (also known as Blue Meanies), or Pan. tropicalis. These strains are often referred to as "zoo-doo" and spread through zoo compost originating from elephant and hippopotamus dung. Regardless of the mystery surrounding its origin, Thai Elephant Dung mushrooms grow exclusively on one type of dung: the precious Thai dung1.

Unique Substrate and Cultural Significance:
The Thai people consider Thai dung to be the "perfect alchemist" that transforms elephant dung into Thai Elephant Dung Psilocybe Cubensis, also known as the "mushroom of illumination". The special relationship between this psychoactive species and elephant dung is intriguing, especially in a country where Ganesha, the elephant-headed Hindu god of beginnings, is worshipped.
Thailand, known as "the land of smiles," has a long history with magic mushroom tourism. In the late 1960s, it was common for restaurants to serve P. subcubensis omelettes or shakes. The Thai natives traditionally refer to these mushrooms as "hed keequai," which translates to "mushroom which appears after water buffalo defecates." The unique exotic substrate on which Elephant Dung mushrooms grow likely contributes to their popularity and cultural significance1.

Descendants and Potency:
The Thai Elephant Dung Strain has given rise to sub-strain descendants, including the powerful Koh Samui Super strain (aka KSSS) and the Thai Ban Huan magic mushroom. Many Thai strains exhibit moderate to **high potency**, making them suitable candidates for microdosing. Reviews of Thai Elephant Dung mushrooms describe a dynamic, euphoric experience, with a fast and powerful come-up, plenty of giggles, and a great afterglow. The nutritive quality of the elephant dung substrate directly affects the psilocybin levels, contributing to the potency of Thai cubensis mushrooms1.

In summary, the Thai Elephant Dung strain is a sought-after delight for cultivators, offering a unique connection to Thai culture, potent effects, and a fascinating history of emergence from elephant dung1. Remember that this is for information purposes only.

Sources:

1. https://microzoomers.co/strains/thai-elephant-dung-strain/
2. https://mushly.com/thai-elephant-dung-magic-mushrooms
3. https://mushly.com/z-strain-vs-thai-elephant-dung-magic

Enigma

The **Enigma** Cubensis strain is a fascinating and unusual variant of the popular psychoactive species Psilocybe cubensis.

Mutation and Propagation:
Enigma Cubensis is not a distinct species but rather a mutant form of Psilocybe cubensis.
It is characterized by its unique growth pattern: when it begins to fruit, it forms bluish blobs of fungal tissue instead of typical mushroom caps.
These blobs never produce spores and must be propagated entirely by cloning. In other words, Enigma doesn't follow the usual mushroom life cycle1.

Appearance and Growth:
Enigma pins (early growth stages) resemble ordinary Psilocybe cubensis pins.
However, instead of developing caps, they continue to grow larger and merge together, forming dense masses of fungal tissue.
These masses may resemble brains, cauliflower, or even the plant cauliflower itself.
The bluish coloration adds to their unusual appearance.
Despite their unconventional shape, Enigma blobs can be used in the same way as regular psychoactive mushrooms and can be preserved through drying or immersion in honey1.

Effects and Trip Experience:
Enigma's trip effects are essentially the same as other Psilocybe cubensis strains.
Users typically experience a combination of altered mood, altered perception, and altered thought patterns.
The altered perception, often associated with hallucinations, varies depending on the dosage. While some claim that different strains produce qualitatively different trips, others believe that a cube is a cube, and the primary difference lies in potency.
Enigma doesn't stand out for having any distinctive style; it remains a novelty product due to its bizarre growth form1.

Potency: Above average

Legal Considerations:
It's essential to note that possession or use of the psychoactive substance psilocybin is illegal in most jurisdictions.
Penalties can be severe, so it's crucial to be aware of the laws in your area1.

In summary, the Enigma Cubensis strain is a captivating anomaly in the world of magic mushrooms, offering both intrigue and potency despite its unconventional appearance1.
Remember this is for information purposes only.

Sources:
1. https://healing-mushrooms.net/enigma-cubensis
2. https://tripsitter.com/magic-mushrooms/strains/enigma/
3. https://fungi.org/cultivation-tips/enigma-cubensis-blob-mutation/

Entheogen Explosion

(Scientifically known as Psilocybe Cubensis, **Entheogen Explosion**) is a variation of the P. Cubensis mushroom strain created through cross-breeding many generations of different P. Cubensis strains. The result is a stable variation of the P. Cubensis strain with very robust and large fruiting bodies1.

Origin and Creation:
Entheogen Explosion was developed by selectively breeding various P. Cubensis strains. The goal was to create a strain with desirable characteristics, including robust growth and potent psychoactive effects.

Appearance:
The fruiting bodies (mushrooms) of Entheogen Explosion are typically larger than average.They exhibit the classic features of P. Cubensis, including a conical to bell-shaped cap, off-white gills, and a bluish ring around the stem when bruised.

Psychoactive Properties:
Like other P. Cubensis strains, Entheogen Explosion contains the psychoactive compounds psilocybin and psilocin.
When consumed, these compounds produce hallucinogenic effects, altered perception, and changes in mood and thought patterns.

Cultivation:
Entheogen Explosion can be cultivated using standard methods for growing P. Cubensis mushrooms. It responds well to various substrates, including grain-based spawn and bulk substrates.

Potency: very potent

Popularity:
Entheogen Explosion is considered one of the most sought-after magic mushrooms by many enthusiasts.
Its potency and robust growth make it appealing to both beginners and experienced cultivators.

Availability:
Entheogen Explosion spores are available for purchase from various online vendors. Cultivators can use these spores to grow their own mushrooms at home.
In summary, Entheogen Explosion Magic Mushrooms offer a unique combination of potency, size, and stability. Whether for personal exploration or cultivation, they continue to captivate those interested in the world of psychedelic fungi!23

Sources:
1. https://psilocybintrippymushrooms.store/product/entheogen-explosion-magic-mushrooms/
2. https://www.trippinbros.com/product/entheogen-explosion-magic-mushrooms/
3. https://massiasexotics.com/product/entheogen-explosion-magic-mushrooms/

Escondido

The **Escondido strain** of Psilocybe cubensis is a remarkable variety of magic mushrooms with a rich history and unique characteristics. The Escondido strain was collected in the small coastal town of Puerto Escondido in the Southern Mexican state of Oaxaca. This region has a centuries-long tradition of cultivating entheogenic mushrooms for both physical and spiritual healing.
The indigenous shamans in this area have used local mushrooms, including the Escondido strain, in their sacred ceremonies for generations. Notably, the famous shaman Maria Sabina is believed to have used Escondido mushrooms in psychedelic rituals. Maria Sabina welcomed Westerners, including Timothy Leary, John Lennon, and Aldous Huxley, to partake in these ancient ceremonies[1].

Appearance and Cultivation:
Escondido mushrooms are a beginner-friendly strain to work with. They grow both quickly and in dense clusters. Their average potency makes them accessible for various users. Cultivators often use rye grain as the substrate for growing Escondido mushrooms. When cultivated, they exhibit a unique spiritual energy that sets them apart from other strains[1].

Spiritual Experiences and Microdosing:
Users of the Escondido strain often report powerful spiritual experiences.
These mushrooms can foster a deep connection with the natural world and a sense of oneness with all living things. For many, the Escondido strain serves as a gateway to a new way of thinking about life and existence. Additionally, it is a popular choice for microdosing, providing access to flow states, improved concentration, mood regulation, and creative problem-solving[1].

Historical Significance:
The Wassons, American amateur mycologists, were the first Westerners to participate in the centuries-old mushroom ceremonies led by Maria Sabina. Maria Sabina used various mushrooms, including the Escondido strain, during these sacred rituals. The Wassons' writings and research played a crucial role in introducing mushrooms to mainstream culture and sparking interest in their spiritual and healing properties[1].

Potency and Psilocybin Content:
While exact potencies can be challenging to find online, the Oakland Hyphae organization provides valuable information. Escondido mushrooms are known for their **average potency**. Their psilocybin content contributes to their ability to induce profound experiences[1].

In summary, the Escondido strain offers a bridge between ancient traditions and modern exploration, inviting users to connect with the spiritual realm and explore new dimensions of consciousness[1]. This is for Information purposes only.
Sources:
1. https://tripsitter.com/magic-mushrooms/strains/escondido/
2. https://ryzobioscience.com/escondido-mexico-mushroom-spores/
3. https://microzoomers.co/strains/escondido-psilocybe-cubensis/

EQ-Ecuador

The **Ecuador** cubensis strain, also known as the Ecuadorian magic mushroom, refers to the Ecuadorian strain of the widely known species of the psilocybin-containing mushroom Psilocybe cubensis. While the Ecuadorian cubensis does not appear to be morphologically or characteristically different from Psilocybe cubensis, it is arguably one of the most majestic of all Psilocybes1.
Here are some key points about the Ecuador cubensis strain:

Appearance and Identification:
The Ecuadorian cubensis strain shares its appearance with Psilocybe cubensis.
Its large size, bell-shaped cap with a golden color, well-formed and persisting ring, and bluing reaction of the stem and veil upon bruising make it easily recognizable.
The cap starts as conical or bell-shaped with a central knob (umbo) and eventually expands to become convex or flat-topped.
The flesh of this species demonstrates a bluing reaction when damaged or bruised, a common feature among psilocybes. The gills are narrow, close, and attached to the stem with a notch at the point of attachment1.

Potency and Effects: Above Average
The main difference that sets apart the Ecuador cubensis from other psilocybin mushroom species is its psilocybin and psilocin content.
Ecuador cubensis is suggested to be one of the **strongest hallucinogenic psilocybin-containing mushrooms.**
Users can expect effects such as altered mood, altered perception, and altered thought patterns. As with any psychedelic substance, responsible use and safety precautions are essential1.

Cultivation:
The Ecuadorian cubensis strain is an excellent choice for beginners.
It produces large, beautiful fruits with generous flushes.
Cultivators find it relatively easy to grow on various substrates.
Its robust morphology makes it suitable for various climates2.
In summary, the Ecuador cubensis strain offers both aesthetic appeal and potent psychedelic effects, making it a sought-after choice for those exploring the world of magic mushrooms1. This is for information purposes only.

Sources:
1. https://healing-mushrooms.net/ecuador-cubensis
2. https://mushly.com/ecuador-mushrooms
3. https://thehigh.guide/voice-memo-trip-report-ecuador/
4. https://microzoomers.co/strains/ecuador-strain/
5. https://tripsitter.com/magic-mushrooms/strains/

F+ strain

The **Florida White** (F+) strain, also known simply as "F+," is a mild variety of Psilocybe cubensis. Let's explore the details of this strain:
Origins and Names:
The **F+ strain** is sometimes referred to as **"Florida Strain,"** **"Florida White,"** or simply "**F-Strain.**"
Despite its ease of cultivation and potent mushrooms, it is not as popular as some other strains12.

Cultivation and Appearance:
F+ produces large fruits and is relatively easy to grow.
Its appearance is similar to other Psilocybe cubensis strains, with a bell-shaped cap and a golden color.
The confusion surrounding this strain arises from its various names, but there appears to be no significant difference between them1.

Potency and Effects: mild potency
F+ is considered an average to below average potency strain.
It is a good option for first-time trippers, as the trip tends to be more manageable than with other strains.
The psychedelic effects include vivid visuals, profound philosophical insight, and an enjoyable body high.
While potent, F+ provides waves of relaxation and calm throughout the trip1.

In summary, the Florida White (F+) strain offers a mild yet enjoyable psychedelic experience, making it suitable for both beginners and experienced users1. This is for information purposes only.

Sources:

1. https://tripsitter.com/magic-mushrooms/strains/florida-white/
2. https://tripsitter.com/magic-mushrooms/strains/
3. https://mushly.com/florida-white-f

Fatass

The **Mystery Fatass** magic mushroom strain is a rare and potent variant of Psilocybe cubensis known for its distinctive characteristics. Let's explore the details of this intriguing strain:

Appearance and Origins:
The Mystery Fatass strain is recognized for its chunky chode stems and golden caps.
Its origins remain unknown, but it has been on the market for several decades.
These mushrooms are notoriously difficult to source and often come with a higher price tag compared to other strains.
The name "Fatass" refers to the mushrooms' unique appearance: they are very short and have thick, fat stems1.

Cultivation and Challenges:
Growing Mystery Fatass mushrooms is considered one of the more challenging options among Psilocybe cubensis strains.
These mushrooms often abort before reaching maturity, making them a test of patience and skill for experienced growers.
Despite the challenges, the payoff can be rewarding for those looking to try something new1.

Effects and Potency: Above Average
While an official lab test of the psilocybin content for the Fatass strain is not available, anecdotal reports suggest that it has more kick than your average cube shroom.
Some mycologists debate whether a strain's genetics truly determine its potency. Growing conditions, including substrate, humidity, and light, play a significant role in determining a mushroom's actual potency.
Although not officially entered in the Psilocybin Cup, the Mystery Fatass strain is believed to be above average in potency.
Users experience intense effects, including auditory and visual enhancements, without feeling overwhelmed1.

Availability and Bag Appeal:
Due to its rarity, Mystery Fatass mushrooms are difficult to find and are often sold by specialized vendors.
The strain's bag appeal is exceptional, with its unique appearance and promise of a potent experience1.

In summary, the Mystery Fatass strain offers both intrigue and challenge for cultivators, making it a sought-after choice for those seeking a distinctive and potent psychedelic experience1. Information purposes only.

Sources:
1. https://tripsitter.com/magic-mushrooms/strains/fatass/
2. https://magicshroomsshopusa.com/product/mystery-fatass-magic-mushrooms/
3. https://trippychemist.com/product/mystery-fatass-magic-mushrooms/

Fiji Cube

The **Fiji Mushroom** Strain, also known as Fiji Cubensis, is a remarkable variety
of Psilocybe cubensis initially discovered in the Fiji Islands.

Appearance and Identification:

Fiji mushrooms are notable for their distinctive golden-brown caps.
The cap shape is typically conical or bell-shaped, often with a distinguishing nipple-like
structure on the top.
The cap color ranges from golden-brown to light brown, with dark brown or black spots.
Underneath the cap, the gills are creamy-white.
The stem is usually white and slender, sometimes displaying a slight blue hue near the
base. When identifying Fiji mushrooms, look for specific characteristics such as size,
shape, color, and the presence of the nipple-like structure on the cap1.

Potency and Dosage: Very Potent

Fiji mushrooms are considered one of the most potent strains of Psilocybe cubensis.
They contain high levels of psilocybin and psilocin.
However, the potency can vary due to environmental factors such as temperature and
season.
Recommended dosages depend on experience level:
For beginners, starting with around 1 gram is advisable, gradually increasing as needed.
More experienced users may take up to 4 grams for a more intense experience.
Caution is essential, as consuming too much of any psychedelic substance can lead to
adverse reactions1.

Effects and Benefits:

Fiji mushrooms produce a range of powerful hallucinogenic effects:
Visual and auditory hallucinations. Distorted sense of time and space. Altered states of
consciousness. In some medical settings, Fiji mushrooms could potentially treat conditions
such as depression, anxiety, and addiction. While the effects can vary based on dose and
individual sensitivity, they are generally considered a safe and natural way to explore
altered states of consciousness. Fiji mushrooms are generally more intense than other
strains of Psilocybe cubensis but less potent than species like Psilocybe azurescens and
Psilocybe cyanescens1.

Cultivation and Harvesting:

Fiji mushrooms can be cultivated both indoors and outdoors.
Cultivation difficulty is moderate. Their elegant appearance and potent effects make them
a sought-after choice for those exploring the world of magic mushrooms1.

In summary, the Fiji Mushroom Strain offers both elegance and potency, making it a
fascinating addition to the realm of psychedelic experiences1. Information purposes only.

Sources:
1.   https://thickspores.com/mushrooms/fiji-4/
2.   https://goldenteachersstore.com/product/buy-fiji-cubensis/
3.   https://wayofleaf.com/shrooms/best-cubensis-strain

Fuzzy Balls

The **Fuzzy Balls** mushroom strain is a private variant of Psilocybe cubensis known for its exceptional potency. Here are some key points about this intriguing strain:

Potency: **Very Potent**
The Fuzzy Balls strain is considered one of the most potent among Psilocybe cubensis varieties.
A sample of Fuzzy Balls submitted in the Spring 2021 Psilocybin Cup tested at an impressive 3% total tryptamine level.
This includes 0.94% psilocybin and 0.16% psilocin12.

Appearance:
While specific details about its appearance are not widely available, the name "Fuzzy Balls" suggests that it may have unique characteristics.
Unfortunately, there is limited information about its physical features beyond its remarkable potency1.

Cultivation and Availability:
Due to its rarity and exceptional potency, the Fuzzy Balls strain is difficult to find and is often sold by specialized vendors.
Cultivating Fuzzy Balls mushrooms may be challenging, but the payoff can be rewarding for those seeking a distinctive and powerful psychedelic experience1.

In summary, the Fuzzy Balls strain offers both intrigue and potency, making it a sought-after choice for those exploring the world of magic mushrooms1. Remember this is for information purposes only.

Sources:

1. https://tripsitter.com/magic-mushrooms/strains/
2. https://magic-mycology.com/the-top-5-most-potent-p-cubensis-magic-mushrooms/
3. https://www.mushiesnow.com/mushrooms/fuzzy-balls-mushroom

Georgia USA

The **Georgia**, USA region is indeed a fascinating place for mushroom enthusiasts, and it hosts a variety of mushroom species, including the renowned Psilocybe cubensis. Here are some key points about the Georgia strain of Psilocybe cubensis:

Origins and Popularity:
The Georgia strain of Psilocybe cubensis is believed to have originated from the coast of Georgia, USA.
While its exact originator remains unknown, it has become a popular choice among cultivators and psychonauts alike.

Appearance and Characteristics:
The Georgia strain shares the typical appearance of Psilocybe cubensis:
Golden-brown caps that darken toward the center and become lighter at the rim.
Medium to large size. White, slender stems.
Its consistent potency and reliable effects make it a favorite among those exploring the world of magic mushrooms.

Potency: average: Average

Effects and Trip Experience:
The Georgia strain provides a classic psychedelic experience associated with Psilocybe cubensis.

Users often report:
Visual enhancements: Colors appear more vibrant, patterns may emerge, and objects may breathe or shift.
Euphoria: A sense of well-being and happiness.
Introspection: Deep thoughts and insights.
Connectedness: A feeling of unity with nature and the universe.

Cultivation and Availability:
Cultivating the Georgia strain is relatively straightforward, especially for those experienced in growing Psilocybe cubensis.
Spore syringes and genetics for the Georgia strain are available from various vendors.

In **summary**, the Georgia strain of Psilocybe cubensis offers a reliable and enjoyable psychedelic experience, making it a sought-after choice for both beginners and seasoned psychonauts1. Remember this is for information purposes only.

Sources:
1. https://magic-mycology.com/the-ultimate-guide-to-psilocybin-mushroom-strains-varieties-origins-and-effects/
2. https://mushly.com/learn/psilocybe-cubensis-in-georgia/
3. https://blog.curativemushrooms.com/psilocybe-cubensis-strains
4. https://thegentrycollection.com/the-ultimate-guide-to-amazonian-cubensis-strain-everything-you-need-to-know/
5. https://healing-mushrooms.net/psilocybe-cubensis-strains

Golden Emperor

The **Golden Emperor** mushroom strain, scientifically known as Psilocybe cubensis, is a remarkable member of the psilocybin-containing mushroom family. Let's explore the intriguing details of this potent strain:

Origins and Classification:
The Golden Emperor strain belongs to the greater Psilocybe cubensis species, which includes over 100 different species of psychoactive fungi.
While strains like Golden Teachers are more well-known, the Golden Emperor remains somewhat less famous but equally exciting. Golden Emperors share their lineage with the renowned Golden Teachers strain, resulting in similar potency and effects. Like their parent strain, Golden Emperor mushrooms are reliable for both introspective journeys and microdosing1.

Appearance and Characteristics:
Golden Emperor mushrooms exhibit a golden-brown cap that sets them apart.
Their overall appearance is similar to other Psilocybe cubensis strains, with a bell-shaped cap and a bright color. The stem is typically white and slender, sometimes showing a slight blue hue near the base. These mushrooms are known for their reliable potency and consistent effects1.

History and Development:
Golden Emperor mushrooms were derived from the Golden Teachers strain, one of the most famous in the shroom world.
The spore vendor Sporeslab is credited with isolating and developing the Golden Emperor strain, making them the best source for obtaining it.
While Golden Teachers have been around since the 1980s, the Golden Emperor strain emerged more recently. The term "Golden Teachers" originally referred to Psilocybe cubensis as a whole due to the common occurrence of gold-colored sport caps in this species. The exact origin of the original Golden Teachers sample remains unconfirmed, but it's believed to have come from somewhere in the Gulf region of the United States1.

Potency and Tryptamine Content: Above Average
Golden Emperor mushrooms, like most psychoactive fungi, contain three active ingredients: psilocybin, psilocin, and baeocystin.
Although limited tests exist for Golden Emperor mushrooms, the data is growing.
Analysis suggests that Golden Emperor shrooms are above average in potency, matching anecdotal reports and experiences.
Sporeslab estimates the average tryptamine content of Golden Emperor mushrooms to be around 1.8%, nearly double the common content for this species1.

Effects and Trip Experience:
Users often report a euphoric and uplifting mood, accompanied by vivid visual hallucinations and a heightened sense of connection to their surroundings.
Effects typically set in within 30 to 60 minutes after consumption and can last for several hours.
Golden Emperors provide a strong experience without necessarily pushing users into uncharted psychedelic dimensions.

Whether for deep introspection or creative exploration, these mushrooms offer a meaningful journey2.

In summary, the Golden Emperor strain combines reliability, potency, and a touch of mystery, making it a sought-after choice for those seeking insightful and meaningful trips1. Remember this is for information purposes only.

Sources:

1. https://tripsitter.com/magic-mushrooms/strains/golden-emperor/
2. https://www.shroomhub.io/shop/golden-emperor-magic-mushrooms/
3. https://medium.com/@mystickybuds/orissa-trinity-and-bluey-vuitton-magic-mushroom-strains-review-1c1a8d7d0d5a
4. https://shroomgarden.co/product/golden-emperor-mushrooms/

Golden Halo

The **Golden Halo** mushroom strain, scientifically known as Psilocybe cubensis, is a unique and intriguing variety within the world of magic mushrooms.

Origins and Stabilization:
The Golden Halo strain hasn't been around for long, but it's gaining popularity among cultivators due to its favorable genetics.
Originally discovered by Steve W in a horse pasture in Jamaica, the strain produces golden/rust-colored spores unlike any other.
The original spore samples of this strain were unstable, making it challenging to produce dense flushes of mushrooms.
However, a group of mycologists from the Shroomery forum worked together to stabilize the strain, resulting in a more reliable and consistent variety.
Now, Golden Halo genetics are available from vendors that ship to various countries, including the United States, Canada, the United Kingdom, and mainland Europe[1].

Appearance and Characteristics:
Golden Halo mushrooms are medium to large in size.
They have large, flat golden-colored caps that darken toward the center and become lighter at the rim. The stems are long, relatively thin, and white.
While it's possible to produce dense clusters of mushrooms in the first and second flush, production becomes sparse in subsequent flushes.
The strain's average potency is comparable to other well-known strains like Golden Teacher and the Lipa Yai strain1.

Effects and Trip Experience:
Golden Halo is a good strain for beginner psychonauts due to its consistent and average potency, reducing the chances of taking too much (especially for inexperienced users).
The effects include light visual stimulation, good closed-eye hallucinations, and feelings of euphoria.
While not the strongest strain, Golden Halo provides a pleasant trip, creative flow, and overall happy vibes1.

Potency: Average

Cultivation and Availability:
Cultivating Golden Halo mushrooms is relatively easy due to their stable genetics.
The strain grows well on substrates such as rye grain, bird seed, BRF, and vermiculite.

In summary, the Golden Halo strain combines stability, ease of cultivation, and pleasant effects, making it a sought-after choice for both beginners and experienced psychonauts1. Information purposes only.

Sources:

1. https://tripsitter.com/magic-mushrooms/strains/golden-halo/
2. https://inoculatetheworld.com/product/golden-halo-isolated-spore-syringe/
3. https://mushroom.cat/golden-halo-mushroom/

Golden Teacher

The **Golden Teacher** mushroom strain, often referred to as GT, is an iconic and widely cultivated variety of Psilocybe cubensis. Let's explore the fascinating details of this well-known and spiritually enriching strain:

Origins and Popularity:
The Golden Teacher strain has been a staple in the world of home mushroom cultivation since the 1970s.
Its name reflects the light brown to golden-yellow caps that distinguish it from other strains of Psilocybe cubensis.
Golden Teachers have gained popularity due to their reliable growth, resistance to contamination, and consistent effects.

Appearance and Characteristics:
Golden Teacher mushrooms exhibit:
Medium to large size: Their caps can reach several inches in diameter.
Golden-brown to yellowish color: The caps are often adorned with darker spots.
Conical or bell-shaped caps: These gradually expand as the mushrooms mature.
White, slender stems: The stems may exhibit a slight blue hue near the base.
Their appearance is both distinctive and beautiful.

Potency: Average

Effects and Trip Experience:
Golden Teachers provide a balanced and insightful psychedelic experience:
Euphoria: Users often feel a sense of well-being and happiness.
Introspection: Deep thoughts and self-reflection.
Visual enhancements: Colors appear more vibrant, patterns emerge, and objects may breathe or shift.
Connectedness: A feeling of unity with nature and the universe.
The trip duration is typically two to four hours, making it suitable for beginners.

Cultivation and Availability:
Golden Teachers are relatively easy to grow compared to other strains.
They fruit well on various substrates and even in suboptimal conditions.
Spore syringes and genetics for Golden Teachers are available from various vendors.

In summary, the Golden Teacher strain offers a reliable and spiritually fulfilling psychedelic experience, making it a favorite among mushroom growers and enthusiasts12. Remember this is for information only.

Sources:

1. https://healing-mushrooms.net/golden-teacher
2. https://thickspores.com/mushrooms/golden-teacher/
3. https://www.shroomer.com/golden-teacher-mushrooms/

Great White Monster

The **Great White Monster** strain is a relatively new and fascinating variant of Psilocybe cubensis, known for its unique characteristics.

Origins and Genetic Makeup:
The Great White Monster strain is a hybridization of the Puerto Rican strain and the classic A-Strain.
It was discovered "accidentally" by a mushroom cultivator known as NHMI.
The strain resulted from an albino/leucistic mutation caused by accidental exposure to quaternary reactive ammonium siloxane.
This mutation was isolated and stabilized until reliable spore samples were produced, leading to the birth of the "Great White Monster" strain.

Distinctive Features:
The Great White Monster strain produces massive ghostly-white mushrooms.
Most of the fruits are leucistic, meaning they are mostly white but capable of producing pigment. However, during sporulation, the strain can release completely white spores (like an albino) or rusty-colored spores similar to the Golden Halo strain.
This unique trait sets it apart from other Psilocybe cubensis strains.

Potency and Psilocybin Content:
The Great White Monster strain is rated as having "**average**" potency.
It contains approximately 0.50% to 0.90% total tryptamines, including psilocybin, psilocin, and baeocystin. While not the strongest strain, it offers a reliable and enjoyable psychedelic experience.

Cultivation and Characteristics:
Great White Monster is an aggressive and contamination-resistant colonizer.
It can grow in an unoptimized environment.
However, it is a slow fruiter, taking almost twice as long as a typical cube strain for the mushrooms to reach maturity.
Cultivators who are patient and attentive can expect large fruits with above-average potency.

Availability:
Spore samples and genetics for the Great White Monster strain are available from vendors such as Southwest Shroomery.

In summary, the Great White Monster strain combines unique appearance, reliable potency, and maximum bag appeal for those who appreciate patient cultivation and distinctive mushrooms1. Remember that this is for information purposes only.

Sources:

1. https://tripsitter.com/magic-mushrooms/strains/great-white-monster/
2. https://magic-mycology.com/product/great-white-monster/
3. https://www.magicmushroomsdispensary.ca/product/great-white-monster-magic-mushrooms/
4. https://www.themagicdispensary.com/great-white-monster-mushroom-revealing-its-unique-potency-and-effects/

Guadalajara

The **Guadalajara** Mushroom Strain, also known as Guadalajara Cubensis, is a remarkable variety of Psilocybe cubensis originating from the Guadalajara region of Mexico. Let's explore the intriguing details of this strain:

Appearance and Characteristics:
The Guadalajara strain is characterized by its unique appearance:
Light golden-brown color: The caps exhibit a rich caramel hue, setting them apart from other strains.
Gentle thinness of stems: The stems are slender and elegant.
These features make Guadalajara mushrooms especially attractive for home cultivation.

Spiritual Significance:
Guadalajara mushrooms have a rich history in ancient spiritual practices.
Indigenous people in the region used them to open their minds and engage with their ancestors.
These shrooms hold a special place in the hearts of those who use magic mushrooms for spiritual purposes.

Cultivation and Fruiting:
The Guadalajara strain is a hearty fruiter.
While the first flush tends to be standard, the second and third flushes are especially dense and may sometimes produce a few large mushrooms ("absolute units").

Potency and Psilocybin Content: Above Average
While exact psilocybin content is not widely available, trip reports suggest significant effects.
Most reports involving Guadalajara mushrooms describe out-of-body experiences and moderate to heavy visual hallucinations.
Based on this information, the estimated total tryptamine levels fall somewhere between 0.9% and 1.8% of the dried weight.

In **summary**, the Guadalajara Mushroom Strain combines unique appearance, spiritual significance, and reliable potency, making it a sought-after choice for both home growers and those seeking meaningful psychedelic experiences12.

Sources:
1. https://tripsitter.com/magic-mushrooms/strains/guadalajara/
2. https://goldenteacherspores.org/magic-mushroom-strain-info/guadalajara-magic-mushroom-psilocybe-cubensis-is-a-species-of-psychedelic-mushroomo/
3. https://magic-mycology.com/product/guadalajara/
4. https://www.magicmushroomsdispensary.ca/product/guadalajara-mexico-magic-mushrooms/

Gulf Coast

The **Gulf Coast Mushroom** Strain, also known as Guadalajara Cubensis, is a remarkable variety of Psilocybe cubensis originating from the Gulf Coast region of the United States. Let's explore the intriguing details of this strain:

Appearance and Characteristics:
The Gulf Coast strain is characterized by its unique appearance:
Light golden-brown color: The caps exhibit a rich caramel hue, setting them apart from other strains.
Gentle thinness of stems: The stems are slender and elegant.
These features make Gulf Coast mushrooms especially attractive for home cultivation.

Spiritual Significance:
Gulf Coast mushrooms have a rich history in ancient spiritual practices.
Indigenous people in the region used them to open their minds and engage with their ancestors.
These shrooms hold a special place in the hearts of those who use magic mushrooms for spiritual purposes.

Cultivation and Fruiting:
The Gulf Coast strain is a hearty fruiter.
While the first flush tends to be standard, the second and third flushes are especially dense and may sometimes produce a few large mushrooms ("absolute units").

Potency and Psilocybin Content: Average
While exact psilocybin content is not widely available, trip reports suggest significant effects.
Most reports involving Gulf Coast mushrooms describe out-of-body experiences and moderate to heavy visual hallucinations.
Based on this information, the estimated total tryptamine levels fall somewhere between 0.50% and 0.90% of the dried weight.

In **summary**, the Gulf Coast Mushroom Strain combines unique appearance, reliable potency, and maximum bag appeal for those who appreciate distinctive mushrooms and meaningful psychedelic experiences1.

Sources:

1. https://tripsitter.com/magic-mushrooms/strains/gulf-coast/
2. https://www.shamanmushroomspores.com/product/gulf-coast-mushroom-spores/
3. https://mushly.com/gulf-coast-mushrooms

Hanoi

The Hanoi Mushroom Strain, also known as Hanoi Cubensis, is a remarkable variety of Psilocybe cubensis that has an interesting history and several desirable traits. Let's explore the intriguing details of this strain:

Origins and Discovery:
The Hanoi strain was collected by none other than the legendary "Mushroom" John Allen during his travels through Southeast Asia in the 1990s. It was discovered just outside of the city of Hanoi, the second-largest city in Vietnam. Some sources even suggest that the Hanoi mushroom was found far earlier, on a small rural farm outside of Hanoi, growing in a pile of livestock manure and straw in the early 1900s. While the exact origins remain mysterious, John Allen was likely the first to bring it back to the West, where its spores would be domesticated and introduced to the market.

Characteristics and Cultivation:
The Hanoi strain is well-rounded and known for several desirable traits:

Potency: Expect **above-average** potency from this strain, although formal tryptamine testing has not yet been performed.

Visual Effects: The effects are highly visual, producing powerful waves of euphoria.
Ease of Cultivation: Hanoi mushrooms are easy to grow and can cope well with unstable growing environments.

Yield Potential: When cultivated correctly, Hanoi produces excellent yields of medium-sized mushrooms across several flushes.
Beginner-Friendly: It can be grown without too much equipment or specialized knowledge, making it an excellent choice for beginners.

Appearance:
Hanoi mushrooms have large brown caps that are rounded when young.
During maturity, the caps open, creating large brown "dinner plates."
The stems are long, white, and even in thickness throughout their length.

Potency and Psilocybin Content:
While formal tryptamine testing is lacking, we estimate the total tryptamine levels of this strain to fall somewhere between 0.9% and 1.8% of the dried weight.
The effects are highly visual and tend to produce powerful waves of euphoria.
Interestingly, Hanoi is surprisingly calming when consumed in low doses, with light visual distortion such as blurred outlines and faint geometric patterns.
In **summary**, the Hanoi Mushroom Strain combines mystery, potency, and ease of cultivation, making it a sought-after choice for both beginners and experienced psychonauts1.

Sources:

1. https://tripsitter.com/magic-mushrooms/strains/hanoi/
2. https://ryzobioscience.com/hanoi-mushroom-spores/
3. https://microzoomers.co/strains/vietnamese-psilocybe-cubensis/

Hawaiian

The **Hawaiian** Mushroom Strain, also known as Hawaiian Cubensis, is a remarkable variety of Psilocybe cubensis. Let's explore the intriguing details of this strain:

Origins and Popularity:
The Hawaiian strain is considered a "typical" Psilocybe cubensis mushroom in terms of its appearance and growth habits.
It is hard to differentiate from many other popular mushroom strains on the market.
Once dried, it's virtually impossible to tell them apart from most other magic mushrooms1.

Appearance and Characteristics:
Hawaiian mushrooms have large brown caps that are rounded when young.
During maturity, the caps open, creating large brown "dinner plates."
The stems are long, white, and even in thickness throughout their length.

Potency and Psilocybin Content: **Average**
While formal tryptamine testing is lacking, we estimate the total tryptamine levels of this strain to fall somewhere between 0.9% and 1.8% of the dried weight.
The effects are highly visual and tend to produce powerful waves of euphoria.
Interestingly, Hanoi is surprisingly calming when consumed in low doses, with light visual distortion such as blurred outlines and faint geometric patterns.

In **summary**, the Hawaiian Mushroom Strain combines mystery, potency, and ease of cultivation, making it a sought-after choice for both beginners and experienced psychonauts1. Remember this is for information purposes only.

1. **Sources**:
   https://www.bing.com/search?q=Hawaiian+mushroom+strain&FORM=bngcht&toWww=1&redig=FC79CEA91B7B4C9D9C9AE9C5A7BD08E5
2. https://mushly.com/psychedelic-mushrooms/pes-hawaiian-mushrooms
3. https://tripsitter.com/magic-mushrooms/strains/hawaiian/
4. https://completemyco.com/blogs/complete-university/strain-highlight-pes-hawaiian
5. https://shroombudz.com/product/hawaiian/

Hillbilly

Hillbilly Cubensis is a cultivated strain of Psilocybe cubensis, which is a well-known psychoactive mushroom. Although it was originally found growing wild in the American South, it is rumored to grow wild almost everywhere that any P. cubensis can. Hillbilly Cubensis has a distinct orange color, especially in the center of its cap. It looks more or less like most other cubes, although its cap is slightly smaller. Beginners attempting to forage Hillbilly mushrooms should be cautious, as they have a close look-alike called the Deadly Galerina. Foraging experience and attention to detail are essential to differentiate between the two species.
Here are some key points about Hillbilly Cubensis:

Identification & Description:
Hillbilly Cubensis looks similar to most other Psilocybe cubensis mushrooms, but its cap is a distinct orange color, especially in the center.
It can be found growing in the wild, so foragers should be cautious due to the presence of look-alike species like the Deadly Galerina.
The overall appearance of Hillbilly Cubensis is typical for a cube, and it falls under the category of "little brown mushrooms" (LBMs), which includes various unrelated mushrooms that can be confusing to identify.

Potency: Average

Trip Effects:
The effects of taking Hillbilly Cubensis are similar to other Psilocybe cubensis strains.
Users generally report a gentler and friendlier high compared to typical strains, with more laughter and fewer visuals.
It is sometimes recommended as a good magic mushroom for beginners, but individual experiences can vary based on set, setting, dosage, and personal biochemistry1.
Remember that responsible use and proper identification are crucial when dealing with any psychoactive mushrooms. Always exercise caution and seek reliable information before consuming any wild mushrooms.

Sources:

1.   https://healing-mushrooms.net/hillbilly-cubensis
2.   https://cbdincubator.com/psychedelics/hillbilly-mushroom/
3.   https://tripsitter.com/magic-mushrooms/strains/hillbilly/

Hillbilly Pancake

The **Hillbilly Pancake** strain is a rare genetic off-shoot of the original Hillbilly
strain of Psilocybe cubensis. Here are some key details about this unique strain:

Appearance:
The Hillbilly Pancake strain produces mushrooms with distinct features.
These mushrooms have short stems and flat, "pancake-like" caps.
The caps are umbilicate, meaning they have a depressed (concave) center.
Due to this central depression, the caps can sometimes resemble donuts more than
pancakes.

Potency: below average
Unlike some other potent strains, the Hillbilly Pancake strain isn't particularly strong. It
produces similar levels of psilocybin and psilocin as its mother strain, the original Hillbilly.
The total tryptamine content in dried samples of the Hillbilly Pancake strain is less than
0.60%.
While it won't blow your mind, it's an excellent choice for those seeking a "microdose"
mushroom or something rare and completely unique-looking.

History:
The origins of the Hillbilly Pancake strain are somewhat unclear.
It is believed to be an isolated mutation of the original Hillbilly strain.
The original Hillbilly strain was discovered in the 1990s when a sample was collected
in Arkansas by a user known as "Hillbilly."
Although overshadowed by more potent strains, the Hillbilly strain gained renewed
popularity in 2022 when it won the title of "Microdose Champion" in a Psilocybin Cup.

In **summary**, the Hillbilly Pancake strain offers a unique appearance and is suitable for
those interested in microdosing or growing something rare and distinctive.

Sources:

1.   https://tripsitter.com/magic-mushrooms/strains/hillbilly-pancakes/
2.   https://tripsitter.com/magic-mushrooms/strains/hillbilly/
3.   https://tripsitter.com/magic-mushrooms/strains/hillbilly-pumpkin/

Hillbilly Pumpkin

The **Hillbilly Pumpkin** strain is a genetic offshoot of the original Hillbilly strain of Psilocybe cubensis. While it's not famed for its potency, producing less than 0.60% total tryptamines, it has some unique characteristics that make it fascinating:

Appearance:
The Hillbilly Pumpkin strain is renowned for its utterly bizarre fruits.
The mushrooms are large and round, often resembling small pumpkins.
The white stems are usually thicker than the caps, which are light brown and have distinct wavy edges.
If you're looking for a super-potent strain, Hillbilly Pumpkin isn't the choice for you. However, if you're dabbling with the idea of microdosing or wish to grow something unlike any other cube on the market, it's the perfect choice1.

History:
The original Hillbilly strain has been around since the late 1990s.
A frequent Mycotopia user known as "Hillbilly" collected and tamed the strain in Arkansas, in the Southern United States.
The Hillbilly strain occasionally throws out a fatass mushroom in a flush.
It's believed that a cultivator named "Mycology Mage" isolated spores from a large pumpkin-shaped fatass phenotype and created the Hillbilly Pumpkin strain from there.
The Hillbilly Pumpkin strain is up there with some of the most bizarre strains of Psilocybe cubensis1.

Potency & Psilocybin Content: Below Average
The Hillbilly Pumpkin strain isn't potent in terms of psychoactive compounds.
It's ideal for people who want to microdose.
The mother strain (Hillbilly) even won a spot as the "Microdose Champion" in the Spring 2022 Oakland Hyphae Psilocybin Cup1.

In **summary**, the Hillbilly Pumpkin strain offers a distinctive psychedelic experience and is perfect for those interested in microdosing or growing something truly unique.

Sources:
1. https://tripsitter.com/magic-mushrooms/strains/hillbilly-pumpkin/
2. https://healing-mushrooms.net/hillbilly-cubensis
3. https://1upmaps.com/hillbilly-pumpkin-mushrooms-strain/

The Honduran

Honduran Magic Mushrooms (also known as Honduran Cubensis) are a fascinating variety of Psilocybe cubensis mushrooms. Here's what you need to know about this strain:

Background and Characteristics:
Honduran Magic Mushrooms are known for their ease of cultivation and resilience.
They grow readily, resist contamination, and adapt well to fluctuations in climate, making them an excellent choice for beginners.
Originally found off the coast of Honduras, these mushrooms have yellowish-brown caps that taper to a point and thin stems of average length.
Their effects are fairly balanced and include visual distortions, a sense of internal introspection, and vibrations1.

Habitat:
The natural habitat of Honduran Magic Mushrooms is the Bay Islands off the coast of Honduras.
These islands provide the ideal environment for their growth and proliferation1.

Taxonomy and Naming:
Genus: Psilocybe
Species: Cubensis
Common Name: Honduran Magic Mushrooms1.

Potency: Above Average

Physical Description:
Caps: Yellowish-brown caps that are pointed on top.
Gills: Spore print produces spores.
Stipe (Stem): Thin white stems of average length with gentle curves.
Honduran Magic Mushrooms are also resistant to temperature fluctuations and contamination, making them beginner-friendly1.

In **summary**, if you are looking for a magic mushroom strain that is easy to grow and offers a balanced psychedelic experience, the Honduran Magic Mushrooms might be a great choice!1. This is for information only.

Sources:

1. https://frshminds.com/psilocybin-mushroom-species-guide/psilocybe-cubensis/honduran-magic-mushrooms/
2. https://tripsitter.com/magic-mushrooms/strains/mexicube/
3. https://tripsitter.com/magic-mushrooms/strongest/
4. https://tripsitter.com/magic-mushrooms/strains/

Huautla aka Huautla Oaxaca Strain

The **Huautla** strain of Psilocybe cubensis is closely associated with the spiritual realm and has a rich history rooted in traditional healing practices. Here are some key points about this fascinating strain:

Origin and Spiritual Significance:
The Huautla strain hails from the Sierra Mazateca in central Mexico, specifically near the village of Huautla de Jimenez.
For centuries, the Mazatec people have used hallucinogenic mushrooms for healing ceremonies, and the Huautla Oaxaca strain is at the center of this tradition.
It is considered slightly **below average** in terms of potency but maintains some stunning hallucinogenic effects and a notoriously gentle nature.
People have reported that it feels like a potent THC edible in lower doses1.

Appearance and Cultivation:
Huautla mushrooms grow tall and thin with a reddish-golden conic to hemispheric cap that can reach up to 50 mm in diameter.
Beginner shroom growers appreciate this strain for its vigor, resilience to contamination, and bountiful flushes.
It's an excellent choice for those who want to feel like an expert grower without much experience.

Historical Significance:
The Huautla strain gained fame after an article titled "Seeking the Magic Mushroom" was published in Life Magazine in 1957. The article featured the American banker and amateur ethnomycologist Robert G. Wasson, who experienced a "velada" (ceremony) with the renowned Mazatec healer Maria Sabina in Huautla. Wasson sent samples of mushrooms he collected in Huautla (believed to be the original source of the Huautla strain) to friends and researchers.
Later, Albert Hofmann identified and synthesized the active ingredients, psilocin and psilocybin, from these very mushrooms.
Maria Sabina, also known as "Saint Mary of the Holy Mushrooms," used hallucinogenic mushrooms as part of her healing ceremonies, but she faced persecution from the authorities. Despite challenges, her work continues to inspire people worldwide1.

In **summary**, the Huautla strain is a fascinating and spiritually significant mushroom strain with a rich history that intertwines traditional healing practices, scientific discovery, and cultural exploration12. This is for information only.

Sources:
1. https://tripsitter.com/magic-mushrooms/strains/huautla/
2. https://www.shamanmushroomspores.com/the-history-of-huautla-magic-mushrooms/
3. https://budlab.co/why-the-huautla-magic-mushroom-is-a-must-try-shroom/
4. https://www.mushlovegenetics.com/mushroom-spores/huaulta-mushroom-spores/

Inca Star Gazer Mushroom

Also known as the **Stargazer** Mushroom, is a strain of Psilocybe cubensis that has captured the imagination of mushroom enthusiasts. Let's explore some key details about this intriguing strain:

Origins and History:

The Stargazer Mushroom strain is believed to have originated in the foothills of the Andes Mountains, particularly around the Inca ruins at Machu Picchu.
Its name evokes images of ancient civilizations and mystical stargazing practices. However, the exact history and lineage of this strain remain somewhat mysterious and shrouded in legend1.

Cultivation and Effects:

Stargazer Mushrooms are a variety of Psilocybe cubensis, known for their potency and general ease of cultivation. Cultivating this strain involves obtaining spores and creating a sterile environment for successful growth. The effects of Stargazer Mushrooms are consistent with other Psilocybe cubensis strains, including hallucinations, altered perception, and changes in mood and thought patterns2.

Paul Stamets and J.S. Chilton:

While some sources attribute the popularity of Stargazer Mushrooms to Paul Stamets and J.S. Chilton, it's essential to clarify that they did not specifically feature this strain in their book "The Mushroom Cultivator" in 1983.
Stamets and Chilton did write about several strains of cubensis, but they were named based on their place of origin (e.g., Amazonian, Ecuadorian, Matias Romero, Misantla, and Palenque). The specific mention of the Incan Stargazer strain as we know it today is not found in their work3.

Creating New Strains:

Mycologists can create new strains by testing the compatibility of mycelia from different pre-existing strains. A strain represents a group of mushrooms that share inherited physical characteristics but are not so different as to represent a new mushroom species. While Stargazer may indeed be a distinct mushroom strain, the specifics can vary based on the breeder and the spores' source3.

In **summary**, the Inca Star Gazer Mushroom remains a captivating mystery, blending ancient legends with modern cultivation techniques. Its name alone invites us to gaze at the stars and explore the depths of our consciousness!31

Sources:

1. https://magic-mycology.com/product/stargazer/
2. https://www.seattlemet.com/discover/magic-mushrooms/stargazer-mushroom/
3. https://doubleblindmag.com/stargazer-mushroom/

Jack Frost

The **Jack Frost** strain is a captivating variant of Psilocybe cubensis, known for its unique appearance and impressive psychedelic properties.

Appearance:
Jack Frost gets its name from the aesthetics of its fruiting bodies.
It is a ghostly-white albino strain of Psilocybe cubensis.
The mushrooms produced by Jack Frost have flat caps that curl upwards, resembling a blanket of fine white spores.
The overall appearance is reminiscent of frost or snow, creating an otherworldly and beautiful effect1.

Parentage and Origins:
While the exact origin of Jack Frost remains somewhat mysterious, it is believed to be a cross between two well-known and highly popular strains:
Albino Penis Envy (APE): A potent and visually striking strain.
True Albino Teacher (TAT): Another albino strain with unique characteristics.
The combination of these two strains resulted in the creation of Jack Frost, which stands out due to its pure white coloration23.

Effects and Potency: Average
The effects of Jack Frost are likely similar to those of other Psilocybe cubensis strains. While biochemistry can vary between strains, the distinction in effects may be overshadowed by other factors such as the user's mindset and setting.
Potency can vary among different strains, and Jack Frost is no exception.
Although it tested with only a high-average psilocybin concentration in the two instances it was analyzed, anecdotal reports suggest that it might be well above average in potency. Users should exercise caution with dosing, as unexpectedly large doses can lead to unpleasant or even dangerous side effects. Starting with a smaller dose and adjusting as needed is advisable2.

Cultivation:
Jack Frost falls into the intermediate category in terms of cultivation difficulty.
It can be somewhat picky about temperature, so maintaining stable and slightly warmer temperatures is essential for optimal yield.
Gentle handling is crucial for those who prefer a truly white mushroom, as rough handling can lead to blue bruising (common in Psilocybe cubensis) and a bluish appearance in dried specimens2.

In **summary**, Jack Frost is not only visually stunning but also offers a unique psychedelic experience. Its ghostly appearance and potential potency make it a sought-after strain among mushroom enthusiasts and cultivators21.

Sources:
1. https://tripsitter.com/magic-mushrooms/strains/jack-frost/
2. https://healing-mushrooms.net/jack-frost
3. https://goldenteacherspores.org/magic-mushroom-strain-info/jack-frost-magic-mushroom-psilocybe-cubensis/
4. https://realitysandwich.com/jack-frost-mushrooms/

Jalisco (Mexican)

The **Jalisco** strain of Psilocybe cubensis is a lesser-known but intriguing variety of magic mushrooms. Let's delve into the details of this strain:

Origin and Background:
The Jalisco strain is believed to originate from the Jalisco region in Mexico.
Like many other Psilocybe cubensis strains, it has a rich history rooted in traditional indigenous practices. Indigenous cultures in Mexico have used magic mushrooms for centuries in their spiritual ceremonies and healing rituals.

Characteristics:
While specific physical characteristics of the Jalisco strain may vary, it shares common features with other cubensis mushrooms.
These mushrooms typically have a conic to hemispheric cap, which can reach a diameter of around 50 mm.
The stem is usually white and may exhibit some variations.
Cultivating the Jalisco strain is considered moderate in terms of difficulty.

Potency and Psilocybin Content: Average to above average
Unfortunately, there is no quantitative data available specifically for the potency of the Jalisco strain.
However, anecdotal reports suggest that this mushroom is potent.
Mycologists emphasize that optimal growing conditions and proper harvesting play a crucial role in determining potency.
Typical cubensis mushrooms contain anywhere from 0.5% to 1% psilocybin content in dry weight. Without specialized lab testing, it's challenging to precisely measure the psilocybin content of home-grown shrooms.

Cultivation:
The Jalisco strain is suitable for both beginners and experienced cultivators.
It responds well to various substrates, including rye grain, manure, BRF, PWS, and concentrated flour. If you're interested in growing the Jalisco strain, you can find spore samples from various vendors.

In **summary**, the Jalisco strain offers a unique psychedelic experience, and its origins in Mexico connect it to ancient traditions and cultural practices1. If you decide to explore this strain, may your journey be enlightening and transformative!

Sources:
1. https://tripsitter.com/magic-mushrooms/strains/mexicana/
2. https://tripsitter.com/magic-mushrooms/strains/palenque/
3. https://magic-mycology.com/the-ultimate-guide-to-psilocybin-mushroom-strains-varieties-origins-and-effects/

Jedi Mind F***

The **Jedi Mind F***** (JMF) strain of Psilocybe cubensis is a captivating and enigmatic variety of magic mushrooms. Let's explore the intriguing aspects of this strain:

Potency and Effects: Average
Despite its epic name, JMF doesn't quite live up to the level of potency that its reputation suggests.
Analytical data currently available on this mushroom places JMF within the standard range considered average for Psilocybe cubensis strains.
However, many trip reports online describe intense visual and auditory hallucinations, feelings of euphoria, and introspection associated with JMF.
While it might not be a full-blown "mind fuck," it still offers a unique psychedelic experience1.

Cultivation Difficulty:
JMF is a stubborn strain to cultivate.
It is not as resistant to contamination as many beginner-friendly strains.
Additionally, JMF is slower to fruit, requiring patience and attention during the growing process.

Origins and Name:
The name "Jedi Mind F***" draws inspiration from the Star Wars universe.
In Star Wars lore, the Jedi are warrior monks who use the Force to influence thoughts and emotions subtly.
JMF shrooms are associated with powerful effects on the mind, leading to their unique name.
While the Jedi Mind Fuck strain hasn't been around as long as some other classic strains, it emerged in the early 2000s.
Its origins remain somewhat mysterious, with various stories suggesting genetic off-shoots or wild discoveries by mycologists1.

Cultivation Recommendations:
JMF responds well to rye grain as a substrate.
If you're interested in growing JMF, you can find spore samples from various vendors.

In **summary**, while JMF may not be the mind-bending experience its name implies, it still offers a fascinating journey into altered perception and introspection.

Sources:
1. https://tripsitter.com/magic-mushrooms/strains/jedi-mind-fuck/
2. https://psychedelicspotlight.com/a-misnomer-in-mushrooms-the-jedi-mind-fuck-strain/
3. https://mushroomsporestore.com/the-science-behind-jedi-mind-fuck-mushroom-spores-strain-and-psyche/
4. https://healing-mushrooms.net/jedi-mind-fuck

Jesus Christ Super Strain

Jesus Christ Super Strain of Psilocybe cubensis is renowned for its potent effects, which can vary from person to person. Here are some common effects reported by users:

Visual Distortions and Hallucinations:
Users often experience vivid visual alterations, such as:
Color enhancement: Colors appear more vibrant and intense.

Patterns and shapes: Walls, surfaces, and objects may display intricate patterns, fractals, or geometric shapes.
Morphing and breathing: Objects may seem to shift, warp, or breathe.

Euphoria and Emotional Intensity:
Many users report a profound sense of joy, interconnectedness, and emotional openness. The experience can be deeply introspective, leading to insights about one's life, relationships, and purpose.

Spiritual and Mystical Experiences:
Some users describe encounters with a sense of unity with the universe, akin to spiritual or mystical states.
Themes of interconnectedness, divine presence, and cosmic understanding may emerge.

Time Distortion:
The perception of time can become altered. Minutes may feel like hours, and hours like minutes.

Body Sensations:
Users may feel a sense of lightness, warmth, or energy flowing through their bodies.
Some report physical sensations like tingling or waves of energy.

Enhanced Creativity and Insight:
The altered state of consciousness can lead to creative breakthroughs, new perspectives, and problem-solving abilities.

Ego Dissolution:
Some users experience a dissolution of the ego—the sense of self—leading to feelings of interconnectedness with all existence.

Intensity and Set and Setting:
The effects can be intense, so a supportive and safe environment (the "set and setting") is crucial.
The mindset and emotional state of the user significantly influence the experience.
Remember that individual responses vary, and some users may have challenging or difficult trips. Always approach psychedelics with respect, caution, and proper preparation. If you choose to explore the Jesus Christ Super Strain, do so in a responsible and informed manner.

The Jesus Christ Super Strain is a specific variety of Psilocybe cubensis, a species of psychedelic mushroom known for its psychoactive compound psilocybin. Psilocybin is renowned for inducing altered states of consciousness, often accompanied by profound insights, introspection, and even mystical experiences1.

The name "Jesus Christ Super Strain" likely stems from the potent and transformative experiences reported by users, drawing parallels to spiritual and divine encounters. This strain shares the general characteristics of Psilocybe cubensis mushrooms. They typically have a pale to golden-brown cap with a distinctive conical shape that flattens with age. The undersides of the caps feature dark gills that mature to a purplish-brown color, while the stem is slender and white, often displaying a bluish hue where damaged.

Potency:

The strain is said to be **highly potent,** containing varying levels of psilocybin, which contributes to its reputation for inducing intense experiences. Throughout history, cultures around the world have used psychedelic substances, including Psilocybe cubensis, as tools for spiritual exploration and connection. The super strain is no exception. Users have reported experiences that are deeply introspective, emotionally charged, and sometimes even visionary. Many describe encounters with a sense of unity with the universe, experiences of ego dissolution, and a feeling of interconnectedness with all life forms. The name "Jesus Christ Super Strain" could suggest a perceived ability of the mushroom to facilitate experiences akin to those of spiritual figures like Jesus Christ, who is associated with profound teachings and spiritual insights. Some users claim to have encountered archetypal and divine symbols during their experiences, leading them to believe in a higher purpose and interconnectedness of all existence. It's important to note that these experiences are highly subjective and can vary greatly from person to person.

Summary:

While some individuals may interpret their encounters through a religious or spiritual lens, others might view them as purely psychological phenomena or extensions of their subconscious thoughts and feelings1.

 The Jesus Christ Super Strain of Psilocybe cubensis exemplifies the intriguing intersection of psychedelics, spirituality, and personal experiences. Its name suggests a potential for profound, transformative encounters that evoke parallels to spiritual figures and teachings. Remember that these experiences are highly subjective and can vary greatly from person to person. While some individuals may interpret their encounters through a religious or spiritual lens, others might view them as purely psychological phenomena or extensions of their subconscious thoughts and feelings1.

Sources:

1. https://mycologynow.com/mystical-mushrooms-jesus-christ-super-strain/
2. https://www.spores101.co/jesus-christ-super-strain.html
3. https://www.fungiculturestore.com/product-page/jesus-christ-super-strain

John Allen Strain

The **Allen** Psilocybe Cubensis strain holds a special place in the captivating world of magic mushrooms. Let's unravel the legacy of this strain, which is named after the ethnomycologist "Mushroom" John Allen1.

Origins and Discovery:
The Allen strain is believed to be an offshoot of the renowned Thai strain.
Its roots trace back to a curious find in a sample of elephant dung several decades ago.
Mushroom John Allen, an adventurous explorer of shroom strains, discovered it during his travels through Southeast Asia, primarily Thailand, in the 1990s.
Mushroom John collected various samples during his explorations, inadvertently sowing the seeds for the future of magic mushroom exploration1.

Distinct Characteristics:
The Allen Psilocybe Cubensis strain is revered for its unique traits:
Rapid colonization times: It quickly takes over its substrate during cultivation.
Distinct bulbous caps: These caps flatten out with astonishing speed as the mushrooms mature.
Mushroom John's reputation as a renowned explorer of shroom strains worldwide further enhances the mystique surrounding the Allen strain.
Other strains he discovered include Ban Hua Thanon, Burma, Cambodian, Corumba, Hanoi, Kathmandu, Malaysian, Thai (from which came the lipa-yai and pink-Buffalo), and many others1.

Potency: Average

Cultivation and Appeal:
For beginners, the Allen Psilocybe Cubensis strain proves to be an excellent choice.
It offers rapid colonization and robust resistance to mold and disease.
Cultivators embarking on the art of mushroom cultivation witness the magic of mycelium and the transformation of the substrate into flourishing mushrooms.
The legacy of the original stock collected by Mushroom John persists to this day, as vendors continue to cultivate and distribute these unique lineages by obtaining spores from various sources1.

In **summary**, the Allen strain, with its intriguing history and captivating characteristics, continues to enchant both growers and users in the world of magic mushrooms1.

Sources:
1. https://mushly.com/learn/allen-psilocybe-cubensis-unraveling-the-legacy-of-mushroom-johns-discovery/
2. https://frshminds.com/psilocybin-mushroom-species-guide/psilocybe-cubensis/allen/
3. https://microzoomers.co/strains/allen-strain/

Kathmandu

The **Kathmandu strain** (KATH) is a fascinating Psilocybe cubensis variety with several distinctive features. Let's explore this mysterious Nepalese strain. The exact origin of the Kathmandu strain remains somewhat mysterious.
It was collected near the capital of Nepal, Kathmandu, but the identity of the first collector remains unclear. Some speculate that the famous entomologist John Allen discovered it during his travels in search of new specimens. However, there is no definitive proof to support this claim. Nepal has a rich history of psychedelic use, with naturally occurring psychedelics being commonplace in rural areas. From psychoactive honey to hallucinogenic plants and mushrooms, Nepal has long been associated with spiritual exploration. Despite the lack of detailed information about its origins, Kathmandu's presence in Nepal aligns with the country's tradition of seeking spiritual enlightenment through natural substances1.

Overview:
Kathmandu is a well-balanced and easy-to-grow strain, making it an excellent choice for beginners venturing into mushroom cultivation. Unlike some strains that excel in specific areas, Kathmandu offers a harmonious combination of attributes:
Fast colonization: It quickly takes over its substrate during cultivation.
Contamination resistance: It is forgiving and less prone to contamination.
Ease of fruiting: Kathmandu produces decent yields without requiring excessive effort.
Medium-sized fruiting bodies: The mushrooms have a long pale stem and a large tan-colored cap.
Ease of spore collection: Collecting spores from mature mushrooms is straightforward.
Overall, Kathmandu provides a balanced experience for growers and users alike1.

Potency and Effects:
While precise potency data is unavailable, trip reports suggest that Kathmandu falls within the **above-average potency range**. Estimated combined psilocybin and psilocin levels (dried weight) are between 0.9% and 1.8% based on various reports.
Users describe effects similar to other potent strains, including bodily vibrations, light visual stimulation, and an overwhelming sense of calm. Kathmandu has been compared to strains like South American, Albino Melmac, and Penis Envy1.

Genetic Relatives:
The Kathmandu strain is believed to be derived from the Chitwan strain.
It shares similarities with another regional strain called Orissa India.
Both Kathmandu and Chitwan exhibit comparable potency and appearance, but Kathmandu is considered easier to grow due to its excellent contamination resistance and aggressive colonization speed12.
In summary, the Kathmandu strain offers a well-rounded and intriguing psychedelic experience, making it an excellent choice for novice cultivators and curious explorers alike.
Sources –
1. https://tripsitter.com/magic-mushrooms/strains/kathmandu/
2. https://tripsitter.com/magic-mushrooms/strains/chitwan/
3. https://www.lilshopofspores.com/cgi/display.cgi?item_num=4140&title=-Psilocybe-cubensis-Kathmandu-Spores

Keepers Creepers

The **Creeper** mushroom strain, also known as Keepers Creepers, has an intriguing history and remains somewhat mysterious.

Origins and Controversy:
The Creeper mushrooms were first sold by a Shroomery user known as "The Keeper." However, there's considerable debate about whether the Creeper strain truly deserves the title of a unique strain or not. The Keeper faced criticism for allegedly rebranding existing mushroom strains and significantly increasing their prices. Some speculate that Keepers Creepers might actually be a rebranded version of the Cambodian strain, while others suggest similarities to the Hawaiian or Tasmanian strains1.

Appearance:
Creeper mushrooms have caps that are the same width as their stems.
The caps exhibit bright golden colors, while the stems are pale.
When touched prior to drying, the pale stems easily bruise blue. This bluing is an indicator of psilocybin content in the magic mushrooms23.

Potency and Effects:
Despite the controversy surrounding its origins, Creeper mushrooms are considered **average** in potency. Users describe the trip produced by Creeper mushrooms as unlike anything else they've experienced.
Some trip reports suggest that the experience can be a bit "darker" than other strains, with a tendency to quite literally "creep up on you."
Whether this perception is influenced by the mushroom's name or other factors remains a topic of speculation1.

Cultivation and Cost:
Creeper mushrooms are suitable for beginner cultivation.
Recommended substrates include rye grain or brown rice flour.
Vendors like Ralphsters Spores, Premium Spores, Spore Store, and Hidden Forest Spore Store offer Creeper spores. The original name "Keepers Creepers" has been dropped by most vendors, and they now sell them simply as "Creepers" without the obnoxiously high price tag1.

Psilocybin Content:
Creeper mushrooms are considered slightly **above average** in terms of potency.
The average tryptamine content (psilocybin and psilocin) is estimated to be around 1.3%, but individual results may vary. Unfortunately, no samples of Creeper shrooms were entered into the 2021 Psilocybin Cup, so we cannot use those results as a resource to determine potency1.

In **summary**, the Creeper strain remains a subject of debate, but its unique appearance, effects, and moderate potency make it an interesting addition to the world of magic mushrooms! For information purposes only.

Sources:
1. https://tripsitter.com/magic-mushrooms/strains/creepers/
2. https://psychedelicsadventure.com/product/creeper-magic-mushrooms/
3. https://frshminds.com/psilocybin-mushroom-species-guide/psilocybe-cubensis/keepers-creeper-magic-mushrooms/
4. https://shroomystore.com/?product=creeper-magic-mushrooms

Koh Samui

The **Koh Samui** strain of Psilocybe cubensis is a captivating and unique variety of magic mushrooms. Let's explore the fascinating aspects of this strain:

Origins and Debate:
Koh Samui mushrooms are associated with the beautiful island of Koh Samui in Thailand. There's some debate about the exact species of these mushrooms:
Most commonly, Koh Samui refers to a particular strain of Psilocybe cubensis that was collected from the island by the amateur mycologist Mushroom John Allen in the 1990s. However, there's also a separate species called Psilocybe samuiensis, which contains psilocybin but is not commonly found online.
Some experts even place Koh Samui mushrooms under the Mexicanae genus rather than Psilocybe cubensis due to their rhomboid-shaped spores and ability to grow sclerotia (compact growth in the mycelium containing food reserves).
Despite the debate, most experts still consider Koh Samui mushrooms to be a strain of Psilocybe cubensis1.

Potency: Average

Characteristics:
Koh Samui mushrooms are known for their:
Fast-growing mycelium: They colonize substrates rapidly.
Contaminant resistance: They are forgiving and less prone to contamination.
Dense clusters: Although not very tall, they proliferate in thick clusters.
These mushrooms have been used in traditional Thai medicine to treat various ailments, including fatigue, anxiety, and depression. They are also believed to improve cognitive function and memory.
The high from Koh Samui mushrooms is formidable but not the strongest available. Users experience strong visual hallucinations, energy, and euphoria.
Quantitative analysis suggests an average psilocybin content of around 0.63%1.

Cultivation and Availability:
Koh Samui mushrooms are beginner-friendly and grow well on rye grain substrates.

In **summary**, the Koh Samui strain offers a balanced and intriguing psychedelic experience, making it a favorite among both cultivators and psychonauts.12

Sources:

1. https://tripsitter.com/magic-mushrooms/strains/koh-samui/
2. https://lordofspore.com/product/psilocybe-cubensis/koh-samui-super-strain/
3. https://completemyco.com/blogs/complete-university/strain-highlight-koh-samui-ss
4. https://goldenteacherspores.org/magic-mushroom-strain-info/koh-samui-magic-mushroom-psilocybe-cubensis/

KSSS

The **Koh Samui Super Strain** (KSSS) is an exotic variety of Psilocybe
cubensis mushrooms that has captured the interest of psychonauts and cultivators alike.
Let's delve into the intriguing aspects of this strain:

Origins and Debate:
The KSSS strain is associated with Koh Samui, a beautiful island in Thailand.
There's some debate about the exact species of these mushrooms:
Most commonly, KSSS refers to a particular strain of Psilocybe cubensis that was
collected from Koh Samui by the amateur mycologist Mushroom John Allen in the 1990s.
However, there's also a separate species called Psilocybe samuiensis, which contains
psilocybin but is not commonly found online.
Some experts even place KSSS mushrooms under the Mexicanae genus rather than
Psilocybe cubensis due to their rhomboid-shaped spores and ability to
grow sclerotia (compact growth in the mycelium containing food reserves).
Despite the debate, most experts still consider KSSS mushrooms to be a strain of
Psilocybe cubensis1.

Potency: Average

Characteristics:
KSSS mushrooms are known for their:
Fast-growing mycelium: They colonize substrates rapidly.
Contaminant resistance: They are forgiving and less prone to contamination.
Dense clusters: Although not very tall, they proliferate in thick clusters.
These mushrooms have been used in traditional Thai medicine to treat various ailments,
including fatigue, anxiety, and depression. They are also said to improve cognitive
function and memory.
The high from KSSS mushrooms is formidable but not the strongest available. Users
experience strong visual hallucinations, energy, and euphoria.
Quantitative analysis suggests an average psilocybin content of around 0.63%1.

Cultivation and Availability:
KSSS mushrooms are beginner-friendly and grow well on rye grain substrates.

In **summary**, the Koh Samui Super Strain offers a balanced and intriguing psychedelic
experience, making it a favorite among both cultivators and curious explorers.12

Sources:
1. https://tripsitter.com/magic-mushrooms/strains/koh-samui/
2. https://myyco.com/product/koh-samui-super-strain-liquid-culture/
3. https://mushroom-growing.com/ksss-mushroom/
4. https://unclekief.co/unveiling-the-magic-your-complete-guide-to-ksss-spores-and-cultivating-the-ultimate-fungi-experience/
5. https://microzoomers.co/strains/kho-samui-super-strain/

KSSS Peyote

The **KSSS Peyote** Mushroom, also known as the Koh Samui Super Strain Peyote, is a unique and sought-after variety of Psilocybe cubensis. Let's explore some key details about this intriguing strain:

Origin and Name:
The KSSS Peyote Mushroom is believed to have originated from the island of Koh Samui in Thailand.
Its name is inspired by the appearance of its fruiting bodies, which tend to resemble peyote buttons (the small, round, and dense cacti known for their psychoactive properties).

Characteristics:
The KSSS Peyote strain shares lineage with the Koh Samui Super Strain (KSSS), which is highly sought after in the mycology community.
The mushrooms themselves are small, round, and dense, with light brown caps that may develop white spots.
Unlike some other strains, KSSS Peyote does not readily drop spore prints. Therefore, spores must be collected directly from the gills using clean and sterile spore swabs.

Cultivation and Research:
When you buy KSSS Peyote spores, they are considered "active spores" meant for microscopy purposes only.
Researchers and enthusiasts use these spores for microscopy research to study their unique characteristics.
The strain's rarity and difficult-to-acquire spores make each swab valuable for scientific exploration.

Potency: Average to above Average

Disclaimer:
It's essential to note that KSSS Peyote spores are not for cultivation or germination purposes. Shipping of these spores is unavailable to certain states (such as California, Idaho, and Georgia) due to legal restrictions.

In **summary**, the KSSS Peyote Mushroom offers a fascinating blend of rarity, unique appearance, and scientific interest. Remember that these spores are for research purposes only, and their cultivation is strictly prohibited.12

Sources:
1.　https://sonoranspores.com/product/ksss-peyote-swabs/
2.　https://www.spores101.co/peyote-ksss.html
3.　https://mushroom-growing.com/ksss-mushroom/

La Primavera –

The La Primavera strain of Psilocybe cubensis is a lesser-known variety that has its origins in Italy. Unfortunately, detailed information about this specific strain is limited.
(I will update this strain when more info become available.)

Leucistic Golden Teacher (LGT)

Leucistic Golden Teacher is a fascinating variant of the Psilocybe cubensis mushroom strain. Let's delve into the details:

Origin and Discovery:
LGT is believed to have been discovered in the 1980s on a farm in Georgia.
It is a mutation of the original Golden Teacher variant, which is already well-known for its psychedelic properties[12].

Appearance:
Unlike the typical Golden Teacher, LGT exhibits leucism, not albinism.
Leucism results in a loss of pigment in the fruiting bodies (mushrooms), leading to pale-white traits.
The gills of LGT can vary from whitish to purple-brown.
Clear spores distinguish LGT from true albino strains[3].

Cultivation and Effects:
Cultivating LGT follows similar methods as other Psilocybe cubensis strains.
The potency of LGT is comparable to that of the regular Golden Teacher.
Users report psychedelic effects such as altered perception, enhanced visuals, introspection, and a sense of wonder.
LGT offers a unique twist for those seeking a different experience within the Golden Teacher family[42].

Potency: Average

In **summary**, Leucistic Golden Teacher mushrooms provide an intriguing variation on the classic Golden Teacher strain, inviting psychonauts to explore their magical properties. [42].

Sources:
1. https://lordofspore.com/product/psilocybe-cubensis/golden-teacher-luecistic/
2. https://medium.com/@LeucisticGoldenTeacherMushroom/an-insight-into-leucistic-golden-teacher-mushrooms-b8c50cc3e695
3. https://inoculatetheworld.com/product/leucistic-golden-teacher-lgt-isolated-syringe/
4. https://www.shroomery.org/forums/showflat.php/Number/24252629

Liberty Cap

The **Liberty Cap** (Psilocybe semilanceata) is one of the planet's most potent psilocybin-containing mushroom species. Although small and sometimes elusive, these mushrooms pack a punch, producing waves of intense euphoria and vivid closed and open-eye visuals1. Here are some key points about the Liberty Cap strain:

Names and Iconic Appearance:
The Liberty Cap goes by several names, including **Witches Hats, Wizard Caps, Snow Caps, Blue Legs, and Pixie Caps**.
Its iconic appearance features a distinct nipple on the top of its conical cap.
The dark brown gills and light brown, thin stems propel the small cap above the grass line where they grow.

History and First Recorded Psilocybin Trip in Europe:
The Liberty Cap has a deep history. It was responsible for the first recorded psilocybin-induced psychedelic trip in Europe.
In 1799, a man accidentally consumed Liberty Caps for breakfast, leading to a powerful psychedelic experience1.

Potency and Effects: **Extremely potent**
Liberty Caps are **strongly psychedelic**. Only a few of these mushrooms are needed to experience a potent psilocybin-induced trip.
After Psilocybe cubensis, the Liberty Cap strain is perhaps one of the most famous and well-known Psilocybe species on the planet, especially in Europe.
Its image is almost as familiar as the Amanita muscaria (Fly Agaric) mushroom and has been used to portray psychedelic mushrooms worldwide.

Availability and Natural Growth:
Liberty Caps cannot be cultivated and are seasonal mushrooms.
They grow in pastures and highlands, often popping up suddenly from beneath tufts of grass.
To experience the power of the Liberty Cap, one must venture into nature to find where they grow.

In **summary**, the Liberty Cap is a small but mighty mushroom with a rich history and a reputation for intense psychedelic effects. Its iconic appearance has been associated with "magic mushrooms" for decades, making it a recognizable symbol in the world of psychedelics1.

Sources:

1. https://tripsitter.com/psilocybe-semilanceata/
2. https://thehigh.guide/mushroom-strain-liberty-cap/
3. https://doubleblindmag.com/mushrooms/types/psilocybe-cubensis-magic-mushrooms/
4. https://doubleblindmag.com/mushrooms/types/liberty-caps/

Lipa Yai (Thai)

Lipa Yai is a Thai strain of the Psilocybe cubensis species. Although it might not be as well-known as some other strains, it has its own unique characteristics and history. Let's explore the fascinating aspects of the Lipa Yai strain:

Origins and Discovery:
The Lipa Yai strain was collected by the legendary Mushroom John Allen during his travels through Southeast Asia in the early 1990s.
Mushroom John Allen is responsible for collecting dozens of popular strains that are still in circulation today. Lipa Yai was discovered in a small town called Lipa Yai, which is located in Thailand. It is closely related to the famous Koh Samui strain, as both were collected around the same area.

Appearance and Growth:
Lipa Yai mushrooms share similarities with the Koh Samui strain but have a few key differences. While Koh Samui is famous for producing "fatasses" (short, stumpy mushrooms), Lipa Yai has a higher affinity for producing tall, slim fruiting bodies.
The caps of Lipa Yai mushrooms are saucer-like, ranging from light to dark brown.
Despite their slimmer appearance, Lipa Yai mushrooms are medium to large in size.

Potency and Effects:
Lipa Yai is said to have **average potency,** but there are conflicting reports.
Some users claim it is just as potent as Koh Samui, while others describe it as average. Unfortunately, until more analytical data is published, the true psilocybin content of Lipa Yai remains uncertain. Testing suggests an average potency of approximately 0.66% psilocybin, 0.05% psilocin, and 0.75% total tryptamines (psilocybin + psilocin + baeocystin + other related compounds).

Cultivation and Availability:
Lipa Yai mushrooms are relatively easy to cultivate.
Spore samples are available from various vendors, including Spores 101, Ralphsters, and The Magic Mushrooms Shop.

Spiritual and Recreational Use in Thailand:
Lipa Yai, along with other Thai strains of Psilocybe cubensis, has been used spiritually and recreationally in Thailand for centuries.
Despite being technically illegal, people in Thailand still consume these mushrooms openly, especially in the southern island regions.
During the famous annual Full Moon Party on Koh Phangan's beach, thousands of people consume Lipa Yai and Koh Samui mushrooms under the moonlit sky.

In **summary**, Lipa Yai is an underrated strain with a rich history and unique characteristics. Its close relationship with the Koh Samui strain and its popularity in Thailand make it a fascinating addition to the world of magic mushrooms. 12
Sources:
1.	https://tripsitter.com/magic-mushrooms/strains/lipa-yai/
2.	https://www.en.psilosophy.info/species/psilocybe_cubensis_thailand_lipa_yai.htm
3.	https://www.spores101.co/lipa-yai-thai-mushroom-spores.html

Lightwave

Lightwave is a unique hybrid that combines the characteristics of two other potent strains: Albino A+ and Tidalwave. Let's explore this fascinating strain:

Origins and Genetics:
Lightwave is the result of a cross between Albino A+ and Tidalwave.
Albino A+ is a leucistic variety, known for its reduced pigmentation and distinct appearance. Tidalwave mushrooms are a hybrid of Penis Envy and B+, making them one of the most potent varieties ever tested12.

Appearance:
While specific details about the appearance of Lightwave mushrooms may vary, they likely exhibit a blend of characteristics from their parent strains.
Albino A+ contributes its leucistic features, while Tidalwave adds its potency and unique visual appeal.

Psychedelic Effects:
As a hybrid, Lightwave is expected to offer a psychedelic experience characterized by:
Mesmerizing Visuals: Users may experience intense visual distortions and hallucinations.
Introspection: Deep self-reflection and insights.
Euphoria: Feelings of joy and interconnectedness.
Heightened Creativity: A boost in creative thinking.
Due to its parentage, Lightwave could be a powerful strain for those seeking a transformative journey32.

Potency and Caution: possibly very potent
Lightwave's potency likely combines the psilocybin levels of Albino A+ and Tidalwave.
Users should approach this strain with caution, especially if they are new to psychedelics.
Starting with a smaller dose is advisable to gauge individual sensitivity and response3.

Cultivation:
Growing Lightwave mushrooms may require some expertise due to their unique genetics.
Cultivators should consider factors like substrate, humidity, and temperature to optimize growth.
Patience and attention to detail are essential for a successful cultivation process3.

In **summary**, the Lightwave mushroom strain offers a blend of potency, visual allure, and transformative effects. Whether you're a seasoned psychonaut or a curious explorer, encountering Lightwave mushrooms can be both enlightening and awe-inspiring32. This is for information purposes only.

Sources:
1. https://thickspores.com/product/lightwave-liquid-culture-syringe/
2. https://psychedelicspotlight.com/tidal-wave-mushrooms-your-comprehensive-guide-to-one-of-the-most-potent-varieties-ever-tested/
3. https://magic-mycology.com/the-ultimate-guide-to-psilocybin-mushroom-strains-varieties-origins-and-effects/

Lizard King

The **Lizard King** is a strain of Psilocybe cubensis, a species of magic mushrooms. It has an intriguing history and unique characteristics. Here's what we know about the Lizard King strain:

Origins and Conflicting Stories:
The Lizard King strain has several conflicting stories associated with its discovery.
Some sources claim it was discovered by a mycologist who called himself the "Lizard King."
Others suggest it was named in honor of Jim Morrison, the charismatic frontman of The Doors, who referred to himself as the "Lizard King."
The strain's original habitat was a mixture of dung and wood, which adds to its mystique.

Physical Characteristics:
Lizard King mushrooms have a typical cube shape but stand out due to their very pale stems.
The caps are usually beige, and their shape can make them appear more substantial than their actual size.

Effects and Potency:
Lizard King is a typical Psilocybe cubensis strain in terms of effects.
Users can expect alterations in mood, thinking style, and perception.
It is reputed to have less "body load" (physical effects) than most P. cubensis varieties. As with any mushroom strain, trip experiences can vary significantly based on individual factors.

Potency:
Lizard King is considered **medium to high potency** compared to other cubes.
However, actual testing for average psilocybin content remains unclear.

In **summary**, the Lizard King strain is a fascinating addition to the world of magic mushrooms, with its unique history and reported effects. As always, caution and responsible use are essential when exploring any psychedelic substance.

Sources:
1. https://healing-mushrooms.net/lizard-king
2. https://completemyco.com/blogs/complete-university/strain-highlight-lizard-king
3. https://psychi.com/mushrooms/what-are-lizard-king-mushrooms/
4. https://www.floweravedc.com/post/lizard-king-magic-mushroom-strain-profile-and-review

Madagascar

Madagascar strain of magic mushrooms, also known as Psilocybe cubensis Madagascar, is an intriguing variety within the world of psilocybin-containing fungi. Let's explore the key details about this strain:

Appearance and Characteristics:
Madagascar mushrooms belong to the species Psilocybe cubensis, which is one of the most common magic mushroom species.
While there are various strains within the Cubensis species, each with unique characteristics, the Madagascar strain stands out for its specific features.
Unfortunately, detailed information about the visual appearance of the Madagascar strain is not readily available in the sources. However, it likely shares some common traits with other Cubensis strains, such as medium-sized mushrooms with domed caps and varying colors.

Potency and Effects:
The potency of Madagascar mushrooms can vary, but they typically fall within the **average range** for Psilocybe cubensis strains.
Users of Madagascar report effects consistent with other psilocybin-containing mushrooms:
Altered perception, Visual distortions, Euphoria, Introspection. As with any psychedelic substance, individual experiences may vary based on factors like dosage, set, and setting.

Cultivation and Availability:
Psilocybe cubensis mushrooms, including the Madagascar strain, are widely cultivated by enthusiasts and researchers.
Spores for the Madagascar strain are available from various vendors, allowing cultivators to explore this unique variety.
Cultivation methods for Cubensis strains are well-documented and accessible for home growers.

In **summary**, the Madagascar strain offers a familiar yet intriguing experience for those interested in exploring altered states of consciousness. Whether you're a seasoned psychonaut or a curious explorer, encountering Madagascar mushrooms can lead to moments of introspection and wonder.12.

Sources:

https://www.psychedelicpassage.com/psychedelic-mushroom-strains-by-potency-30-popular-varieties/
https://magic-mycology.com/the-ultimate-guide-to-psilocybin-mushroom-strains-varieties-origins-and-effects/
https://www.leafly.com/strains/madagascar
https://reliablespores.com/product/madagascar-spore-syringe/

Makilla Gorilla

Makilla Gorilla mushroom strain is a relatively new cultivated variety of Psilocybe cubensis. Here are some key points about this intriguing strain:

Origins and Genetics:
Makilla Gorilla was developed through crossbreeding two other strains: Albino Penis Envy (APE) and Melmac.
Both APE and Melmac are themselves derived from the famous Penis Envy strain, known for its potency and distinctive appearance (due to its narrow cap that resembles a phallus).
Unlike its ancestors, Makilla Gorilla doesn't inherit the phallic appearance, but it does share some genetic lineage with them1.

Appearance:
Makilla Gorilla mushrooms produce large fruiting bodies.
The stem is thick, meaty, and often bruised blue.
The cap is moderately sized and has a pale caramel color.
Interestingly, the flesh of this mushroom is unusually dense, which means it's essential to use a scale rather than eyeballing doses to ensure accurate measurements1.

Effects:
Makilla Gorilla is reputed to be very visual, likely due to its potency and density.
Like most Psilocybe cubensis strains, it alters mood, fosters different thought patterns, and causes hallucinations (especially at higher doses).
Users may experience a "body high" and other effects, which can vary based on dose size, mindset, setting, and individual biochemistry1.

Potency and Dosage: High Potency
The prospect of a giant mushroom that is also **unusually potent** can be both exciting and intimidating.
Any degree of intensity, from microdosing to heroic doses, is possible with any psilocybin mushroom, provided the dose is right.
With high-potency strains like Makilla Gorilla, it's crucial to be cautious not to take too much. Accidental high doses can lead to unexpected side effects.
Taking less than desired is safer than accidentally taking too much, especially with a mushroom as potent as Makilla Gorilla1.

In **summary**, Makilla Gorilla is a fusion of genetics from Albino Penis Envy and Melmac, resulting in a highly potent strain that offers deep psychedelic experiences. Whether you're seeking visual distortions or a profound journey, this unique strain might be worth exploring! Remember this is for information purposes only.

Sources:
1.   https://healing-mushrooms.net/makilla-gorilla
2.   https://thinkmushrooms.ca/makilla-gorilla-mushroom-review/
3.   https://3amigos.co/shop/dried-magic-mushrooms/makilla-gorilla/

Malabar India

The **Malabar** India strain of Psilocybe cubensis is a sought-after variety known for its impressive characteristics. Let's explore the fascinating aspects of this strain:

Origins and Discovery:
The Malabar India strain was originally collected from the southwestern Malabar Coast of India.
The first sample was supposedly found growing in elephant dung.
Spore samples have been circulating the market since the early 1990s, gaining popularity among amateur and commercial cultivators.

Appearance and Yield:
Malabar India mushrooms aren't particularly remarkable unless they reach enormous sizes.
They have golden brown caps and long, white, moderately thick stems associated with "a typical cube."
Some home cultivators have grown mushrooms that weigh as much as 250 grams fresh, and cultivators at Sporeslab have reported fruits weighing over one pound (453 grams) wet.

Potency and Psilocybin Content:
The Malabar strain is rated as "**above average**" in potency.
It can produce between 0.90% and 1.80% total tryptamines.
Users can expect vivid visual distortions, an intense body high, and deep introspection from a three-gram dose.

Cultivation and Availability:
Malabar India spore samples can be purchased from major vendors across the United States, Canada, and Europe.
It is considered a good choice for both beginner and experienced cultivators due to its impressive yield potential and respectable psilocybin content.

In **summary**, the Malabar India strain stands out for its large fruits and above-average potency. Whether you're a new or seasoned cultivator, this strain offers a rewarding psychedelic experience. 123

Sources:
1. https://tripsitter.com/magic-mushrooms/strains/malabar/
2. https://healing-mushrooms.net/malabar-mushroom
3. https://microzoomers.co/strains/malabar-coast-cubensis/

Malaysian

The **Malaysian** strain of Psilocybe cubensis is a unique and intriguing variety known for its distinctive characteristics. Let's explore what makes this strain special:

Appearance:
Malaysian mushrooms have wavy, cream-white stems with rounded golden-brown caps. As they mature, white spots on the caps give them an almost toadstool-like appearance, although these spots fade over time.
The veils hide the gills of these mushrooms until the very last minute, giving the caps a dome-like look that can seem almost alien.

Potency and Effects: Average
The potency of the Malaysian strain is roughly average compared to other Psilocybe cubensis strains.
However, Malaysian mushrooms often break their own rules:
Some produce large, flat caps, defying typical expectations.
Changes in pigmentation and even albino shrooms have been observed from a single genetic sample.
Occasionally, you might encounter underpowered mushrooms or others that seem to deliver an intense experience with just a few grams.

History and Origins:
The Malaysian strain's history remains mysterious.
Allegedly, a mycologist named MJshroomer was the first to collect and domesticate this strain.
The strain's introduction to the Western world is shrouded in secrecy, and spores can still be difficult to find due to Malaysia's strict drug laws.

Potency and Psilocybin Content:
The Malaysian strain is inconsistent in terms of potency.
Analytical data is limited, but available testing suggests it falls within the average potency range for Psilocybe cubensis.
In a Spring 2022 Psilocybin Cup, a sample of the Malaysian strain had a psilocybin content of 0.81% and a psilocin content of 0.03%. The total tryptamine content (including related compounds) was 0.85%.

In **summary**, the Malaysian strain offers an exciting and unpredictable nature, making it a fascinating addition to the world of magic mushrooms. Whether you encounter large, flat caps or unexpected variations, the Malaysian strain keeps cultivators and enthusiasts intrigued.123

1. **Sources:**
2. https://tripsitter.com/magic-mushrooms/strains/malaysian/
3. https://goldenteacherspores.org/magic-mushroom-strain-info/malaysian-magic-mushroom-psilocybe-cubensis/
4. https://tripsitter.com/magic-mushrooms/strains/stropharia/
5. https://www.psychedelicpassage.com/psychedelic-mushroom-strains-by-potency-30-popular-varieties/

Martinique Cubensis

Martinique is a fascinating Psilocybe cubensis magic mushroom species originating from the Caribbean Island of Martinique. Here are some key details about this unique strain:

Identification and Origins:
The Martinique Cubensis is suspected to be none other than the naturally growing Psilocybe yungensis.
It is distinguishable by its orangish color and grows in large numbers.
The cap of the Martinique Cubensis remains conical at maturity, featuring an eye-catching and pronounced nipple-like umbo (though less prominent than the P. mamillata).
This magic mushroom thrives on decomposing wood stumps, wood debris, and in environments like coffee plantations and cloud forests at altitudes of 1000 to 2000 meters1.

Habitat and Climate:
The creole-speaking island of Martinique has a tropical climate with remarkably constant hot and humid weather year-round.
These optimal conditions make it a perfect habitat for the Martinique Cubensis to flourish.
Martinique, known as the "island of iguanas and flowers," boasts fertile volcanic land, lush vegetation, and a tortuous relief1.

Potency and Effects: Below Average
The Martinique Cubensis has a mild to moderate potency.
Reports suggest that it induces a dreamy state of mind with a very relaxing body high.
Consumed by the Mazatecs Indians of Oaxaca for entheogenic purposes, it is referred to as the "genius mushroom" or the "divinatory mushroom".
Its transcending powers make it a sacred strain for psychedelic journeys, similar to other sacred teonanacatl species like P. mexicana1.

Microdosing Potential:
Due to its milder potency, the Martinique Cubensis can be a good candidate for discovering the benefits of micro-dosing.
If you're looking for a smooth day-to-day partner to enhance your performance at work or improve your overall mood, this islander mushroom may add a touch of magic to your routine1.

In **summary**, the Martinique Cubensis offers a unique blend of tropical origins, moderate potency, and relaxing effects. Whether you're seeking a sacred journey or exploring micro-dosing, this magic mushroom has something to offer! 123

Sources:
1. https://microzoomers.co/strains/martinique-cubensis/
2. https://originmushrooms.life/product/martinique/
3. https://buymushroomonlineus.com/product/martinique/

Matias Romero

The **Matias Romero** strain of Psilocybe cubensis is a fascinating variety with a mysterious history. Let's delve into the intriguing aspects of this strain:

Origin and Enigma:
The Matias Romero strain is named after the Mexican village of Matias Romero where it was supposedly collected.
However, little is known about the exact origin or where the first sample was isolated.
Some believe it is one of the oldest strains on the market, allegedly cultivated for generations somewhere in the rainforests of Southern Mexico.

History and Lineage:
The strain's history is shrouded in mystery, adding to its appeal for cultivators and users.
It's unclear whether the spores were collected from a wild strain and isolated in a lab or bred using another strain named after the founder: PF Classic.
Debate exists about whether there is a unique strain with the name Matias Romero or if users confuse it with the original PF Classic. Both mushrooms look very similar.

Potency and Trip Experience:
The potency of the Matias Romero strain is **average**, but individual experiences can vary significantly.
Growing conditions and substrate play a major role in determining potency.
Some claim that the real Matias Romero strain is rare but produces a trip experience unlike any other.

Availability and Cultivation:
Finding the Matias Romero strain can be challenging due to its scarcity.
Spore samples are available from vendors such as Ralphsters Spores, The Spore Depot, and Shayana Shop.

In **summary**, the Matias Romero strain remains an enigma, making it an intriguing addition to the world of magic mushrooms. Whether it truly holds ancient origins or not, its mysterious history continues to captivate cultivators and enthusiasts alike. 123

Sources:

1. https://tripsitter.com/magic-mushrooms/strains/matias-romero/
2. https://mushly.com/matias-romero-vs-malabar-mushroom
3. https://markpsychedelic.com/product/matias-romero-magic-mushrooms/
4. https://mushly.com/matias-romero-vs-pesa

Mazatepec

The **Mazatepec** strain of Psilocybe cubensis is a fascinating variety with a rich history and unique characteristics. Let's explore what makes this strain special:

Origins and Discovery:
The Mazatepec strain comes from the Mazatec people of Mexico, specifically the Sierra Mazateca region.
These indigenous people have a long history of using magic mushrooms, including Psilocybe cubensis, in their spiritual and healing ceremonies.
The strain was named after the Mazatec people, who have a deep cultural connection to these mushrooms.

Appearance and Effects:
Mazatepec mushrooms have typical Psilocybe cubensis characteristics:
Golden-brown caps with white spots.
Long, slender stems.
The effects of Mazatepec are often described as spiritual, with beautiful hallucinations and fewer bodily symptoms compared to most P. cubensis strains.
Users report a sense of connection, introspection, and sometimes deep personal insights during their trips.

Potency and Cultivation:
Mazatepec is considered slightly **less potent than average** for Psilocybe cubensis.
It is a good option for beginners or anyone interested in spiritual exploration.
Cultivating Mazatepec mushrooms follows similar methods as other P. cubensis strains.

In **summary**, the Mazatepec strain offers a unique and potentially transformative psychedelic experience, connecting users to the rich cultural heritage of the Mazatec people.12345

Sources:

1. https://healing-mushrooms.net/mazatapec
2. https://fungimaps.com/learn/mazatapec-mushroom-strain/
3. https://completemyco.com/blogs/complete-university/strain-highlight-mazapatec
4. https://pnwspore.com/product/mazatapec/
5. https://tripsitter.com/magic-mushrooms/strains/mazatapec/

Mckennaii or Makenna 2

The **McKennaii** strain is a Psilocybe cubensis mushroom named in honor of the legendary psychedelic lecturer, author, and psychonaut, Terence McKenna. Terence McKenna is well-known for his popular theory known as the "Stoned Ape Theory," which links psychedelic substances to human evolution1.
Here are some key details about the McKennaii strain:

Appearance:
The McKennaii strain features medium-sized bell-shaped caps that flatten out as they mature.
Its stems are above-average in thickness and often exhibit waviness or slight curvature.
When dried, these mushrooms can take on intense blue hues along the stem and parts of the cap. The cap may also turn purplish after sporulation.

Potency and Characteristics:
The McKennaii strain boasts **above-average potency** and impressive colonization speeds.
It is a resistant strain that can thrive in an unoptimized environment, making it suitable for beginner growers or commercial cultivators.
Large yields are possible over several dense flushes before the colony succumbs to mold.

Cultivation:
The McKennaii strain is easy to grow and quick to colonize.
It can be cultivated using substrates such as rye grain or brown rice flour (BRF).
In summary, the McKennaii strain is a versatile and potent Psilocybe cubensis variety, making it popular among both cultivators and psychonauts1. If you're interested in exploring its effects, it's worth considering for your next mushroom-growing adventure!

Sources:

1. https://tripsitter.com/magic-mushrooms/strains/mckennaii/
2. https://www.bing.com/search?q=mckennaii+strain&FORM=bngcht&toWww=1&redig=19097BB6CF3044418ECC48876E515B24
3. https://completemyco.com/blogs/complete-university/strain-highlight-mckennaii
4. https://healingmaps.com/mckennaii-mushrooms-psilocybe-cubensis/
5. https://gwellamushrooms.com/blogs/magazine/mckennaii-mushrooms

Melmac

The **Melmac** Mushroom (also known as the Melmac strain) is a variety of Psilocybe cubensis, one of the world's most popular psychoactive mushrooms. Let's explore the intriguing aspects of this strain:

Origin and Name:
The name "Melmac" is likely a playful reference to the old TV show "ALF", where the title character was a rather aardvark-like space alien from the planet Melmac.
The idea behind naming this mushroom "Melmac" is that it's "out of this world."

Distinct Characteristics:
Melmac mushrooms have a unique appearance:
Their stems are thick, contorted, and wavy.
The caps are often split and wavy, with a golden-brown color.
While not resembling the phallic appearance of the Penis Envy strain, Melmac has its own distinct look.
It stands out among other Psilocybe cubensis strains due to deliberate breeding efforts to stabilize an interesting variation within the original genetics of the early Penis Envy stock.

Effects and Potency: Above Average
The trip effects of Melmac are generally similar to any other psilocybin mushroom.
Users can expect mood enhancement, altered thinking, and hallucinations.
Unpleasant side effects (such as nausea and vomiting) are common, but serious problems are rare.
As with any psychedelic substance, responsible use and adherence to safety guidelines are crucial.

Cultivation and Availability:
Melmac mushrooms are relatively easy to cultivate.
Spore samples are available from various vendors, but always be aware of local laws regarding psilocybin-containing mushrooms.

In **summary**, the Melmac strain offers an intriguing and potentially transformative psychedelic experience. Whether you're a curious explorer or an experienced psychonaut, Melmac mushrooms provide a unique journey. Remember to approach them with respect and mindfulness. 123

Sources:
1.   https://healing-mushrooms.net/melmac-mushroom
2.   https://tripsitter.com/magic-mushrooms/strains/melmac/
3.   https://doubleblindmag.com/melmac-mushroom-strain/

Menace

The **Menace** strain of Psilocybe cubensis is a type of magic mushroom known for its potency and ability to reliably elicit transcendent experiences. Here are some key points about the Menace variety:

Origin: The Menace strain traces its origins back to a farm or pasture in Texas1. It has been around for quite some time, with posts about it dating back to the late 2000s and early 2010s.

Characteristics:
Yield: Menace mushrooms tend to have a great yield.
Colonization: They colonize quickly.
Mycelium: Menace mushrooms have rhizomorphic mycelium.
Fruiting Bodies: They often produce quite large fruiting bodies2.
Effects:
Visual Hallucinations: Menace mushrooms induce intense visual hallucinations.
Insights: Users may experience profound insights during their trips.

Potency: **Above Average**

Overall, the Menace strain is considered a potent variety within the Psilocybe cubensis family, making it a sought-after choice for those seeking transformative psychedelic experiences2. If you're interested in exploring this strain, be sure to research further and approach it with care and respect.
For more detailed information, you can explore resources like the Shroomery Message Board or other mycology-related platforms1. Remember to exercise caution and follow safe practices when working with any psychedelic substances.

Sources:

1. https://www.shroomery.org/forums/showflat.php/Number/27514443
2. https://frshminds.com/psilocybin-mushroom-species-guide/psilocybe-cubensis/psilocybe-cubensis-menace-magic-mushrooms/

Mestizo

Mestizo magic mushrooms are derived from the Mexicube strain and possess effects that elicit spiritual or mystical states of consciousness. Here are the key details about this intriguing strain:

Physical Description:
Caps: Mestizo cubensis produces medium-sized, tan caps that are darker brown towards the center. As the mushrooms mature, the caps may become discolored and turn black due to spore production.
Stems (Stipes): The stems are moderately thick and cylindrical. They can vary in appearance, with some being tall and skinny (resembling Tasmanian strains) and others fat and thick (similar to Brazilian strains).

Growth Characteristics:
Colonization: Mestizo is known for its fast colonizing ability, allowing it to quickly spread through a substrate.
Fruiting: It is also relatively fast fruiting, forming dense patches of mushrooms.

Potency: Above Average

Effects:
Mestizo cubensis shares similarities with other Mexican species. When consumed, it can lead to:
Spiritual States: Users may experience spiritual or mystical states of consciousness.
Out-of-Body Experiences: In some cases, Mestizo mushrooms may even induce out-of-body experiences.

In **summary**, Mestizo magic mushrooms offer a unique journey for those seeking altered perception and introspection. As with any psychedelic substance, approach them with respect and mindfulness.

Sources:
1. https://frshminds.com/psilocybin-mushroom-species-guide/psilocybe-cubensis/psilocybe-cubensis-mestizo-magic-mushrooms/
2. https://tripsitter.com/magic-mushrooms/strains/
3. https://www.psychedelicpassage.com/psychedelic-mushroom-strains-by-potency-30-popular-varieties/

Mexican Dutch King

Mexican Dutch King is a remarkable strain of Psilocybe cubensis, known for its robust growth, potency, and distinct appearance. Let's explore the key details about this fascinating mushroom strain:

Origin and Cultivation:
Origins: The Mexican Dutch King strain originates from Mexico. However, it has been cultivated in the Netherlands for many years, earning its own name.

Appearance:
Caps: Mexican Dutch King produces medium to large golden-colored caps.
Stems: The stems are thick and sturdy, making it a favorite among cultivators.
Mycelium: The rhizomorphic mycelium of Mexican Dutch King is extremely aggressive and quickly colonizes substrates.
Fruiting: It is a fast and prolific fruiter, making it an easy and fruitful strain to grow.

Potency:
Mexican Dutch King mushrooms have an **above-average potency**. They contain approximately 0.90% to 1.80% total tryptamines, including psilocybin, psilocin, baeocystin, and related alkaloids.
The balanced psychedelic experience provided by MDK makes it a sought-after strain.

Commercial History:
In the Netherlands, Mexican Dutch King was developed as a commercial strain for sale in "Smart Shops" before psilocybin mushrooms became illegal in the country.
Despite the legal restrictions, Mexican Dutch King spores and magic truffles remain popular.

Cultivation:
Recommended Substrate: BRF (Brown Rice Flour) or Rye Grain.
Suitable for Beginners: Mexican Dutch King is an excellent all-around strain suitable for beginner cultivators, keen mycologists, and commercial growers alike.
Big Yields: With minimal equipment, experience, and time, growers can achieve big yields of potent mushrooms.

In **summary**, Mexican Dutch King is a versatile strain that combines Mexican origins with Dutch cultivation expertise. Whether you're a beginner or an experienced cultivator, this strain offers a rewarding journey into the world of magic mushrooms.

Sources:
1. https://tripsitter.com/magic-mushrooms/strains/mexican-dutch-king/
2. https://psilocybincircus.com/psilocybe-cubensis/spore-syringe/mexican-dutch-king/
3. https://mycologynow.com/psilocybe-cubensis-mexican-dutch-king-origins/

Mexicube

Mexicube is a variety of Psilocybe cubensis mushrooms, which naturally
contain psilocybin and psilocin, making them psychedelic. Here are the key details about
this sought-after shroom strain:

Origin and History:
Name: The name "Mexicube" combines "Mexi-" (originating from Mexico) and "-cubes"
(indicating that it belongs to the Psilocybe cubensis species).

Development: An amateur mycologist named Mr. G is credited for developing this strain.
The original spore sample was collected somewhere around Oaxaca, Mexico.

Ancient Use: Magic mushrooms have been used in Mexico and parts of Central America
for more than 2,000 years, particularly within cultures like the Aztecs living around Oaxaca.
These mushrooms were lovingly referred to throughout history as "teotlnanacatl," which
roughly translates to "food of the gods."

Size:
Mexicube mushrooms are known for their relatively large size.

Potency:
They are considered **average** in terms of psychedelic potency compared to other
Psilocybe cubensis samples.

Appearance:
 Mexicube is one of the only members of the Mexican cubensis strains that produce light-
colored spots on the caps as they grow, resembling features seen in Amanita
muscaria mushrooms.

Psilocybin Content:
While there isn't enough analytical data to precisely quantify the average potency of
Mexicube, the total tryptamine content (including psilocybin, psilocin, and related
tryptamines) is estimated to fall somewhere between 0.5% and 1%.
Keep in mind that the potency of magic mushrooms can vary significantly based on
growing conditions. Two samples of the same strain grown under different conditions can
register radically different psilocybin and psilocin levels1.

In **summary**, Mexicube mushrooms have a rich history and continue to be highly sought-
after due to their link to ancient psychonauts of Mexico and Central America. Approach
them with respect and curiosity, as each strain offers its own unique journey into altered
states of consciousness.

Sources:

1. https://tripsitter.com/magic-mushrooms/strains/mexicube/
2. https://tripsitter.com/magic-mushrooms/strains/mexicana/

Mississippi

Mississippi Shrooms, also known as the Mississippi strain, refer to a genetically isolated strain of Psilocybe cubensis (magic mushrooms). Here are the key details about this intriguing strain:

Origins and Characteristics:
Harvest Location: The Mississippi strain was originally harvested near the Mississippi River, which suggests it is closely related to other strains from the same region.
Related Strains: It shares similar growth habits and potency with the Acadian Coast and Dixieland strains.
Mystery Origins: Unfortunately, little is known about the specific origins or who should be credited for the development of this popular strain.
Appearance: Mississippi shrooms grow with some large mushrooms interspersed with smaller ones.
Resistance: This strain is relatively resistant to mold and disease.

Potency and Psilocybin Content:
The psychedelic potency of the Mississippi strain is **roughly average** compared to other Psilocybe cubensis strains.
While there isn't enough analytical data to provide an accurate average potency, it is estimated that the strain contains somewhere in the ballpark of 0.5% to 0.9% total tryptamine content (by dried weight).

Variations and Genetic Relatives:
Given the limited information available about the Mississippi strain, it's difficult to say with certainty what strains are directly related to it.
Strains obtained from samples growing around the same region as the Mississippi strain include the Acadian Coast and Dixieland strains.

In **summary**, the Mississippi strain remains somewhat mysterious, but its ubiquity and unique characteristics make it an interesting choice for those exploring the world of magic mushrooms. Approach it with curiosity and respect, and happy growing!

Sources:
1. https://tripsitter.com/magic-mushrooms/strains/mississippi/
2. https://tripsitter.com/magic-mushrooms/strains/
3. https://tripsitter.com/psilocybin-cup/

Moby Dick

Moby Dick is a fascinating and relatively new variation in the world of Psilocybe cubensis mushrooms. Let's delve into the details of this magical mushroom:

Genetic Origins:
The Moby Dick strain was created through a deliberate crossbreeding experiment involving two distinct cubensis varieties: Albino A+ and Golden Teacher.
By meticulously combining the desirable traits of both parent strains, breeders aimed to develop a new and distinctive variety of Psilocybe cubensis1.

Distinctive Characteristics:
What sets Moby Dick mushrooms apart is their striking lack of pigment, particularly evident in the caps.
The caps exhibit a light blue hue, reminiscent of a zombie or a corpse submerged in water.
Unlike traditional cubensis strains, Moby Dick caps have a tendency to tear prematurely, adding to their enigmatic allure.
The stems of these mushrooms are robust and meaty, boasting an ivory coloration with a base adorned in white down1.

Ease of Cultivation:
Despite their unconventional appearance, Moby Dick mushrooms are prized for their ease of cultivation and robust growth habits.
Whether grown by novice or experienced cultivators, these mushrooms thrive under a variety of conditions, making them an accessible choice for growers seeking a unique and rewarding cultivation experience1.

Psychedelic Effects:
Moby Dick mushrooms promise a novel and exhilarating psychedelic experience.
Their potent effects, combined with their distinctive appearance, transport users on a journey of exploration and self-discovery.
Embark on an adventure into the unknown and unlock the secrets of Moby Dick mushrooms, where every trip is a voyage into uncharted waters1.

Conclusion:
Moby Dick mushrooms represent a captivating fusion of genetics and a testament to the ingenuity of cultivators in the realm of mycology.
With their unique appearance, potent effects, and ease of cultivation, these mushrooms have carved out a niche in the world of psychedelic exploration.
Whether you're a seasoned enthusiast or a curious novice, Moby Dick mushrooms offer a tantalizing glimpse into the endless possibilities of the fungal kingdom1.

In **summary**, Moby Dick mushrooms are a remarkable addition to the diverse world of psilocybin-containing fungi, inviting curious minds to explore their mysteries and embark on transformative journeys.

Sources:
1.   https://mushly.com/moby-dick-magic-mushrooms

Na Muang

Na Muang mushroom strain is an interesting variety of Psilocybe cubensis, known for its unique origins and characteristics. Here's what we know about this strain:

Origin and Discovery:
The Na Muang strain was discovered by mycologist John Allen in Thailand.
It was found growing on water buffalo dung in rice paddies on the Thai island of Koh Samui.
The name "Na Muang" refers to the specific location where it was found12.

Physical Characteristics:
Cap: The cap of Na Muang mushrooms is light yellow in color.
Stem: The stem is typically around 5 cm long and 2 cm thick. It is wider at the base than at the apex.
The strain produces enormous fruiting bodies, similar to other strains from the same region3.

Cultivation and Effects:
Cultivators have reported that Na Muang is a solid producer with good yields.
Its inoculation/incubation period is relatively fast.

Potency: Above Average
In terms of potency, some users believe that Na Muang mushrooms are 1.25 to 1.4 times stronger than the popular Golden Teacher (GT) strain1.
However, individual experiences may vary, and it's essential to approach any psychedelic substance with caution and respect.
In summary, the Na Muang strain offers a unique combination of origin, size, and potential potency. 132

1. **Sources**:
   https://www.reddit.com/r/shrooms/comments/me12yd/anything_special_about_na_muang_shrooms/?rdt=37959
2. https://1upmaps.com/the-ultimate-magic-mushroom-strain-list/
3. https://frshminds.com/psilocybin-mushroom-species-guide/psilocybe-cubensis/nua-muang-magic-mushrooms/
4. https://www.shroomery.org/forums/showflat.php/Number/12282151

Natal Super Strain

Psilocybe natalensis, also known as the **Natal Super Strength** mushroom, is a fascinating strain within the Psilocybe genus. Let's explore the key details about this potent and intriguing mushroom:

Taxonomy and Origin:
Discovery: Psilocybe natalensis was taxonomically described in 1995 by mycologists Jochen Gartz, Michael Smith, Derek Reid, and Albert Eicker.
Native Habitat: This species is native to pastures in the Natal region of South Africa.

Appearance and Potency: Above Average
Hygrophanous Caps: The caps of P. natalensis are hygrophanous, meaning they can change color. Initially brown, they can turn white as they dry.
Bluing Reaction: When bruised or disturbed, the stems and caps of Natal Super Strength mushrooms exhibit a vivid blue bruising reaction.
High Alkaloid Content: These mushrooms contain high levels of psilocybin, psilocin, and baeocystin—naturally occurring psychoactive compounds responsible for their hallucinogenic effects.

Growing Characteristics:
Similar to Psilocybe cubensis: P. natalensis is closely related to Psilocybe cubensis. Their DNA sequences reveal this close relationship, and the alkaloidal concentration in P. natalensis is comparable to that in P. cubensis.
Resilience to Contamination: Natal Super Strength mushrooms are more resilient to molds and contamination than P. cubensis. Their aggressive mycelium actively outcompetes molds.

Cultivation:
Growing Techniques: P. natalensis can be cultivated using the same techniques and substrates as P. cubensis.
Vigorous Growth: This strain exhibits extremely rhizomorphic growth and rapid colonization times.
Leucistic Specimens: In the wild, some collected specimens may appear leucistic or albino.

In **summary**, Psilocybe natalensis, with its high potency and unique characteristics, has captured the attention of growers. Whether you're an experienced cultivator or a curious explorer, Natal Super Strength mushrooms offer a fascinating journey into altered states of consciousness. Remember that this is for information purposes only.

Sources:

1. https://thethirdwave.co/psilocybe-natalensis-mushrooms/
2. https://www.bing.com/search?q=natal+super+strain+mushroom+synopsis&FORM=bngcht&FORM=bngcht&FORM=bngcht&FORM=bngcht&FORM=bngcht&toWww=1&redig=898340793964482E9CB531AE0A0A8A2E
3. https://www.myshrooms.co.za/product/natal-super-strength/
4. https://www.mushroomnetwork.co.za/shop/spore-prints/spore-prints-natal-super-strength/

Nutcracker

Nutcracker (scientifically known as Psilocybe Cubensis Nutcracker) is a distinct isolated variation of the Yeti strain. Its name originates from the uniquely textured cap that humorously resembles a nutsack, which was the original name given to this P. cubensis isolation. Nutcracker mushrooms are not to be taken lightly, as they pack a punch in terms of potency1.
Here are some key details about the Nutcracker strain:

Origin and Isolation:
The Nutcracker strain emerged in 2020 when a mycologist named Myco Clay isolated a mutation from a Yeti culture.
After more than 15 generations, this genetic variant became a unique and highly sought-after phenotype1.

Appearance:
The Nutcracker P. Cubensis is characterized by exceptionally wrinkled caps, severe bruising, ridges, bumps, and wavy blue cap edges.
At maturity, the cap measures between 25-65 mm in diameter, transitioning from a convex to a broad convex, and eventually to a plane shape.
The stem ranges from 20-85 mm in length, revealing white flesh that turns blue when bruised, sometimes with subtle green undertones.
Some stems may retain occasional remnants of a partial veil, forming a web-like ring around the outermost underside cap area.
The gills exhibit an adnate to adnexed attachment and transition from opalescent white to dark blue as they mature.
Notably, this strain produces translucent or albino spores, adding another unique aspect to its genetic composition1.

Cultivation:
Nutcracker mushrooms are considered easy to average to grow.
Environmental conditions play a crucial role in achieving full canopy flushes.
Various methods can be used for cultivation, including fruiting directly from the bag or using a more hands-on approach with grain spawn and a manure-based substrate1.

Potency: Above Average

In **summary**, the Nutcracker Magic Mushroom stands out due to its distinctive appearance and potent effects. Whether you're a beginner or an experienced cultivator, Nutcracker mushrooms offer a unique and sought-after experience!12

Sources:

1. https://magic-mycology.com/product/nutcracker/
2. https://thefunguys.co/product/nutcracker-dried-mushroom/
3. https://moneymaverickpro.com/nutcracker-mushroom-strain-understanding-its-unique-characteristics/

Oak Ridge

Psilocybe Cubensis Oak Ridge, commonly known as the 'Nuclear Mushroom,' is a naturally occurring variant of the Psilocybe cubensis species found near a former nuclear weapons complex in Oak Ridge, Tennessee1. Let's explore the key aspects of this intriguing strain:

Origins and Scientific Research:
Discovery: The Oak Ridge strain originates from Oak Ridge, Tennessee, which played a crucial role in the development of atomic bombs during World War II.
Radiation-Free: Extensive scientific research confirms that Psilocybe Cubensis Oak Ridge contains no trace amounts of mercury or nuclear irradiation1.
Adaptive Cultivation: The mushrooms were discovered in enriched soils and equine dung, signifying their adaptive cultivation methods.
Natural Variant: While it was initially speculated to be a product of atomic mutation, further research supports the hypothesis that it is a naturally occurring variant of Psilocybe cubensis1.

Appearance and Identification:
Cap Shape: Psilocybe cubensis Oak Ridge displays a convex to broadly convex cap that becomes plane as it matures.
Color: The cap color varies, and the mushrooms exhibit a blue bruising reaction when disturbed.
Unique Adaptations: This strain's adaptations to its environment provide insights for future conservation efforts and serve as a model for spore dispersal and mushroom sustainability1.
Cultivation and Potential Use:
Cultivation: Oak Ridge is an easy-to-cultivate strain, making it suitable for both beginner and experienced growers.

Potency: Average

Potential Therapeutic Use: While the cultural and medical applications of this strain are yet to be fully explored, its discovery near a location of historical importance has sparked interest among researchers and enthusiasts.
Model for Conservation: Psilocybe cubensis Oak Ridge's unique adaptations could inform future conservation efforts for other mushroom species1.

In **summary**, the Oak Ridge strain, with its radiation-free origins and intriguing characteristics, offers a fascinating journey into the world of psilocybin mushrooms. As research continues, we may uncover more about its potential therapeutic benefits and cultural significance.

Sources:
1. https://thickspores.com/mushrooms/oak-ridge-mushroom-strain/
2. https://inoculatetheworld.com/product/oakridge-cubensis-spore-syringe/
3. https://magic-mycology.com/oak-ridge/

Old Dirty Penis Envy

Old Dirty Penis Envy (ODPE), also known as Nuclear Mushroom, is a unique strain of Psilocybe cubensis that has garnered attention for its distinct characteristics. Let's delve into the key aspects of this intriguing mushroom strain:

Origins and Genetic Isolation:
Discovery: ODPE was initially isolated and stabilized by a mycologist named Joshua.
Distinct Traits: ODPE displays abundant flushes and compact, stout structures, accompanied by intriguing and enjoyable unique traits.
Color Variation: Its coloring is distinct, ranging from deep browns to blondes and even hints of green12.

Appearance and Cultivation:
Cap Shape: ODPE mushrooms exhibit a convex to broadly convex cap that becomes plane as they mature.
Blue Bruising: When bruised or disturbed, both the stems and caps of ODPE mushrooms display a vivid blue bruising reaction.
Adaptive Cultivation: The strain's adaptations to its environment provide insights for future conservation efforts and serve as a model for spore dispersal and mushroom sustainability.
Easy to Cultivate: ODPE is an easy-to-cultivate strain, making it suitable for both beginner and experienced growers3.

Potency and Effects: Above Average
High Alkaloid Content: ODPE contains high levels of psilocybin, psilocin, and baeocystin, which are naturally occurring psychoactive compounds responsible for its hallucinogenic effects.
Unique Experience: Users report intriguing and enjoyable experiences with ODPE, making it a sought-after strain for those seeking a distinctive journey into altered states of consciousness.

Availability:
ODPE mushrooms are available for purchase online, allowing enthusiasts to explore their unique properties and enjoy their effects4.

In **summary**, Old Dirty Penis Envy (ODPE) stands out for its genetic isolation, distinct appearance, and potent effects. Whether you're a mycology enthusiast or an adventurous psychonaut, ODPE offers a fascinating exploration into the world of magic mushrooms. Remember to approach them with respect and mindfulness.

Sources:
1. https://www.trypadvizor.com/strains/albino-pe-8e5gz
2. https://basidiumequilibrium.com/product/old-dirty-penis-envy-isolated-plate/
3. https://shroomok.com/gallery/odpe-old-dirty-penis-envy-strain
4. https://shroombros.co/product/old-dirty-penis-envy-magic-mushrooms/
5. https://basidiumequilibrium.com/product/old-dirty-penis-envy-spore-swab/

Orissa India

Orissa India Shroom Strain, also known as Orissa India, is a cultivated strain of Psilocybe cubensis, one of the most popular hallucinogenic mushroom species in the world. Let's explore the key aspects of this intriguing strain:

Origins and Characteristics:
Discovery: Orissa India was initially discovered in Odisha (previously called Orissa), which is located near Nepal and Bihar, India.
Large Mushroom Size: This strain is known for producing some of the largest mushrooms among all Psilocybe cubensis strains.
Potency: Orissa India mushrooms are notoriously potent, making them one of the strongest varieties.
Preferred Substrate: They thrive when growing in elephant dung, which can result in the production of unusually large mushrooms.

Potency and Psilocybin Content: Very Potent
Most users who consume this strain report that the psychedelic experience is more intense than most other strains.
While the average potency for Orissa India is not clear, it's well above 1.5% and could even be as high as 3% total tryptamine content (including psilocybin and psilocin). For reference, the average total tryptamine content for magic mushrooms (Psilocybe cubensis) is around 0.5-0.9% by weight.

Cultivation:
Orissa India is an easy-to-cultivate strain, making it suitable for both beginner and experienced growers.

In **summary**, Orissa India mushrooms offer a fascinating journey into altered states of consciousness. Whether you're a mycology enthusiast or a curious explorer, approach them with respect and mindfulness.

Sources:
1. https://tripsitter.com/magic-mushrooms/strains/orissa-india/
2. https://healing-mushrooms.net/orissa-india
3. https://shafaa.ca/product/orissa-india-magic-mushrooms/

Pacific Blue Liberty Cap

Pacific Blue Liberty Cap (also known as Psilocybe semilanceata) is a unique and intriguing variant of the classic Liberty Cap mushroom. Let's explore the key details about this captivating fungus:

Identification and Appearance:
Psilocybe semilanceata, commonly known as the Liberty Cap, is a small and potent hallucinogenic mushroom. The Pacific Blue strain is an uncommon but not necessarily rare color variant of the Liberty Cap. It exhibits unusual bluish tones and has a more hemispheric cap shape compared to the typical Liberty Cap.
The blue coloration is most apparent in young specimens and in mushrooms growing under shady conditions1.

Psilocybin Content and Effects: Very Potent
The potency of Psilocybe semilanceata (including the Pacific Blue variant) is attributed to its high psilocybin content. Psilocybin is the chemical compound responsible for its psychedelic effects. Users of Liberty Caps typically experience subtle visual changes, altered perception, and a sense of euphoria. Walls may appear to breathe, and patterns can become more vivid. It's essential to approach any psychoactive substance with respect and caution, including mushrooms containing psilocybin. Legal restrictions also apply in most jurisdictions23.

Habitat and Geographic Distribution:
Liberty Cap mushrooms are commonly found in British Columbia and other regions with temperate climates.
In North America, you can find these mushrooms west of the Cascade mountain range from Northern California and into the Pacific Northwest, including British Columbia. They also grow in grassland habitats throughout Europe, including countries like Ireland, France, Holland, Norway, and Switzerland2.

Legal Considerations:
The legality of Liberty Cap mushrooms is a hot-button issue and often causes confusion. Under federal law, they are illegal in most states due to their psilocybin content. However, there are some exceptions. For example, in places like Oregon and Colorado, recent legislative changes have made possession of small amounts of psilocybin mushrooms a low-priority offense2.

In **summary**, the Pacific Blue Liberty Cap is a captivating mushroom with its bluish tones and potent effects. Remember to approach psychedelic substances responsibly and be aware of legal regulations231.

Sources:
1. https://sporeworks.com/Psilocybe-semilanceata-Pacific-Blue-Liberty-Cap-Spore-Print-Microscopy-Kit.html
2. https://www.shroomer.com/liberty-cap-mushrooms/
3. https://thinkmushrooms.ca/psilocybe-semilanceata-information-potency-effects-and-dosages/
4. https://en.wikipedia.org/wiki/Psilocybe_semilanceata

Palenque Mexico

Palenque Mexico Strain is a potent variety of Psilocybe cubensis that was discovered outside of the town of Palenque in southern Mexico (hence the name). This strain is noted for producing tall, slender fruiting bodies with above-average potency. The mushrooms have triangular-shaped, conical, caramel-colored caps that become darker towards the center1.
Here are some key details about the Palenque Mexico strain:

History:
The first sample of the Palenque Mexico strain was discovered growing near the town of Palenque in southern Mexico.
Palenque, also known as "Lakamha" in the ancient Itza language, has been inhabited for thousands of years by the Mayan people who likely consumed Psilocybe cubensis and other psilocybin-producing mushrooms for religious purposes.
Spore samples of Palenque Mexico have been circulating the market since the early 2000s, and they are now available from reliable spore vendors globally.

Potency and Psilocybin Content:
The Palenque Mexico strain is considered to have **above-average potency**.
These mushrooms produce tryptamine levels of between 0.90% and 1.80%, which puts them on par with strains such as Malabar India, some Penis Envy variants, and the Mexican Albino strain.

Cultivation:
While Palenque Mexico can be difficult to cultivate, those with experience growing psychedelic and gourmet mushrooms shouldn't have too many issues.
Creating an optimum growing environment can lead to several dense flushes of potent mushrooms before the colony eventually succumbs to mold.
Palenque Mexico mushrooms are famous for being prolific sporulators, allowing large quantities of spores to be collected from mature mushrooms.

If you're looking for an exotic Mexican cubensis strain that's a little different from the norm, Palenque Mexico is worth exploring. Its unique characteristics and rich history make it a fascinating addition to the world of magic mushrooms.

Sources:
1.   https://tripsitter.com/magic-mushrooms/strains/palenque/
2.   https://tripsitter.com/magic-mushrooms/strains/mexican-albino/
3.   https://thefungidude.com/2023/05/11/palenque-mushrooms/

Panaeolus Bisporus

Also known as **Copelandia bisporus**, is a rare and widely distributed little brown mushroom. Here are some key details about it:

Description:
Cap: Measures 15-30 mm, tan to gray, fading to black sometimes when covered with spores. It has a defined ring zone and can be somewhat globe-shaped or bell-shaped to convex. The margin is often torn and pedaled, and the cap is smooth, not viscid. As it ages, it becomes slightly wrinkled and pitted. Dark grey-brown when drying and whitish.
Gills: Adnexed (narrowly attached), tightly packed, mottled gray to jet black, with white edges.
Stem: White, fibrous, 65-120 mm long, 2-3 mm thick, hollow, translucent gray. It bruises heavily blue where bruised.
Spores: Jet black, elliptical, measuring 12-14 x 8-10 x 6-7.5 µm. They are smooth and opaque, elongated with a germ pore straight off the end.
Habitat: Saprotrophic, found on grasses.
Microscopic features: Two-spored basidia (18-23 × 8-10 µm), cheilocystidia are bottle-shaped and clear (20-30 µm), metuloids with yellow-brown walls (40-55 × 12-15 µm), some with excreted crystals1.

Distribution:
Panaeolus bisporus has been found in various locations, including Hawaii, Southern California, North Africa, Spain, and Switzerland.
It prefers the dung of buffalo and cattle, sometimes occurring in manured soil but is rare. Notably, it was originally known from Morocco and Africa, and later discovered in abundance in a lawn near Bern, Switzerland2.

Psychoactive Properties:
Panaeolus bisporus contains the hallucinogen psilocybin.
It shares macroscopic similarities with other mushrooms like Panaeolus tropicalis, Panaeolus cambodginiensis, and Panaeolus cyanescens, but can be differentiated using a microscope due to its two-spored basidia1.

Sources:
1.   https://en.m.wikipedia.org/wiki/Panaeolus_bisporus
2.   https://www.shroomery.org/12482/Panaeolus-bisporus
3.   https://files.shroomery.org/attachments/19865548-Panaeolus%20bisporus%20-%20an%20adventitious%20fungus%20in%20central%20Europe,%20rich%20in%20psilocin.pdf

Panaeolus Subbalteatus

The fascinating **Panaeolus subbalteatus**, also known as **Panaeolus cinctulus**. This mushroom holds a special place in the world of psilocybin-containing fungi.

Common Names:
Banded Mottlegill
Weed Panaeolus
Belted Panaeolus
Subbs

Distribution:
Panaeolus subbalteatus is widely distributed and quite common.
According to American naturalist and mycologist David Arora, it holds the title of the most common psilocybin mushroom in California1.

Appearance:
Cap: Ranges from 1.5 to 5.5 centimeters in diameter.
When young, it is hemispherical to convex, later becoming broadly umbonate or flat. The cap color is striking cinnamon-brown when moist and turns soot-black when wet. The outer band is usually darker.
Gills: Initially cream-colored, they later mottle to dingy brown and eventually turn soot-black. The gill edges are white and slightly fringed but darken with maturity2.
Spore Print: Jet black.
Stipe (Stem): Varies from 2 to 10 centimeters in length and 2 to 9 millimeters in thickness. It can be reddish-brown to whitish, pruinose, and longitudinally white-fibrillose. The stipe may twist vertically down its entire length.
No veil remnants are present2.

Ecology:
Panaeolus subbalteatus is a coprophilic (dung-inhabiting) species.
It also thrives in other habitats, including:
Lawns, Haystacks, Compost heaps, Riding stables
Stable shavings of woodchips, hay, and manure3.

Edibility:
This mushroom is psychoactive due to its psilocybin content.
However, it's essential to exercise caution and follow legal guidelines when considering its use. The name "subbalteatus" refers to the dark outer band on the cap, derived from Latin words meaning "somewhat" and "girdled." So, if you encounter this banded mottlegill during your explorations, appreciate its unique features and its role in the natural world! 23
Sources:
1.   https://www.inaturalist.org/guide_taxa/636080
2.   https://en.m.wikipedia.org/wiki/Panaeolus_cinctulus
3.   https://www.erowid.org/plants/mushrooms/mushrooms_cultivation24.shtml
4.   https://www.chemeurope.com/en/encyclopedia/Panaeolus_subbalteatus.html
5.   https://www.inaturalist.org/taxa/179099-Panaeolus-subbalteatus

Panama

Panama Mushrooms, scientifically known as Psilocybe cubensis Panama, are a popular strain of magic mushrooms known for their unique appearance, potent effects, and rich cultural history. Here are the key details about this intriguing strain:

Appearance:
Panama magic mushrooms have a classic mushroom shape.
Their caps can vary in color from light brown to darker brown.
The caps often have a distinct dome shape and may exhibit characteristic cracking or splitting as they mature.
The stems are usually white or light brown.

Potency: Average
Panama magic mushrooms are known for their potency.
They contain high levels of psilocybin, the naturally occurring psychedelic compound responsible for their psychoactive effects.
As a result, Panama magic mushrooms are often sought after by experienced psychonauts and those seeking intense and profound psychedelic experiences.

Cultivation:
Panama is an easy-to-cultivate strain, making it suitable for both beginner and experienced growers.
It produces medium to large fruits with bold caps.
The strain is prolific sporulator, allowing large quantities of spores to be collected from mature mushrooms.

In **summary**, Panama magic mushrooms offer a fascinating journey into altered states of consciousness. Whether you're a mycology enthusiast or an adventurous psychonaut, and remember this is for information purposes only.

Sources:
1. https://mushly.com/psychedelic-mushrooms/panama-mushrooms
2. https://mushly.com/panama-vs-red-boy
3. https://mushly.com/panama-vs-pf-classic
4. https://mushly.com/mexicana-vs-panama

Paraguay

Paraguay Shrooms, also known as the Paraguay strain, are a type of psilocybin mushrooms originating from Paraguay. Although there isn't much information available about this strain, it's relatively hard to find and often underrated. However, those who have experienced it note that it is surprisingly strong for a mushroom that receives little attention.

Here are some key points about the Paraguay strain:

Potency and Effects: Above average

Paraguay shrooms are far more potent than most other strains.

Users report intense visions and fervent visual hallucinations when consuming this strain. While the typical tryptamine level in magic mushrooms hovers between 0.5% and 1% by weight, the Paraguay strain likely has a potency between 1% and 3%—possibly even double the average potency.

Cultivation:

Paraguay is an easy-to-cultivate strain, making it suitable for both beginner and experienced growers.

The mushrooms are known for being prolific sporulators, allowing large quantities of spores to be collected from mature specimens.

In **summary**, if you come across Paraguay Shrooms, consider giving them a try. Their unique characteristics and potency make them a fascinating addition to the world of magic mushrooms.

Sources:

1. https://tripsitter.com/magic-mushrooms/strains/paraguay/
2. https://goldenteacherspores.org/magic-mushroom-strain-info/paraguay-magic-mushroom-psilocybe-cubensis/
3. https://driedmagicmushroomspores.com/product/buy-paraguay-magic-mushroom-online/

Panther Amanita

The fascinating **Panther Amanita** (Amanita pantherina), also known as the Panther
Cap or False Blusher. This mushroom is a close relative of the more famous Amanita
muscaria, but it packs a stronger punch in terms of its psychoactive properties. ♠

Appearance:
The Panther Cap has a striking appearance:
Its cap ranges from 1.5 to 5.5 centimeters in diameter.
When young, it is hemispherical to convex, later becoming broadly umbonate or flat.
The cap color is a captivating cinnamon-brown when moist, turning soot-black when wet.
The outer band is usually darker.
The gills start cream-colored, mottling to dingy brown, and eventually turning soot-black.
Their edges remain white and slightly fringed.
The spore print is jet black.
The stipe (stem) varies from 2 to 10 centimeters in length and 2 to 9 millimeters in
thickness. It can be reddish-brown to whitish, pruinose, and longitudinally white-
fibrillose. No veil remnants are present1.
Unlike the iconic red-and-white Amanita muscaria, the Panther Cap sports earthy tones
that blend into its natural surroundings.

Psychoactive Properties:
The Panther Cap contains higher concentrations of ibotenic acid and muscimol than its
more famous cousin.
These compounds are responsible for the psychoactive effects experienced by those who
consume this mushroom.
While it may not be as recognizable as the storybook Amanita muscaria, the Panther Cap
certainly commands attention due to its potency1.

Remember that if you encounter the Panther Amanita during your explorations, appreciate
its unique features and respect its power. As with any psychoactive substance, caution
and responsible use are essential. 12

Sources:
1.   https://amanitamushrooms.com/blogs/articles/history-behind-amanita-pantherina
2.   https://en.m.wikipedia.org/wiki/Amanita_pantherina
3.   https://www.acslab.com/mushrooms/amanita-pantherina-mushrooms

Psilocybe Allenii

Also known as **Psilocybe cyanofriscosa,** is a fascinating mushroom with intriguing properties. Let's dive into the details:

Description:
P. allenii is a small, classic-looking brown mushroom. It has a cheerful appearance and distinct features:
Cap: Ranges from 2 to 4.5 centimeters across, bell-shaped, without a central bump or pronounced wavy edges. When moist, the cap is sticky to slimy and light, possibly orangish-brown. Dry specimens fade to yellowish-brown or buff. It bruises blue.
Gills: Attached but narrow. Initially reddish-brown, aging to dark gray-brown with mottling. The gill edges are paler than the faces.
Stem: Medium to tall, thin, white (bruises blue), and has a faint, hairy ring zone.
Spores: Elliptical, smooth, and purple-brown, purple-gray, or purple-black.
Habitat: Typically found fruiting from mulch and wood chips in urban or suburban areas. It's common within 50 miles of the Pacific Coast, especially around San Francisco, California. P. allenii never occurs more than 100 miles from the coast and fruits in larger groups during autumn and winter1.

Psychoactive Properties:
As a bluing species in the genus Psilocybe, P. allenii contains the psychoactive compounds psilocin and psilocybin. People consume it recreationally for its hallucinogenic effects.
It closely resembles Psilocybe cyanescens, but macroscopically, it lacks the wavy cap margin2.

Discovery and Naming:
P. allenii was initially considered a variant of P. cyanescens and unofficially named Psilocybe cyanofriscosa due to its common sightings around the San Francisco Bay Area.
In 2012, mycologist John W. Allen discovered its distinctiveness and introduced it to science. The species was then officially named after him3.

Potential Global Interest:
While lesser-known currently, P. allenii's potent effects could gain global traction as interest in psychedelic plants and fungi grows4.
Remember, when exploring mushrooms, always exercise caution and ensure proper identification.

Sources:
1. https://healing-mushrooms.net/psilocybe-allenii
2. https://en.m.wikipedia.org/wiki/Psilocybe_allenii
3. https://fungushead.com/psilocybe-allenii/
4. https://thethirdwave.co/psilocybe-allenii/

Pearly Gates

Also known as **Pearly White** mushrooms, is a fascinating hybrid within the Psilocybe cubensis family. Let's explore its intriguing characteristics:

Origin and Genetics:
Pearly Gates is a cross between True Albino Teacher (TAT) and Melmac (also known as Homestead Penis Envy).
The strain's name possibly refers to the pearly color of its caps, which are usually a very pretty gray rather than pure white.
Melmac itself is a variant of Penis Envy, contributing to the unique appearance of Pearly Gates12.

Appearance:
Pearly Gates mushrooms have ghostly white bodies with blue-grey, bulbous crowns that grow in tight flushes. The pale color is a legacy of the True Albino Teacher heritage, while the shape resembles a throwback to Penis Envy. The thick stems and narrow, sometimes bulbous caps give them a distinctive and somewhat mammalian appearance13.

Potency and Effects: Above Average
Pearly Gates is reputed to be unusually potent, similar to its two parents.
Testing has shown that it contains much more psilocybin than the average Psilocybe cubensis strain. Users may experience an intense and transformative trip, with effects including cerebral highs, visual hallucinations, and heightened introspection. Interestingly, Pearly Gates is said to come up with unusual speed, sometimes in as little as half an hour1.

Dosage Considerations:
Choosing the right dose is crucial for planning a safe and enjoyable trip.
Pearly Gates is a **high-potency strain**, so users should start with a smaller dose than usual. Remember to start low, go slow, and adjust based on your desired effects.
Dose calculators can provide a ballpark estimate, but fine-tuning through trial and error is essential1.

Growing Difficulty:
Pearly Gates is considered somewhat advanced for growers.
Its slow growth rate and unique characteristics require careful attention during cultivation. Patience and expertise are necessary to cultivate this intriguing strain1.

In **summary**, the Pearly Gates mushroom strain offers a blend of potency, unique appearance, and transformative effects. Whether you're a researcher or a psychonaut, encountering these ghostly white mushrooms can be both awe-inspiring and enlightening13.
Sources:
1.   https://healing-mushrooms.net/pearly-gates
2.   https://shroomwave.com/product/pearly-gates/
3.   https://www.shamanmushroomspores.com/product/pearly-gates-mushroom-spores/
4.   https://mushboyz.com/product/pearly-gates/

PeeP Cubensis

The intriguing world of **Panaeolus subbalteatus**, also known as the Peep Cubensis. However, it's important to note that the Peep Cubensis is not a strain of Psilocybe cubensis; rather, it belongs to the Panaeolus genus. Let's dive into the details:
Panaeolus subbalteatus (Peep Cubensis):
Common Names:
Banded Mottlegill
Weed Panaeolus
Belted Panaeolus
Subbs

Distribution:
Widely distributed and quite common.
Thrives in various habitats, including lawns, haystacks, compost heaps, riding stables, and stable shavings of woodchips, hay, and manure1.

Appearance:
The Peep Cubensis has distinctive features:
Cap: Ranges from 1.5 to 5.5 centimeters in diameter.
Initially hemispherical to convex, later becoming broadly umbonate or flat.
Cinnamon-brown when moist, turning soot-black when wet, with a darker outer band.
Gills: Cream-colored initially, mottling to dingy brown, and eventually turning soot-black.
Edges remain white and slightly fringed.
Spore Print: Jet black.
Stipe (Stem): Varies in length (2 to 10 centimeters) and thickness (2 to 9 millimeters).
Color ranges from reddish-brown to whitish, with longitudinal white-fibrillose texture. No veil remnants are present1.

Psychoactive Properties:
The Peep Cubensis contains psilocybin, making it psychoactive.
Caution and responsible use are essential when considering any psychoactive substance.

Remember that while the Peep Cubensis is not a Psilocybe cubensis strain, it still offers unique characteristics and a place in the natural world. As always, respect its power and follow legal guidelines if you encounter it during your explorations! 1

Sources:
1. https://healing-mushrooms.net/psilocybe-cubensis-strains
2. https://tripsitter.com/magic-mushrooms/strains/pesa/
3. https://psychedelicspotlight.com/a-list-of-the-strongest-psilocybe-cubensis-strains/
4. https://magic-mycology.com/the-ultimate-guide-to-psilocybin-mushroom-strains-varieties-origins-and-effects/

Penis Envy

Penis Envy is one of the most famous and controversial magic mushroom strains in existence. It belongs to the Psilocybe cubensis species and is known for its exceptional potency. Here are some key points about this intriguing strain:

Exceptional Potency:
Penis Envy shrooms are regarded as **one of the strongest Psilocybe cubensis** strains currently known.
Samples of this mushroom have shown combined psilocybin and psilocin concentrations as high as 2.90%, which is 3–6 times more potent than the average Psilocybe cubensis. Only one sample from a strain called Tidal Wave had higher psilocybin levels than Penis Envy (3.82% total tryptamines). Tidal Wave itself is a cross between B+ and Penis Envy genetics.

Distinct Appearance:
The cap on Penis Envy mushrooms remains close to the stem, and the stem is thicker than average, making the shrooms look a lot like a circumcised penis.
Today, dozens of variations and offshoots are derived from the original Penis Envy cultivar.

Mysterious Origins:
The origins of the Penis Envy strain are shrouded in mystery. Some believe the original sample was taken by Terence McKenna during his trip to the Colombian Amazon in the early 1970s.
The strain was further developed by another mycologist named Steven Pollock, who met a tragic end under mysterious circumstances.

In **summary**, Penis Envy mushrooms are renowned for their potency and unique appearance. Whether you're a seasoned psychonaut or a curious explorer, approach them with respect and mindfulness.

Sources:
1. https://tripsitter.com/magic-mushrooms/strains/penis-envy/
2. https://www.medicalnewstoday.com/articles/penis-envy-mushrooms
3. https://www.zoomiescanada.ca/penis-envy-a-closer-look-at-the-strongest-mushroom-strain/
4. https://www.shroomer.com/penis-envy-mushrooms/

Penis Envy #6

Penis Envy #6 is a unique and potent strain of Psilocybe cubensis, a species of magic mushrooms. Here are the key details about this intriguing strain:

Distinct Appearance:
Penis Envy #6 mushrooms are known for their distinctive appearance.
They feature thicker and gnarly stems compared to other Psilocybe cubensis strains.
The caps are rounded and may exhibit a wrinkled or pitted texture.
While the name suggests a phallic resemblance, the true genetic lineage of this strain remains uncertain, fueling various speculations and stories about its origin.

Potency: **Very Potent**
Penis Envy #6 is renowned for its potency.
It contains high levels of psilocybin and psilocin, the naturally occurring psychoactive compounds responsible for its hallucinogenic effects.
Users report intense visions and fervent visual hallucinations when consuming this strain.

Cultivation:
Penis Envy #6 is easy to cultivate, making it suitable for both beginner and experienced growers.
The strain is known for being a prolific sporulator, allowing large quantities of spores to be collected from mature mushrooms.

In **summary**, Penis Envy #6 mushrooms offer a fascinating glimpse into the world of Psilocybe cubensis strains. Whether studying their genetic lineage or simply marveling at their mutant-like appearance, these mushrooms continue to captivate enthusiasts and researchers alike. Approach them with respect and mindfulness.

Sources:
1. https://mushly.com/psychedelic-mushrooms/penis-envy-mushrooms
2. https://www.medicalnewstoday.com/articles/penis-envy-mushrooms
3. https://www.shroomer.com/penis-envy-mushrooms/

Penis Envy Uncut

Penis Envy Uncut (also known as Uncut Penis Envy) is a varietal hybrid of the Penis Envy mushroom strain and the PF Albino. Like other Penis Envy shroom isolations, it has underdeveloped caps, thick dense stipes, and an overall phallic stature[1].

The Penis Envy strain itself is among the most famous and controversial magic mushroom strains in existence. Many regard it to be the strongest Psilocybe cubensis strain currently known. The most notable characteristic of the Penis Envy mushroom is its exceptional potency. Samples of this mushroom have shown combined psilocybin and psilocin concentrations as high as 2.90%, which is 3–6 times more potent than the average Psilocybe cubensis[2]. **It is considered exceptionally potent** compared to other strains within the Psilocybe cubensis family[3].

Interestingly, the Penis Envy mushroom has a distinctive phallic shape. The cap remains close to the stem, and the stem is thicker than average, making the shrooms look a lot like a circumcised penis[2].

Origins:
The origins of this magical mushroom strain are somewhat mysterious and controversial. Some believe that the original sample of Penis Envy was taken by Terence McKenna during his trip to the Colombian Amazon in the early 1970s. The strain was further developed by another mycologist named Steven Pollock, who eventually created the Penis Envy we know today. However, Pollock's death under mysterious circumstances adds intrigue to the story[2].

In **summary**, Penis Envy Uncut is a potent and unique mushroom strain with a fascinating history and distinctive appearance. Its high potency and phallic shape make it stand out among other magic mushrooms[2][1].

Sources:
1. https://microzoomers.co/strains/penis-envy-uncut/
2. https://tripsitter.com/magic-mushrooms/strains/penis-envy/
3. https://www.shroomer.com/penis-envy-mushrooms/

Peruvian

The **Peruvian strain** of magic mushrooms is an ancient and potent psychedelic mushroom variety. Let's explore what makes this strain special:

Origin and Characteristics:
The Peruvian strain was collected from the high-altitude mist-covered pastures of the Peruvian Andes mountains. These pastures receive the perfect combination of sunshine, fertile land, and rainfall, creating an ideal environment for fungi growth. The mushrooms produced by the Peruvian strain have medium-sized, flat, disk-shaped caps that range from light tan to dark brown in color. These caps exhibit noticeable color changes from one flush to the next, making Peru a visually interesting mushroom to grow. The strain colonizes aggressively, fruits quickly, and is a prolific spore producer. It is also extremely resistant to contamination and can produce up to six healthy flushes before succumbing to mold. Aborts are rarely reported among amateur growers[1].

Ancient History:
Evidence suggests that magic mushrooms were an important part of life in pre-Hispanic Peru. Images and carvings of mushrooms have been found on ceramics, textiles, stone, and metal objects from various ancient cultures.

The most abundant and vivid representations of mushrooms were discovered in the art of the Moche culture. These artifacts illustrate the mushroom's use by shamans (curanderos), people of high authority, and sacrificial victims.
Researchers have identified several mushroom species from these artworks, including Calvatia, Psilocybe, Mochella, and Amanita muscaria. The Peru strain could be a direct descendant of an ancient psychedelic mushroom that was used in ritualistic ceremonies over 3000 years ago[1].

Potency and Effects:
The Peruvian strain is said to have above-average potency. Expect moderate to intense visual perceptual changes and a feeling of bodily vibrations.
It's great for stimulating philosophical thought and deep introspection.
The exact psilocybin content of the Peru strain remains unknown, but its effects are highly regarded[1].

In **summary**, the Peruvian strain is a fascinating mushroom with a rich historical background and unique characteristics. Its potency and visual appeal make it a sought-after variety among psychonauts and mushroom enthusiasts[1].

Sources:
1. https://tripsitter.com/magic-mushrooms/strains/peruvian/
2. https://www.psychedelicpassage.com/psychedelic-mushroom-strains-by-potency-30-popular-varieties/
3. https://tripsitter.com/magic-mushrooms/strains/

PESA

The **PESA strain** (also known as **Pacific Exotica Spora Amazonia**) is a variety
of Psilocybe cubensis, a psychedelic mushroom species. Let's explore the key details
about this strain:

Characteristics:
Potency: The PESA strain has **below-average potency** compared to many other
P. cubensis strains1.
Appearance: PESA produces enormous fruiting bodies with caps that can reach a
diameter of over 15 centimeters and stems around 20 centimeters. The caps start as
reddish-brown and become more golden brown as they mature. The stems are yellowish-
white and bruise blue-green when damaged. Due to their hollow stems, the mushrooms'
colossal size often diminishes when dried, but a single dried PESA mushroom can still fill
the palm of a hand1.
Growth Habits: PESA tends to form denser clusters and has darker caps than the classic
Amazon strain. While some debate exists, it's likely that PESA is a genetic isolation from
the original Amazon strain. The original Amazon Cubensis strain was discovered and
brought back to the United States by Terence and Dennis McKenna in the 1970s after a
trip to the rainforest in search of psychedelics1.

Cultivation:
Substrate Recommendation: PESA mushrooms can be cultivated using substrates such
as rye grain, coco coir & vermiculite, BRF cakes, and bird seed1.

History and Origins:
The PESA strain was initially sold by the Pacifica Exotica Spora vendor, which is where it
got its name. The strain name used to include the name of the company that "discovered"
it, but this practice is no longer common.
Some believe that PESA is identical to the more well-known "Amazon
cubensis" or "Amazon strain" mushroom, but there's debate about this. Both strains
produce similar large mushrooms, but PESA has distinct characteristics.
The original Amazon Cubensis strain was discovered during a rainforest trip by the
McKenna brothers and has been used in spiritual ceremonies and healing by native
people in South and Central America for centuries1.

In **summary**, the PESA strain is a unique and large Psilocybe cubensis variety with an
interesting backstory. While its potency may be weaker than some other strains, its rapid
growth and impressive size make it noteworthy among mushroom enthusiasts1.

Sources - https://tripsitter.com/magic-mushrooms/strains/pesa/
https://mushly.com/psychedelic-mushrooms/pesa-mushrooms
https://optimusplant.com/pesa-mushrooms-guide-benefits-cultivation-tips/

PF Albino

 PF Albino is a fascinating variant of the PF Classic strain of Psilocybe cubensis, a type of psychedelic mushroom. Let's delve into the details of this ghostly-white mushroom:

Description:
Appearance: PF Albino is a non-pigmented mutation of the PF Classic strain. While it is almost identical to the original strain, its fruiting bodies are completely white. Imagine ethereal, otherworldly mushrooms emerging from the substrate.

Potency: PF Albino has **mild to average potency** for a magic mushroom. It produces total tryptamine levels between 0.50% and 0.90%1.

Cultivation: Growing PF Albino can be a bit more challenging than other strains in the PF series, but the resulting fruits are truly stunning. Spores for this strain can be obtained from various spore vendors that ship worldwide1.

History:
Robert McPherson, also known as Psilocybe Fanaticus (PF), developed the PF Albino strain. McPherson played a significant role in popularizing the hobby of psychedelic mushroom cultivation. He not only created the PF Classic strain and its variants but also pioneered the commonly used PF-Tek cultivation method.
The exact origin of the PF Albino strain is not widely documented, but it emerged sometime during the late 1980s or early 1990s after McPherson isolated this mutation from his PF Classic strain. PF Albino was initially sold through High Times Magazine and later through McPherson's online spore vendor store, "fanaticus.com"1.

Potency and Psilocybin Content:
PF Albino mushrooms are considered to have **average potency**. While their effects are subtle, they can induce euphoria, insight, and hallucinations. Walls may appear to breathe, and tree branches might take on geometric shapes.
The leucistic (white) appearance of PF Albino mushrooms adds to their mystique, making them a sought-after variety among mushroom enthusiasts1.

In **summary**, PF Albino is a captivating strain with its ghostly-white appearance and ties to the legendary Robert McPherson.

Sources:
1. https://tripsitter.com/magic-mushrooms/strains/pf-albino/
2. https://sporeprinters.com/buy/pf-albino-spores/
3. https://tripsitter.com/magic-mushrooms/strains/pf-classic/

PF Classic

PF Classic, also known as **Psilocybe Fanaticus Classic**, is a strain of Psilocybe cubensis developed by Robert McPherson, who went by the nickname "Psilocybe Fanaticus" (PF). Here are the key details about this strain:

Description:
Physical Variability: PF Classic is a classic cube strain, popular among users but not as commonly grown. Like other P. cubensis strains, it exhibits physical variability. Its stem can be short or tall, thick or thin, spongy or fibrous.

Veil and Spore Release: The veil of PF Classic does not tear until the mushroom is fully mature. Growers can wait until the mushrooms are quite large before harvesting without getting spores everywhere.

Hallucinogenic Properties: P. cubensis, including PF Classic, is one of the most popular hallucinogenic mushrooms in the world. It contains the active compound psilocybin, which induces effects such as euphoria, insight, and hallucinations. These effects are usually subtle, such as walls appearing to breathe or tree branches looking geometric.

Risk and Legal Considerations: While P. cubensis is essentially non-toxic (unless you count psychoactivity itself as a form of toxicity), mild side effects like nausea and excessive yawning are common. More serious problems, including anxiety, can occur. Legal risk is also a concern, as psilocybin is illegal in most jurisdictions1.

Potency: Average

Cultivation:
PF Classic was first isolated in the 1990s. In countries where growing magic mushrooms is legal, cultivators carefully cloned the strain to grow optimally using the PF Tek technique pioneered by Robert McPherson. PF Tek involves growing mushrooms on PF tek cakes.

Summary:
The strain is an excellent choice for beginners, microdosers, and those seeking a milder psychedelic experience. It's suitable for threshold doses during nature walks, social situations, or relaxation after work23. PF Classic is a well-known Psilocybe cubensis strain developed by Robert McPherson, and it offers a unique combination of physical characteristics and moderate psychedelic effects13.

Sources:
1. https://healing-mushrooms.net/pf-classic
2. https://ryzobioscience.com/pf-classic-mushroom-spores/
3. https://tripsitter.com/magic-mushrooms/strains/pf-classic/
4. https://frshminds.com/psilocybin-mushroom-species-guide/psilocybe-cubensis/pf-classic-magic-mushrooms/

PF Redspore

PF Redspore, also known as **Psilocybe Fanaticus** Redspore, is a fascinating variant of the PF Classic strain of Psilocybe cubensis. Let's explore the key details about this unique mushroom:

Origins and Nickname:
The "PF" in PF Redspore stands for "Psilocybe Fanaticus", which is the nickname of Robert McPherson. McPherson is well-known in the mushroom world for his contributions to cultivation techniques and strain development.
McPherson invented the PF Tek technique and developed the PF Classic strain, along with several variations of it.
The Redspore is essentially a red-spored version of the Classic strain. Its spores are not fire-engine red but rather a reddish-brown color. The gills also take on this color once the spores mature.
Interestingly, the spore color of most other Psilocybe mushrooms is purple-black, making the Redspore's reddish-brown spores notably different1.

Potency and Effects: Average
Like the Classic strain, PF Redspore is popular among users for its potency. It contains the active compound psilocybin, which induces effects such as alterations in mood, thought-patterns, and hallucinations.
The effects of PF Redspore are essentially those of psilocybin, which include subtle visual changes and altered perception. Walls may appear to breathe, and patterns can become more vivid.
It's essential to approach any psychoactive substance with respect and caution, including mushrooms containing psilocybin. Legal restrictions also apply in most jurisdictions1.

Cultivation:
PF Redspore, like the Classic strain, can be a bit challenging for growers. However, with proper care, it grows relatively fast.
The strain's unique reddish-brown spores make it a sought-after variety among mycophiles and mushroom enthusiasts1.

In **summary**, PF Redspore is a captivating mutation of the PF Classic strain, characterized by its reddish-brown spores and similar effects to other Psilocybe cubensis mushrooms. Remember to approach psychedelic substances responsibly and be aware of legal regulations12.

Sources:
1. https://healing-mushrooms.net/pf-redspore
2. https://tripsitter.com/magic-mushrooms/strains/pf-redspore/
3. https://sporeprinters.com/buy/pf-redspore/
4. https://psilocybincircus.com/psilocybe-cubensis/spore-syringe/pf-redspore/
5. https://frshminds.com/psilocybin-mushroom-species-guide/psilocybe-cubensis/pf-redspore-magic-mushrooms/

Pink Buffalo

Pink Buffalo Mushroom (also known as Psilocybe cubensis Pink Buffalo) is a unique strain of psychedelic mushrooms.

Origins and Legend:

The Pink Buffalo strain was originally found in Thailand. According to legend, the person who named it discovered the mushrooms in a field where a pink buffalo was grazing. While the pink buffalo part of the story might be more folklore than fact, the strain has become popular internationally.

The Pink Buffalo mushrooms are visually striking due to their deep blue color that develops when the stems are bruised or cut. The caps tend to be a bit dark. Cultivating Pink Buffalo is considered relatively easy compared to other Psilocybe strains12.

Effects and Potency: Above Average

The effects of taking Pink Buffalo are essentially those of any Psilocybe cubensis strain. These mushrooms cause changes in mood, thought patterns, and perception, along with certain physical symptoms.

Ideally, users experience euphoria, insight, and interesting visual hallucinations (especially with higher doses). However, the thoughts and feelings the user brings into the trip influence its direction, so fear or disturbing visions are also possible. Common side effects include nausea, vomiting, and poor coordination. Despite this, psilocybin mushrooms are relatively safe when used responsibly. Pink Buffalo is said to offer a gentler, kinder version of the typical Psilocybe high1.

Potency and Dosage:

Pink Buffalo is one of the more potent P. cubensis strains, although the difference is not dramatic. P. cubensis, in general, falls in the middle range of potency among psilocybin-containing mushroom species.

Dosage depends on the user's intention and whether the mushroom is wet or dry. There are approximately six recognized dosage levels for psilocybin.

Beginners should start with a low dose that still causes hallucinations. More experienced users can try medium or large doses. Above the large dose is the "heroic dose", which can be mind-blowing but potentially challenging. Microdoses are smaller and used therapeutically for mood improvement and insight. Dried mushroom doses are much smaller than equivalent fresh doses. It's essential to err on the side of too little, as higher doses increase the risk of unpleasant or dangerous side effects1.

In **summary**, Pink Buffalo Mushroom is a visually captivating strain with intriguing effects. Remember to approach psychedelic substances responsibly and be aware of legal regulations12.

Sources:
1. https://healing-mushrooms.net/pink-buffalo
2. https://medium.com/@iaskmushroom/pink-buffalo-mushrooms-safe-consumption-and-precautions-83eafab45adf
3. https://mushroom-growing.com/pink-buffalo-mushroom/
4. https://1upmaps.com/the-pink-buffalo-mushroom-strain-guide/
5. https://www.mushiesnow.com/mushrooms/pink-buffalo-mushroom

Plantasia Mystery

Plantasia Mystery is a peculiar strain of Psilocybe cubensis that arrived on the scene sometime in the late 90s to early 2000s. Here are the key details about this intriguing mushroom strain:

Appearance:
Plantasia Mystery mushrooms are medium-sized and look like a "typical cube."
The caps are golden brown and bulbous when young, flattening out and becoming more saucer-shaped as they mature.
How these mushrooms are grown greatly impacts their appearance. When cultivated outdoors, they can look extremely similar to Psilocybe azurescens mushrooms, only larger. They develop a characteristic nipple on the caps and take on a more creamy-yellow coloration.
When cultivated in an artificial environment, they tend to look more like a typical P. cubensis strain, such as Colombian cubensis, although some caps may still produce defined nipples1.

Potency:
The Plantasia Mystery strain has **above-average potency**. Although exact psychedelic tryptamine levels are unknown, it's estimated that this strain produces a combined tryptamine level (psilocybin, psilocin, baeocystin, and other tryptamines) in the region of 0.90% to 1.80%.
While we're yet to see this strain in Oakland Hyphae's Psilocybin Cup, its potential makes it an exciting addition to the world of magic mushrooms1.

Cultivation:
Plantasia Mystery is adaptable to a variety of conditions and climates.
It's relatively contamination-resistant and colonizes the substrate quickly, making it relatively easy to grow.
This strain is a good pick for amateur cultivators who want to explore beyond typical beginner strains like Golden Teacher1.

History and Rumors:
There's a lot of "mystery" surrounding the history of the Plantasia Mystery strain.
Some rumors suggest it's a cross between the two species Psilocybe azurescens and Psilocybe cubensis, but this is unlikely. Plantasia Mystery is simply a strain of P. cubensis that coincidentally looks similar to P. azurescens.
The iconic mycologist Paul Stamets was rumored to have handed out Plantasia Mystery mushrooms as an "Azure" at a mushroom conference in Mexico back in the early 2000s1.

In **summary**, Plantasia Mystery is a captivating strain with its unique appearance and above-average potency. Remember this is for information purposes only.
Sources:
1. https://tripsitter.com/magic-mushrooms/strains/plantasia-mystery/
2. https://tripsitter.com/magic-mushrooms/strains/stropharia/
3. https://mushly.com/psychedelic-mushrooms/plantasia-mystery-mushrooms

Pollock

Steven Hayden Pollock was a mycologist who studied psychoactive mushrooms and published many articles on the potential of mushrooms to treat illness and improve quality of life. One of his significant contributions was the discovery and isolation of a strain of Psilocybe tampanensis that produced sclerotia (also known as "magic truffles") of a size much bigger than previously known. This discovery enabled a means of using psilocybin (the psychoactive compound found in magic mushrooms) in places where magic mushrooms are illegal1.
Here are some key points about the Pollock mushroom strain:

Discovery of Psilocybe tampanensis:
On September 3, 1977, while the Second International Mycological Congress was ongoing in Tampa, Florida, Steven Hayden Pollock and Gary Lincoff discovered a new species of psychoactive mushroom. They named it Psilocybe tampanensis1.
Pollock wrote a book on Magic Mushroom Cultivation in 1977, which included his research on several ways to cultivate magic mushrooms. His method of cultivation in brown rice was later demonstrated to produce mushrooms of high psilocybin content1.

Isolation of High-Potency Strain:
Pollock isolated a strain of P. tampanensis that produced larger sclerotia than previously known. These sclerotia contain high levels of psilocybin.
This discovery allowed for the use of psilocybin in places where magic mushrooms are illegal1.

Business Ventures:
Pollock envisioned creating the first legal medical mushroom research laboratory and estimated he would need about two million dollars to set it up1.
Together with another mushroom enthusiast, Michael Forbes, he founded a company called Hidden Creek in 1979 to sell P. tampanensis sclerotium by mail. Hidden Creek became the largest magic mushroom vendor in the world within the same year1.
Pollock also planted an acre of cannabis to fund his research1.

Other Discoveries:
Pollock traveled to the Amazon and Mexico to study psychoactive mushrooms and discovered three additional species in 1979: Psilocybe armandii, Psilocybe wassoniorum, and Psilocybe schultesii1.
Despite his groundbreaking work, Pollock's life was tragically cut short. On the evening of January 31, 1981, he was murdered1. His contributions to mycology and the study of psychoactive mushrooms continue to be remembered and appreciated.
For more detailed information, you can refer to the Wikipedia page on Steven Hayden Pollock1 or read the article "Blood Spore" by Hamilton Morris in Harper's Magazine2.

Sources:
1. https://en.m.wikipedia.org/wiki/Steven_Hayden_Pollock
2. https://harpers.org/archive/2013/07/blood-spore/
3. https://tripsitter.com/magic-mushrooms/strains/

Psilocybe Azurescens

Let's delve into the fascinating world of **Psilocybe azurescens,** also known as the **Flying Saucer** Mushroom or the Blue Angel.

Psilocybe azurescens: The "Flying Saucer" Shrooms
Appearance: These mushrooms have a caramel-colored cap with a wide saucer-like shape, resembling a miniature flying saucer. The cap often features a distinct nipple on top, which contributes to its whimsical name1.

Potency: **Extremely potent**. Psilocybe azurescens is a small but powerfully psychedelic mushroom. **It is undeniably more potent than your typical Psilocybe cubensis strain**. When consumed, it can produce strong psychedelic effects, including intense waves of energy, euphoria, and prominent closed and open-eye visuals. This potency makes it a favorite among experienced psychonauts, but it's definitely not for beginners1.

Natural Habitat: Psilocybe azurescens grows naturally in a small area of North America, particularly thriving in coastal environments. You can find these mushrooms growing amongst sand dunes within clumps of grass and on rotting wood. Interestingly, they look extremely similar to Psilocybe cyanescens and Psilocybe allenii1.

Cultivation Challenges: While Psilocybe cubensis strains are relatively easy to cultivate indoors, Psilocybe azurescens presents more challenges. Optimal indoor conditions are hard to maintain, and yields tend to be poor. As a result, most people choose outdoor cultivation methods to produce these potent mushrooms. In the wild, they have a unique habitat and require a highly-optimized growing environment to flourish1.

History and Origins: The known history of Psilocybe azurescens is limited. Unlike other species with thousands of years of use, we can trace P. azurescens back to its discovery in 1979. Supposedly, a group of Boy Scouts camping near the Columbia River Delta in Oregon stumbled upon these mushrooms and experienced their potent psychedelic effects. However, there is little concrete evidence to support this story. It's possible that local foragers discovered them earlier but considered them poisonous and inedible until later on1.

In **summary**, Psilocybe azurescens is a remarkable species with its UFO-like appearance, potent effects, and unique natural habitat. Approach it with respect and curiosity, and perhaps you'll catch a glimpse of its otherworldly magic! This is for information only,

Sources:
1. https://tripsitter.com/magic-mushrooms/species/psilocybe-azurescens/
2. https://realitysandwich.com/flying-saucer-mushrooms-guide/
3. https://thethirdwave.co/psilocybe-azurescens/
4. https://www.shroomer.com/flying-saucer-mushrooms/

Psilocybe Cyanescens

Psilocybe cyanescens, commonly known as the **Wavy Cap**, is a species of psilocybin-containing mushroom that grows on wood. Its common name comes from the flat brown caps with characteristic "wavy" edges.

Appearance:
The Wavy Cap has large, flat brown caps that become wavy as they mature. Creamy-colored gills and a white stem make this mushroom particularly attractive. The cap shape resembles a miniature flying saucer, which adds to its allure12.

Potency:
Psilocybe cyanescens is **extremely potent**. It is undeniably more powerful than your typical Psilocybe cubensis strain. When consumed, it can produce strong psychedelic effects, including intense waves of energy, euphoria, and prominent closed and open-eye visuals. Due to its potency, it's not recommended for beginners and should be treated with great respect13.

Natural Habitat:
Psilocybe cyanescens grows naturally in a small area of North America, particularly thriving in coastal environments. You can find these mushrooms growing amongst sand dunes within clumps of grass and on rotting wood. Interestingly, they look extremely similar to Psilocybe cyanescens and Psilocybe allenii1.

Cultivation Challenges:
While Psilocybe cubensis strains are relatively easy to cultivate indoors, Psilocybe cyanescens presents more challenges. Optimal indoor conditions are hard to maintain, and yields tend to be poor. Most people choose outdoor cultivation methods to produce these potent mushrooms. In the wild, they have a unique habitat and require a highly-optimized growing environment to flourish1.

History and Origins:
Psilocybe cyanescens was first described by British mycologist Elsie Maud Wakefield in 1838. Other than this limited information, there's very little in terms of the taxonomic history of this species. It's believed that Psilocybe cyanescens originated in the United States and was later transported to mainland Europe and the United Kingdom1.

In **summary**, Psilocybe cyanescens, with its wavy caps and potent effects, remains a captivating member of the psychedelic mushroom world.

Resources:
1. https://www.bing.com/search?q=psilocybe+Cyanescens+wavy+cap&FORM=bngcht&toWww=1&redig=223DA0B392D043C085121062D1B9B808
2. https://tripsitter.com/magic-mushrooms/species/psilocybe-azurescens/
3. https://thinkmushrooms.ca/psilocybe-cyanescens-information-potency-effects-and-dosages/
4. https://tripsitter.com/magic-mushrooms/species/psilocybe-cyanescens/
5. https://en.m.wikipedia.org/wiki/Psilocybe_cyanescens
6. https://healingmaps.com/wavy-cap-mushrooms-psilocybe-cyanescens/
7. https://realitysandwich.com/flying-saucer-mushrooms-guide/
8. https://thethirdwave.co/psilocybe-azurescens/
9. https://www.shroomer.com/flying-saucer-mushrooms/

Psilocybe Hispanica AKA Spanish

Psilocybe hispanica, also known as the **Spanish Wavy Cap**, is a species of fungus found in the family Hymenogastraceae. Here are some key details about this intriguing mushroom:

Appearance:
Psilocybe hispanica produces small brown mushrooms with conical to convex caps.
The cap diameter ranges from 5 to 10 millimeters (0.2 to 0.4 inches).
The stems are 16 to 25 millimeters (0.6 to 1.0 inches) long and 0.5 to 1 millimeter (0.02 to 0.04 inches) thick1.

Habitat and Distribution:
Psilocybe hispanica is known only from a localized region in Aragon, Spain.
It grows on horse dung in grass fields at elevations of 1,700 to 2,300 meters (5,600 to 7,500 feet) in the Pyrenees mountain range in northern Spain and southwestern France1.

Psychoactive Compound:
Like other psilocybin-containing mushrooms, Psilocybe hispanica contains the psychoactive compound psilocybin.
Psilocybin is responsible for the hallucinogenic effects experienced when consuming these mushrooms.

Historical Significance:
The 6,000-year-old Selva Pascuala rock art near Villar del Humo in Spain suggests that Psilocybe hispanica might have been used in ancient religious rituals.
This rock art provides the oldest evidence of such mushroom usage in prehistoric Europe2.

Taxonomy and Classification:
Psilocybe hispanica was described by Mexican mycologist Gastón Guzmán in 2000 based on specimens collected in northern Spain.
It belongs to the section Semilanceata of the genus Psilocybe due to its thick-walled spores and fruit body that bruises blue when handled.
The specific epithet "hispanica" refers to its origin in Spain1.

In **summary**, Psilocybe hispanica is a fascinating mushroom with a rich history and unique characteristics. Its small size and potent effects make it an intriguing subject for both mycologists and those interested in ancient rituals.

Sources:
1.   https://en.wikipedia.org/wiki/Psilocybe_hispanica
2.   https://en.m.wikipedia.org/wiki/Psilocybin_mushroom
3.   https://www.wikiwand.com/en/Psilocybe_hispanica
4.   https://www.inaturalist.org/taxa/519040-Psilocybe-hispanica

Psilocybe Mexicana

Also known as **Mexican Mushrooms**, is a species of psilocybin-containing mushroom native to North and Central America. Let's explore its history, biology, and other interesting aspects:

History and Biology:
Psilocybe mexicana has been used in indigenous cultural practices for over 2,000 years in areas of North and Central America. Valentina Pavlovna Wasson and her husband Roger Gordon Wasson collected Psilocybe mexicana during their journey around Mexico (1953-1955). They visited Maria Sabina, the Mazatec curandera credited with introducing psilocybin mushrooms to the world. French mycologist Roger Heim characterized the species and cultivated it under laboratory conditions. Swiss chemist Albert Hofmann self-experimented with the mushrooms, extracting and characterizing psilocybin and psilocin in 19581.

Sclerotia Formation:
Psilocybe mexicana, along with P. tampanensis, is known to produce sclerotia—hardened masses of mycelium.
Sclerotia serve as a survival mechanism for the organism during unfavorable conditions (nutrient depletion, drought, freezing, etc.).
These sclerotia are sometimes colloquially referred to as "truffles", although technically this is a biological misnomer. True truffles are reproductive structures with a different function12.

Preferred Habitat:
While Psilocybe mexicana is found near various trees, its preferred habitat is manure-rich grassland. This affinity for similar environments led mycologist Paul Stamets to nickname it the "Mexican liberty cap" due to its resemblance to the liberty cap mushroom (Psilocybe semilanceata)1.

Legality:
In most countries where psilocybin-containing mushrooms are illegal, Psilocybe mexicana is no exception. However, in the Netherlands, the sclerotia of Psilocybe mexicana are legal, even though other psilocybin-containing mushrooms are not.
The Dutch government excluded sclerotia from the ban, considering them weaker than mushrooms. However, their potency may not always align with this perception1.

In **summary**, Psilocybe mexicana has a rich history, fascinating biology, and a unique affinity for manure-rich grasslands. Its role in indigenous practices and its survival strategy through sclerotia make it a captivating member of the psychedelic mushroom world!

Sources:
1. https://doubleblindmag.com/mushrooms/types/psilocybe-mexicana/
2. https://www.shroomery.org/8420/Psilocybe-mexicana-amp-P-tampanensis-sclerotia
3. https://magic-mycology.com/the-ultimate-guide-to-psilocybin-mushroom-strains-varieties-origins-and-effects/
4. https://mushly.com/edible-mushrooms/mexicana-mushrooms

Psilocybe Samuiensis

Also known as the **Samui Mushroom**, is a fascinating psychedelic mushroom found in specific regions of Thailand and Cambodia. Let's explore its characteristics:

Description:
The cap of Psilocybe samuiensis is typically 7–15 mm in diameter, almost convex to conic in shape, and has a small umbonate (nipple-like) projection.
When moist, the cap is reddish-brown, but it becomes lighter brown when dry.
The stipe (stem) is 4.0–6.5 cm high and 1.5 cm thick, equal or slightly bulbous. It is hollow, whitish, and covered with white fibrils.
Both the cap and stipe stain blue when bruised.
The odor and taste are slightly reminiscent of grain meal (farinaceous)[1].

Habitat:
Psilocybe samuiensis was first discovered in Koh Samui, a small tropical island in Thailand. It has also been found in Ranong Province in Thailand and at Angkor Wat in Siem Riap, Cambodia. The mushroom grows scattered to gregarious in rice paddies, but interestingly, it never grows directly on manure.
Fruiting occurs from early July to late August[1].

Chemistry:
Psilocybe samuiensis contains psilocybin and psilocin as its main active compounds.
Analyzed by HPLC and TLC, the fruit bodies contain psilocybin ranging from 0.023% to 0.90% (dry weight) and psilocin ranging from 0.05% to 0.81%.
Baeocystin is also detected at concentrations of 0.01% to 0.05%[1].

Potency is average to less that average.

Local Use:
While some psychoactive species are consumed by both natives and tourists in the region, Chao Samui (local inhabitants of Koh Samui) rarely consume psilocybin-containing fungi.
Local use is usually restricted to local females who do so at the request of foreigners[1].

In **summary**, Psilocybe samuiensis is a rare and unique mushroom with intriguing properties. Its restricted range and cultural context make it a special treat for those interested in the world of psychedelics!

Sources:
1. https://en.m.wikipedia.org/wiki/Psilocybe_samuiensis
2. https://healing-mushrooms.net/psilocybe-samuiensis
3. https://ultimate-mushroom.com/edible/812-psilocybe-samuiensis.html

Psilocybe Semilanceata

Commonly known as the **liberty cap**, is a species of fungus that produces the psychoactive compounds psilocybin, psilocin, and baeocystin. Here are some key details about this fascinating mushroom:

Appearance:
The liberty cap mushrooms have a distinctive conical to bell-shaped cap, reaching up to 2.5 cm (1 inch) in diameter. The cap is yellow to brown, covered with radial grooves when moist, and fades to a lighter color as it matures.
The slender and long stipes (stems) are the same color or slightly lighter than the cap.
The gill attachment to the stipe is adnexed (narrowly attached), initially cream-colored, and later tints purple to black as the spores mature.
The spores are dark purplish-brown, ellipsoid in shape, and measure 10.5–15 by 6.5–8.5 micrometers1.

Habitat and Distribution:
Psilocybe semilanceata grows in grassland habitats, especially wetter areas.
Unlike Psilocybe cubensis, it does not grow directly on dung; instead, it is a saprobic species that feeds off decaying grass roots.
The mushroom is widely distributed in the temperate areas of the Northern Hemisphere, particularly in Europe. It has also been reported occasionally in temperate areas of the Southern Hemisphere1.

Historical Significance:
The earliest reliable history of P. semilanceata intoxication dates back to 1799 in London.
In the 1960s, the mushroom was the first European species confirmed to contain psilocybin.
However, the possession or sale of psilocybin mushrooms is illegal in many countries1.

Potency: extremely High

Taxonomy and Naming:
The mushroom gets its common name from its resemblance to the Phrygian cap.
It was first described by Elias Magnus Fries as Agaricus semilanceatus in 1838.
Paul Kummer transferred it to the genus Psilocybe in 1871.
Panaeolus semilanceatus is a synonym for this species1.

In **summary**, Psilocybe semilanceata is both widely distributed and potent, making it a significant member of the psilocybin mushroom family. Its historical use and unique appearance contribute to its allure!

Sources:
1. https://en.m.wikipedia.org/wiki/Psilocybe_semilanceata
2. https://thinkmushrooms.ca/psilocybe-semilanceata-information-potency-effects-and-dosages/
3. https://www.wikiwand.com/en/Psilocybe_semilanceata
4. https://mushroomsite.com/2020/11/22/psilocybe-semilanceata/

Psilocybe Semperviva

Psilocybe Semperviva, also known as **Psilocybe Subtropicalis**, is a fascinating strain of psychedelic mushrooms. Let's explore the key details about this captivating fungus:

Origin and Classification:
Psilocybe Semperviva was originally classified as a genetic variant of the Mexicana strain. However, recent genetic testing has revealed that it is actually Psilocybe Subtropicalis, not Mexicana12.
Originating in Mexico, Psilocybe Semperviva received its name from its resistance to contamination and decay1.

Appearance:
These mushrooms are medium-sized and resemble a "typical cube."
The caps are golden brown and bulbous when young, flattening out and becoming more saucer-shaped as they mature.
When cultivated outdoors, they can look similar to Psilocybe azurescens mushrooms, only larger, with a creamy-yellow coloration. Indoors, they resemble typical P. cubensis strains but may still produce defined nipples on the caps3.

Potency and Effects:
Psilocybe Semperviva has **above-average potency**. While exact tryptamine levels are unknown, it's estimated to produce a combined tryptamine level (psilocybin, psilocin, baeocystin, etc.) in the range of 0.90% to 1.80%.
Users typically experience subtle visual changes, altered perception, and a sense of euphoria. Walls may appear to breathe, and patterns can become more vivid.
It's essential to approach any psychoactive substance responsibly, considering both the effects and legal restrictions3.

Cultivation:
Psilocybe Semperviva is adaptable to various conditions and climates.
It's relatively contamination-resistant and colonizes the substrate quickly, making it relatively easy to grow.
This strain is suitable for amateur cultivators who want to explore beyond typical beginner strains like Golden Teacher3.

In **summary**, Psilocybe Semperviva (Psilocybe Subtropicalis) is a captivating mushroom strain with unique characteristics. Remember this is for information purposes only.

Sources:
1.   https://sporeprinters.com/buy/psilocybe-subtropicalis-spore-print/
2.   https://sporeprinters.com/buy/psilocybe-semperviva-spores/
3.   https://www.shroomery.org/forums/showflat.php/Number/27070123
4.   https://www.skeletoncrewspores.com/shop/p/semperviva
5.   https://en.m.wikipedia.org/wiki/Psilocybe_hoogshagenii
6.   https://www.shroomery.org/forum

Psilocybe Stuntzii AKA Blue Ringer

Commonly known as **Blue Ringers** or **Stuntz's Blue Legs**, is a weakly psychoactive mushroom found in lawns and pastures in the Pacific Northwest. Although it is not especially popular among recreational users, it has the advantage of fruiting into the winter when growing wild1. Here are some key details about Psilocybe stuntzii:

Description:
Cap: Small to medium-sized, initially conical, becoming nearly flat with a wavy edge as it ages. Variable in color, often yellowish or greenish brown.
Gills: Attached, off-white when young, turning brown with age.
Stem: Medium in length, sometimes thicker at the base, yellowish in color. The distinctive feature is a bluish ring around the stem, which is the remnant of the partial veil.
Spores: Elliptical, purple-brown.
Edibility: Psychoactive.
Habitat: Often found in lawns, pastures, and mulch-beds. Usually fruits in groups.
Range: Found in Washington, Oregon, and California as far south as Los Angeles1.

Effects:
The effects of taking Blue Ringers are essentially the effects of taking psilocybin, a psychoactive substance found in many mushroom species.
Known effects include hallucinations, changes in mood and thought-pattern, nausea, and trouble with coordination and balance.
The experience can vary dramatically depending on the dose, mindset, and surroundings of the user.
Dangerous effects and fatalities are rare but possible, especially in children1.

Potency: Very Weak
Blue Ringers are **much less potent** than most other popular psychoactive mushrooms. They require doses almost ten times the size of that used for P. cubensis to achieve the same effect1.
The blue ring around the stem is a subtle but very distinctive feature, and like many other Psilocybes, this mushroom will bruise blue when handled, although the bruising is not dramatic12. So, if you encounter these Blue Ringers, remember their unique characteristics and approach them with caution!

Sources:

1. https://healing-mushrooms.net/psilocybe-stuntzii
2. https://gwellamushrooms.com/blogs/magazine/blue-ringer-mushrooms
3. https://realitysandwich.com/magic-mushroom-strains/
4. https://www.psychedelicpassage.com/psychedelic-mushroom-strains-by-potency-30-popular-varieties/

Psilocybe Subfimetaria

Also known as **Psilocybe Sierrae**, is a psilocybin mushroom that contains psilocybin and psilocin as its main active compounds. Here are the key details about this mushroom:

Description:
Cap: The cap of P. subfimetaria is 1.5 to 3.5 cm in diameter. It starts as a papillate shape (with a small nipple-like protrusion) and becomes umbonate to broadly convex as it matures. The surface is even or translucent-striate near the margin, and it's viscid when moist due to a thick, separable gelatinous pellicle. The color ranges from pale reddish-brown to ochraceous, and it fades to yellowish olive or ochraceous buff when drying. Velar remnants are often present on the surface, especially around the margin.
Gills: The gills are adnexed, free, or sinuate. They are close, interleaving, and ventricose. Initially whitish clay, they eventually turn dark reddish-brown with an olivaceous hue, with white fimbriate edges.
Spore Print: The spore print is dark purple-brown, with spores measuring (9.5)12.5–15 (16) x 6.5–9.5 μm. The spores are ovoid in front view and ellipsoid in side view, with thick walls and a broad germ pore.
Stipe (stem): The stem is 2–9 cm long and (0.5)2–4 mm thick. It is cylindrical, flexuous, and equal (though sometimes slightly swollen at the base). Initially whitish, it discolours to yellow or yellowish-brown from handling and turns reddish-brown or honey-brown with age. Distinctive blue tones may appear at the base. The stem is covered with whitish fibrils toward the apex and has an apical evanescent fibrillose annulus that develops from a thickly cortinate partial veil.
Odor: Farinaceous (resembling the smell of freshly ground flour).
Taste: Also farinaceous.
Microscopic Features: Basidia are 4-spored, and pleurocystidia are absent. Cheilocystidia are ventricose-fusiform or lageniform with a narrow neck, often flexuous. The gills of P. subfimetaria are adnexed or freely attached, curving up before meeting the top of the stem1.

Habitat and Distribution:
P. subfimetaria is found growing solitary to gregariously on horse or cow dung in grassy areas. It typically appears from September to November.
Interestingly, Psilocybe semilanceata (the liberty cap) may serve as an indicator species for P. subfimetaria, as they both favor similar grasses, soil types, and climatic conditions. The distribution of P. subfimetaria includes Great Britain, Iceland, and much of mainland Europe. However, there have been no confirmed recordings of P. subfimetaria in Asia or the Americas12.

In **summary**, Psilocybe subfimetaria is a psychoactive mushroom that grows exclusively on dung and exhibits distinctive features in its cap, gills, and stem. Its habitat and distribution are relatively widespread, but it remains less common compared to other Psilocybe species1

Sources:
1. https://en.m.wikipedia.org/wiki/Psilocybe_fimetaria
2. https://www.shroomery.org/forums/showflat.php/Number/4397850
3. https://www.shroomery.org/forums/showflat.php/Number/4397850/fpart/all

Psilocybe Tampanensis

Also known as the **Philosopher's Stone Mushroom**, is a very rare psychedelic mushroom in the family Hymenogastraceae. Here are some interesting details about this unique species:

Discovery and Rarity:
Psilocybe tampanensis was originally collected from a sandy meadow near Tampa, Florida, in 1977.
After its initial discovery, the fungus remained elusive in Florida until 44 years later when it was found again.
The original Florida specimen was cloned, and its descendants continue to circulate widely1.

Appearance:
The fruit bodies (mushrooms) produced by Psilocybe tampanensis are yellowish-brown in color.
They have convex to conic caps that can reach diameters of up to 2.4 cm (0.9 in).
The thin stem can grow up to 6 cm (2.4 in) long1.

Psychoactive Truffles:
Psilocybe tampanensis forms psychoactive truffle-like sclerotia.
These sclerotia are known and sold under the nickname "philosopher's stones".
Both the fruit bodies and the sclerotia are consumed by some individuals for recreational or entheogenic purposes12.

Taxonomy and Classification:
The species was scientifically described by Steven H. Pollock and Mexican mycologist Gastón Guzmán in a 1978 Mycotaxon publication.
The type specimen is kept at the herbarium of the Instituto Politécnico Nacional in Mexico.
Guzmán classified P. tampanensis in his section Mexicanae, a grouping of related Psilocybe species characterized primarily by having spores with lengths greater than 8 micrometers1.

In **summary**, Psilocybe tampanensis is a rare and intriguing mushroom species that produces both fruit bodies and psychoactive truffle-like sclerotia. Its discovery and unique properties make it a fascinating subject for mycologists and enthusiasts alike!

Sources:
1. https://en.m.wikipedia.org/wiki/Psilocybe_tampanensis
2. https://tripsitter.com/magic-mushrooms/species/psilocybe-tampanensis/
3. https://wayofleaf.com/shrooms/what-are-philosophers-stone-mushrooms

Puerto Rican

The Puerto Rican mushroom strain is known for its **very potent effects** and extremely rizomorphic mycelium. Here are some key details about this strain:

Discovery and Origin:
The Puerto Rican Cubensis strain was discovered near the town of Canovanas, Puerto Rico.
It is characterized by its large caps and thin stems1.

Effects and Characteristics:
Potency: Users often list the Puerto Rican strain as one of the stronger strains they've tried.
Colonization: The strain exhibits fast and aggressive colonization of substrates.
Fruiting: It produces medium to large fruits during the fruiting stage.
Temperature: Optimal colonization temperatures are 84-86°F, while optimal fruiting temperatures are 74-78°F23.

Challenges:
Due to its rapid colonization, the Puerto Rican strain can sometimes cause overlay, making it a bit more challenging for beginners.
However, once successfully cultivated, it is hard to stop2.

Spore Printing:
The caps of the Puerto Rican cubensis are dome-shaped to flat, making them great specimens for further spore printing1.

In **summary**, the Puerto Rican mushroom strain is prized for its potency, rapid growth, and distinctive appearance. Cultivating this strain requires attention to temperature and substrate conditions, but the rewards are well worth it for experienced growers.

Sources:
1. https://tripsitter.com/magic-mushrooms/strains/
2. https://mushly.com/puerto-rican-mushrooms
3. https://mushly.com/puerto-rican-vs-palenque

Quezon (Philippines)

The **Quezon strain** of magic mushrooms is a unique variety of Psilocybe cubensis that was collected from a garden in Quezon City, Philippines over a decade ago. While most of its growth characteristics are considered standard for the species, what sets this strain apart is its tendency to continue growing to ever larger sizes even after reaching maturity1.

Here are some key points about the Quezon mushroom strain:

Origin and Collection:
The Quezon strain was discovered in Quezon City, which is part of the Philippines.
It was collected more than ten years ago from a garden in the city.

Growth Characteristics:
The Quezon strain belongs to the species Psilocybe cubensis.
While it shares many features with other cubensis strains, its unique trait is its propensity to grow larger even after reaching maturity.
This strain is known for producing large mushrooms.

Distinctive Features:
Although it exhibits standard cubensis characteristics, its ability to continue growing sets it apart.
The Quezon strain is favored by growers who appreciate its potential for impressive mushroom sizes.

In **summary**, the Quezon mushroom strain is a fascinating variation of Psilocybe cubensis that defies the usual growth limits and continues to expand even after reaching maturity1. Its unique features make it an intriguing choice for those interested in cultivating magic mushrooms.

Sources:
1. https://tripsitter.com/magic-mushrooms/strains/
2. https://magic-mycology.com/the-ultimate-guide-to-psilocybin-mushroom-strains-varieties-origins-and-effects/
3. https://www.psychedelicpassage.com/psychedelic-mushroom-strains-by-potency-30-popular-varieties/

Red Boy

The **Red Boy mushroom** strain is a distinct variety of Psilocybe cubensis, known for its unique characteristics and intriguing features. Here's a synopsis of this fascinating strain:

Appearance:
The Red Boy mushrooms have large, meaty stems and beautiful round caps.
Their caps are red and darkish, which makes them quite interesting and visually appealing.
Some describe the caps as resembling a Mexican Sombrero due to their shape1.

Growth and Cultivation:
The strain is generally considered to be a fast grower.
It produces thick stems and gorgeous caps.
Despite its beauty, it is not just a pretty face; the Red Boy strain is also known for its robust growth12.

Spore Coloration:
One of the most distinctive features of the Red Boy strain is its red-tinted spores.
When the mushrooms drop spores, they have a reddish hue, setting them apart from other strains34.

Psychedelic Effects:
Red Boy mushrooms are considered one of the best strains for beginners or those with limited experience.
Their effects are softer and **less intense** compared to many other strains.
While they can be visual, they provide a gentler psychedelic experience1.

Important Note:
It's essential to remember that Red Boy mushroom kits are designed and sold for mycological study purposes only1.

In **summary**, the Red Boy strain offers a unique combination of visual appeal, robust growth, and a softer psychedelic experience, making it an intriguing choice for both cultivators and psychonauts13.

Sources:
1. https://mushly.com/psychedelic-mushrooms/red-boy-mushrooms
2. https://www.mondogrowkits.com/blogs/news/red-boy-the-mutant-shroom
3. https://completemyco.com/blogs/complete-university/strain-highlight-red-boy
4. https://www.magic-mushrooms-shop.com/en/blog/red-boy-magic-mushroom

R44 Cubensis

The R44 strain is one of several hundred known magic mushroom strains that belong to the species Psilocybe cubensis. Although not much information is available regarding its origins, we do know that this strain was first collected somewhere in the Southern United States by Ralph, the owner of Ralphster's Spores1. Unfortunately, due to poor record-keeping, the strain was lost for quite some time and became unavailable from Ralphster's Spores or any other commercial vendor. However, it was later recovered and has since been added back into the Ralphster's Spores lineup.

Here are some key details about the R44 strain:

Characteristics:
The R44 strain is characterized by its thick, dense caps and stems with an off-reddish color.
It stands out as a unique mushroom for aficionados who have tried various strains or those looking for something that won't induce an intense experience at the 3-gram range1.

Potency and Psilocybin Content:
While there are no specific recordings to confirm the potency of the R44 strain, trip reports suggest that its trip intensity is **average**.
Estimated potency places it somewhere in the ballpark of 0.7% to 0.9% tryptamine content (combined psilocybin and psilocin)1.

In **summary**, the R44 strain, once almost lost entirely, offers a unique combination of appearance and moderate potency, making it an intriguing choice for mushroom enthusiasts1.

Sources:
1. https://tripsitter.com/magic-mushrooms/strains/r44/
2. https://magic-mycology.com/the-ultimate-guide-to-psilocybin-mushroom-strains-varieties-origins-and-effects/
3. https://tripsitter.com/magic-mushrooms/strains/

Rosa's Strain

The **Rosas strain** is a unique variety of Psilocybe cubensis, a species of magic mushrooms. While there isn't extensive information available about its origins, it is mentioned as a tribute to an influential person named Rosa[1]. Here are some key points about the Rosas strain:

Appearance and Characteristics:
The Rosas strain exhibits certain characteristics that set it apart from other strains within the Psilocybe cubensis species.
These characteristics include factors like mushroom size, cap color, gill production, and flush vitality.
While specific details about the Rosas strain's appearance are not widely documented, it likely has its own unique combination of these features[1].

Tribute to Rosa:
The Rosas strain is named in honor of someone named Rosa. Unfortunately, further details about this individual are not readily available.
It's common for collectors or enthusiasts to name strains after influential people or as a way to pay homage to someone's contributions to the field of mycology[1].

Availability:
Like many magic mushroom strains, the availability of the Rosas strain may vary over time.
Collectors and cultivators interested in this strain may need to keep an eye out for opportunities to acquire it from reputable sources or spore vendors[1].

In **summary**, the Rosas strain remains somewhat mysterious due to limited documentation, but its unique features and tribute to an influential person make it an intriguing choice for those exploring the world of magic mushrooms[1]. If you come across the Rosas strain, consider it a nod to Rosa's legacy in the mycological community.

Sources:
1. https://tripsitter.com/magic-mushrooms/strains/
2. https://www.psychedelicpassage.com/psychedelic-mushroom-strains-by-potency-30-popular-varieties/
3. https://magic-mycology.com/the-ultimate-guide-to-psilocybin-mushroom-strains-varieties-origins-and-effects/

Rusty Whyte

Rusty Whyte is a psilocybe cubensis strain created in 2014 by shroomery forum member **PastyWhyte**. It is a leucistic phenotype of the Albino A+ and Colombian Rust Spore Cubensis varieties. Here are some details about this unique mushroom strain:

Appearance and Identification:
Rusty Whyte mushrooms are renowned for their dense clusters of medium-sized fruits with cream-colored caps and long, uniform stems.
The caps of these mushrooms are typically cream-colored and medium-sized, and the stems are uniform and long.
They are characterized by their lack of pigmentation and rust-colored spore deposit, which gives them their name.
Rusty Whyte is not found in the wild; it was produced by selective breeding and genetic manipulation.
To identify Rusty Whyte, look for the rust-colored spore deposit and the unique cream-colored caps1.

Leucism in Mushrooms:
Leucism is a condition that causes an organism to be unable to produce pigmentation in its skin, feathers, or fur.
Unlike albinism, leucism does not affect the eyes.
In mushrooms, leucism results in spores retaining their typical pigment, unlike Albino mushrooms with translucent spores.
Rusty Whyte cannot produce melanin in the flesh, but the spores still have a rust color because the mushroom is leucistic1.

Potency and Dosage:
Rusty Whyte is of **moderate potency** compared to other P. cubensis strains.
Effects can be milder than other strains but can still produce strong psychedelic effects.
Recommended dosage varies based on the user's experience level:
Beginners: 1-2 grams for mild psychedelic effects.
Intermediate users: 2-3.5 grams.
Experienced users: 3.5-5 grams.
Start with a low dose and work your way up to gauge the effects, as consuming too much can lead to adverse side effects1.

Cultivation:
Rusty Whyte is cultivated using brown rice flour as the recommended substrate.
It is considered easy to cultivate and provides abundant research material for intermediate spore researchers1.

Psychedelic Effects:
Rusty Whyte mushrooms contain psilocybin, a naturally occurring psychedelic compound.
Users can expect altered perception, enhanced sensory experiences, and changes in thought patterns.

Common effects include:

Visual distortions: Colors may appear more vibrant, patterns may shift, and objects may breathe or warp.

Euphoria: A sense of happiness, contentment, and interconnectedness.

Introspection: Users often engage in deep self-reflection and contemplation.

Enhanced creativity: Some individuals report increased creativity and novel insights.

Spiritual experiences: Rusty Whyte mushrooms are sometimes used in spiritual or ceremonial contexts.

Time distortion: The perception of time may slow down or speed up.

Emotional sensitivity: Users may experience heightened emotions.

Mystical experiences: Some users report feeling connected to a larger universal consciousness.

The specific effects can vary based on individual sensitivity, dosage, set (mindset), and setting (environment).

Dosage and Intensity:

Rusty Whyte mushrooms are considered moderately potent compared to other P. cubensis strains.

Dosage plays a significant role in the intensity of effects:

Low dose: 1-2 grams for mild effects, suitable for beginners.

Moderate dose: 2-3.5 grams for more pronounced effects.

High dose: 3.5-5 grams for intense experiences.

It's essential to start with a low dose, especially for inexperienced users, to gauge individual sensitivity.

Duration:

The effects of Rusty Whyte mushrooms typically last 4 to 6 hours.

The onset occurs within 30 minutes to 1 hour after ingestion.

The peak experience usually happens around 2 to 3 hours after consumption.

Safety and Precautions:

Psychedelics can be intense and emotionally challenging. Users should be in a safe and comfortable environment.

Avoid mixing with other substances, especially alcohol or stimulants.

Individuals with a personal or family history of mental health issues should exercise caution.

Always verify the identity of mushrooms before consumption to avoid accidental ingestion of toxic species.

Remember that individual responses can vary, and it's essential to approach psychedelic experiences with respect and mindfulness. If you decide to explore Rusty Whyte mushrooms, consider doing so in a supportive and informed context.

In **summary**, Rusty Whyte is a fascinating mushroom strain with unique characteristics, making it a favorite among both cultivators and psychonauts23.

Sources:

1. https://thickspores.com/mushrooms/rusty-whyte/
2. https://completemyco.com/blogs/complete-university/strain-highlight-rusty-whyte
3. https://ryzobioscience.com/rusty-whyte-mushroom-spores/

Sandose Domesticate

Sandose strain of magic mushrooms (Panaeolus cambodginiensis), which has piqued the interest of cultivators and psychonauts alike.
Sandose Strain Overview:

Discovery and Origins:
The Sandose strain emerged after mycologist John Allen found specimens of Panaeolus cambodginiensis in Cambodia.
This strain, originally from Thailand, surfaced soon after.
Sandose spores are known for their stability and ease of viewing compared to the Goliath strain.

Macroscopic Characteristics:
Sandose mushrooms are macroscopically identical to Panaeolus bispora.
They grow in grassy pastures on the dung of water buffalo, cattle, and horses in tropical and subtropical climates.
Interestingly, they've also been reported in other climates, including Florida and Mexico.

Ecological Role:
Sandose is an excellent choice for ranches and farmlands due to its ability to quickly decompose dung. As it breaks down dung, it enriches the soil, benefiting the grass that livestock graze on. Ranchers have even noticed reduced dung odor when Sandose fungi are present.

Medicinal Potential:
Beyond its ecological role, Panaeolus cambodginiensis is known for its medicinal properties. It has been associated with quickly relieving migraine headaches.

Microscopic Features:
Spores: Blackish in deposit, smooth, lemon-shaped, measuring 11-16 by 7.5-11 μ.
Basidia: 4-spored (rarely 2-spored).
Cheilocystidia: Irregular in form.
Pleurocystidia: Absent.

In **summary**, Sandose mushrooms combine ecological benefits with potential medicinal value, making them a captivating addition to the world of magic fungi.12

Sources:
1. https://www.mushrooms.com/panaeolus-cambodginiensis-sandose-mushroom-spore-syringe
2. https://en.m.wikipedia.org/wiki/Panaeolus_cambodginiensis
3. https://www.shroomery.org/forums/showflat.php/Number/18611114/fpart/2

Scaly Purple Gym

The **Scaly Purple Gym** strain (Gymnopilus luteofolius) is a unique variety of Psilocybe cubensis, a species of magic mushrooms. Here are some key details about this intriguing strain:

Appearance:
The Scaly Purple Gym mushrooms have caps that are 2-15 cm broad, initially covered with dense, dark red or purple-red scales.
As the mushrooms mature, these scales fade to yellowish-red and then yellow, and they diminish in prominence with age. The surface of the cap sometimes stains blue, especially in younger mushrooms. When growing in clusters, the caps can appear orange due to spore deposition. The flesh of the cap is reddish-yellow, which fades to yellow when cut1.
Gills and Spores: The gills (lamellae) are notched to adnate or slightly decurrent, close together, and exhibit 3 or 4 tiers of lamellulae. Initially yellow, they turn pinkish where bruised and eventually become bright rusty orange as the spores mature.
The spores are bright rusty orange, sometimes collecting on the cap, veil remnants, and wood chips below the cap. Spore measurements are approximately 6-9 x 4.5-5.5 μm, and they are warty and elliptical1.
Stem: The stem (stipe) is 3-10 cm long and 0.4-2.5 cm thick (sometimes up to 4 cm). It is fleshy, equal or enlarged below, and may be tapered at the base when clustered. The center of the stem contains fibrous pith, and it can sometimes become hollow with age. The stem is usually colored the same as the cap, often darker. It may also stain blue, and remnants of the veil can give it a reddish-orange color due to spore deposit1.

Habitat and Distribution:
The Scaly Purple Gym strain is found in both the east and west of North America and is widely distributed.
It grows on decaying wood, including both hardwoods and conifers.
Preferred substrates include older logs, fallen trees, and wood chips.
While it can grow on newly fallen trees, it tends to thrive on older wood1.

Cultivation:
Cultivating the Scaly Purple Gym strain involves similar techniques to other Gymnopilus species. It can be grown indoors (cased) or outdoors (inoculating woodchips). Like other wood-loving mushrooms, it benefits from wood-based substrates23.

Dosage:
Dosage levels for the Scaly Purple Gym strain are as follows:
Level 1: Approximately 1.5 g Level 2: Approximately 2.8 g Level 3: Approximately 4.4 g1

In **summary**, the Scaly Purple Gym strain stands out for its distinctive appearance, including the scaly cap and reddish hues. .
Sources:
1.   https://www.shroomery.org/12467/Gymnopilus-luteofolius
2.   https://www.shroomery.org/forums/showflat.php/Number/6525159
3.   https://www.shroomery.org/forums/showflat.php/Number/7853218

SG30

The **SG30** magic mushroom strain is a fascinating variety of Psilocybe cubensis that has an intriguing history. Here's a synopsis of this unique strain:

Origins and Restoration:
The SG30 strain was brought back to life from a 30-year-old spore sample.
A cultivator known as Shdwstr discovered the spores in an envelope that had been kept in files for almost three decades.
Through gradual rehydration on agar plates, Shdwstr successfully restored the spores and managed to reproduce mushrooms from the sample.
This remarkable feat highlights the resilience of the Psilocybe cubensis species1.

Appearance and Characteristics:
The SG30 mushrooms are relatively average in terms of looks and potency.
They resemble Golden Teachers but are slightly thicker with tall, thick stems comparable to the Penis Envy strain in some instances.
The caps of the SG30 mushrooms are domed, flattening out as they mature, and their edges tend to crack.
Overall, they have a moderate potency, capable of producing intense psychedelic effects in high doses1.

Potency and Psilocybin Content:
The SG30 strain has been rated as "**average potency**".
It produces somewhere in the region of 0.50% to 0.90% total tryptamines.
After consuming SG30 mushrooms, expect a moderately strong body high, intense waves of euphoria, light open-eye visuals, and moderate closed-eye visuals1.

Cultivation and Availability:
SG30 mushrooms are suitable for cultivators and psychonauts of all experience levels.
They can be grown using substrates such as Rye Grain or BRF (Brown Rice Flour & Vermiculite).

In **summary**, the SG30 strain's fascinating history, moderate potency, and unique appearance make it an appealing choice for those interested in exploring the world of magic mushrooms1.

Sources:
1. https://tripsitter.com/magic-mushrooms/strains/sg30/
2. https://ralphstersspores.com/product/sg30/
3. https://tripsitter.com/magic-mushrooms/strains/

South American

The **South American** mushroom strain is a remarkable variety of Psilocybe cubensis, known for its impressive features and unique status. Here's a synopsis of this fascinating strain:

World Record Holder:
The South American shroom strain holds the world record for producing the largest fruiting body of any Psilocybe cubensis strain.
A specimen grown by Shroomery user P. Menace achieved this distinction, surpassing all other strains in terms of sheer size1.

Origins and Collection:
Originally collected in Venezuela, the South American strain has become abundant in regions south of the tropic of Capricorn and in eastern Mexico.
Its name reflects its geographical origin and the rich mycological heritage of South America.
Like other strains from this region, it may have ancestral ties to mushrooms used in religious ceremonies by indigenous tribes hundreds or even thousands of years ago12.

Effects and Potency:
The South American shroom strain contains an **above-average** concentration of psilocybin and psilocin.
Despite its potency, users often report a well-balanced psychedelic experience that isn't as overwhelming as some other high-potency strains.
Comparable to strains like Tapalpa, True Albino Teacher, and Xapuri, it provides a strong yet manageable trip1.

Cultivation:
Cultivating the South American strain is suitable for beginners.
It can be grown using substrates such as Rye Grain or Brown Rice Flour.

In **summary**, the South American mushroom strain combines impressive size with a balanced psychedelic experience, making it a sought-after choice for both cultivators and psychonauts1. If you encounter this strain, appreciate its unique place in the world of magic mushrooms.

Sources:
1. https://tripsitter.com/magic-mushrooms/strains/south-american/
2. https://thinkmushrooms.ca/product/south-american/
3. https://goldenteacherspores.org/product/the-worlds-largest-magic-mushroom-strains-4-pack-special-the-giants-are-here/

Spanish – see Psilocybe hispanica

Starry Night Mushroom

(possibly two versions with the same name. one is a Psilocybe cubensis the other is below)

(Scientifically known as **Omphalotus nidiformis**) is a visually striking and rare variety within the Psilocybe cubensis species. Let's explore its captivating characteristics:

The starry night cubensis strain is a child of two albino penis envy's and is very potent.

Appearance:

The **Starry Night** mushroom truly lives up to its name. Its caps resemble a starry night sky, with deep hues of purples, blues, and blacks1. The cap starts out with a convex shape and then flattens out as it matures. Its surface is smooth and can range in color from deep purple to black, often with hints of blue.

Underneath the cap, you'll find closely packed gills that share the same mesmerizing coloration1.

Habitat:

These captivating mushrooms typically grow in clusters on decaying wood, such as logs or stumps. They thrive especially after rainy periods when the moisture and humidity create the perfect conditions for their growth. The Starry Night mushroom's preference for wood substrate and its striking appearance make it a sought-after find for many mushroom foragers1.

Edibility:

As captivating as the Starry Night mushroom is, **it is not edible** and, in fact, can be toxic if ingested. Its beauty is best appreciated through observation and photography rather than consumption. In this case, it's truly important to admire nature from a safe distance1.

Cultural Significance:

While the Starry Night mushroom may not be on the menu, it holds cultural significance in some parts of the world. In traditional Chinese medicine, it is believed to have medicinal properties and is used in various remedies. Additionally, its unique appearance and mystical allure have inspired folklore and stories in different cultures, adding to its allure1.

Growing Your Own:

For those drawn to the Starry Night mushroom's beauty, cultivating them at home can be an exciting project. While they may not be as commonly cultivated as some edible mushroom species, there are resources and methods available for those interested in exploring the cultivation of these stunning fungi. Creating the right environment, substrate, and conditions can potentially lead to the rewarding experience of observing these remarkable mushrooms up close1.

In **conclusion**, the Starry Night mushroom is truly a marvel of nature, with its captivating colors and alluring presence.

Sources:

1. https://mushroom-growing.com/starry-night-mushroom/
2. https://thickspores.com/product/starry-night-liquid-culture-syringe/

Stropharia

The **Stropharia** magic mushroom strain, specifically referring to Psilocybe cubensis, is an interesting and lesser-known variety. Here are the key details about this strain:

Characteristics:
The Stropharia strain produces relatively large mushrooms.
It is contamination-resistant, making it suitable for beginners.
The mushrooms from this strain have dark coloration, with atypical caps and hollow stems.
Despite its **average potency**, the Stropharia strain compensates with its ability to produce multiple dense flushes1.

Cultivation:
Cultivating the Stropharia strain is considered easy.
It can be grown using substrates such as Rye Grain, BRF (Brown Rice Flour), Coco Coir, and Vermiculite.
Spores of the Stropharia strain are available from various vendors, including Spores 101, Miracle Farms, Sporeslab, and The Magic Mushrooms Shop12.

Potency and Psilocybin Content:
While there isn't much quantifiable information regarding its potency, the Stropharia strain is estimated to have a total tryptamine content of 0.5%–0.9%.
At doses above 2.5 grams, it can produce vivid open and closed-eye visuals, along with intense feelings of excitement and euphoria1.

In **summary**, the Stropharia strain offers a good balance of ease of cultivation, decent potency, and the potential for multiple harvests, making it a suitable choice for both beginners and experienced cultivators1.

Sources:

1. https://tripsitter.com/magic-mushrooms/strains/stropharia/
2. https://driedmagicmushroomspores.com/product/buy-stropharia-magic-mushrooms-online/
3. https://en.m.wikipedia.org/wiki/Stropharia

Suphanburi Goliath

The **Suphanburi Goliath (Panaeolus cambodginiensis)** is a fascinating mushroom strain that has captured the attention of mycologists and cultivators. Let me provide you with a brief overview based on the available information:

Origin: The Suphanburi Goliath strain hails from Thailand, specifically the Suphanburi region.

Growth Characteristics:
Colonization Speed: It colonizes very quickly from spores, germinating in just a few days and fully colonizing in about a week or two1.

Substrate: It can be grown on various substrates, including straight cow dung.

Casing: The casing layer for this strain typically consists of a mix of peat, fine vermiculite, powdered lime, and powdered gypsum.

Fruiting Conditions:
Lighting: Growers have used 6500K fluorescent tube bulbs, placing one on each chamber angled in from the top right on the edge of the lids1.
Fruiting Chamber: A shotgun fruiting chamber or a monotub hybrid can be used.

Flushes:
The Suphanburi Goliath undergoes multiple flushes during its growth cycle. These include tub pinning, bag pinning, tub fruiting, bag fruiting, printing, picking, and drying1.

Remember that successful cultivation involves maintaining proper environmental conditions, cleanliness, and attention to detail. If you're planning to grow this strain, make sure to follow best practices for mushroom cultivation.

Sources:

1. https://www.shroomery.org/forums/showflat.php/Number/14431205
2. https://www.shroomery.org/forums/showflat.php/Number/16064950
3. https://www.shroomery.org/forums/showflat.php/Number/17907680
4. https://www.shroomery.org/forums/showflat.php/Number/13230632

Syzygy

The **Syzygy** magic mushroom strain is a fascinating variety of Psilocybe cubensis that has an intriguing history and cultural significance. Here's a synopsis of this unique strain:

Discovery by Terence McKenna:
The Syzygy strain was discovered, isolated, and sold by the famed Terence McKenna. Terence McKenna is widely regarded as one of the godfathers of psychedelics and made significant contributions to the study of entheogens and altered states of consciousness. He sold spore samples of the Syzygy strain through an online store named after this strain1.

Characteristics:
The Syzygy strain is native to the Amazon in South America.
It is characterized by its convex cap, dark purple-brown spore print, and cylindrical hollow stem.
Despite being considered average in potency, users often report that the trip experience is more intense and introspective than the potency would suggest2.

Cultivation and Availability:
Cultivating the Syzygy strain is suitable for beginners.
It can be grown using substrates such as Rye Grain or Brown Rice Flour.
Spores of the Syzygy strain are available from various vendors, including Ralphsters Spores, Free Spores, and Lil Shop of Spores13.

Potency and Psilocybin Content: Average
While there isn't much formal testing on this relatively obscure magic mushroom strain, anecdotal reports suggest that its potency is consistent.
The estimated total tryptamine content (including psilocybin, psilocin, baeocystin, and other trace tryptamine derivatives) is somewhere between 0.5% and 1%1.

In **summary**, the Syzygy strain, discovered by Terence McKenna, offers a unique blend of history, moderate potency, and introspective effects, making it an intriguing choice for those exploring the world of magic mushrooms12.

Sources:
1. https://tripsitter.com/magic-mushrooms/strains/syzygy/
2. https://thickspores.com/mushrooms/syzygy-mushroom-strain/
3. https://ganjawest.co/product/shrooms-syzygy/

T3 Strain

The **T3 mushroom strain** is an intriguing and somewhat mysterious variety of magic mushrooms. Here's what we know about it:

Origin and Genetics:
The T3 strain is believed to be a genetic offshoot of the Koh Samui strain. Ethnomycologist John W. Allen, also known as "Mushroom John," discovered the Koh Samui strain while traveling in Thailand. The strain was found near the town of Hua Thanon on the island of Koh Samui, which is why it's named after the location. John Allen brought back a spore print of the mushroom to the US and isolated its genetics. The Koh Samui strain has become popular for its high yields, decent potency, and rapid colonization. John Allen also supposedly developed other strains like the Koh Samui Super Strain, which is a genetic offshoot of the original wild strain. Whether the T3 strain is truly a separate offshoot or just a rename of the original Koh Samui strain remains uncertain.

Distinct Growth Patterns:
The T3 strain is named for the three distinct growth patterns that occur between each flush.
Unlike the "original" Koh Samui strain, which occasionally has anomalies in growth patterns, the T3 consistently exhibits these three growth patterns.
This diversity in growth patterns makes the T3 strain interesting and unusual.

Characteristics:
The T3 strain has average potency compared to other Psilocybe cubensis strains.
The estimated total tryptamine levels (including psilocybin, psilocin, baeocystin, and others) fall somewhere between 0.5% and 1% (by dried weight).
While it doesn't yield consistent results for commercial or home growers, it appeals to connoisseurs who appreciate its bizarre and unique nature.

Potency: Average

In **summary**, the T3 strain is a "freak of nature" with unstable genetics, producing three different phenotypes and intriguing growth patterns. It's not your typical magic mushroom strain, but it offers an interesting experience for those who seek it out12.

Sources:
1. https://tripsitter.com/magic-mushrooms/strains/t3/
2. https://www.bing.com/search?q=T3+mushroom+strain+synopsis&FORM=bngcht&toWww=1&redig=669E383EC0F94EC18064E275484F7AF1
3. https://tripsitter.com/magic-mushrooms/strains/
4. https://www.psychedelicpassage.com/psychedelic-mushroom-strains-by-potency-30-popular-varieties/

Tak Mountain Cube

The **Tak Mountain Cube** strain is a fascinating variety of Psilocybe cubensis, a type of magic mushroom. Let's delve into the details:

Origin and Discovery:
The Tak Mountain Cube strain was discovered by the renowned mycologist John Allen during his travels through Southeast Asia in the 1990s.
Allen collected a sample from a patch of what he believed to be water buffalo dung at an elevation of 1000 feet (300 meters) in the Taksin Maharat National Forest Park in Tak, Thailand.
He hypothesized that the strain was introduced from elsewhere in Thailand through spores present in the water buffalo manure spread around the National Forest Park.
The spore samples were propagated in the Netherlands by cultivators, resulting in the stabilized strain we know today.

Characteristics:
Potency: The exact psilocybin and psilocin percentages are yet to be tested, but user reports suggest that the Tak Mountain Cube strain has **average potency** similar to the popular Golden Teacher strain.
Colonization and Contamination: It colonizes slowly but is highly resistant to contamination.
Mushroom Size: The mushrooms themselves are medium to large, with some specimens reportedly reaching weights of over 90 grams.
Growth Environment: This strain loves manure and can produce impressive yields when cultivated properly.
Typical Southeast Asian Traits: The Tak Mountain Cube strain exhibits all the robust traits typical of Southeast Asian strains.

Cultivation:
Substrate Recommendation: It grows well on pasteurized manure or BRF (Brown Rice Flour) substrates.
Beginner-Friendly: While it requires a bit more patience due to slower colonization, it is still considered an easy strain for beginners to cultivate.
Flushes: Expect several healthy, dense flushes.

Availability:
Surprisingly, the Tak Mountain Cube strain is difficult to obtain in Europe, even though it was developed there.

In **summary**, the Tak Mountain Cube strain offers a unique combination of average potency, ease of cultivation, and intriguing growth patterns. If you're looking for a strain that produces large yields and has Southeast Asian characteristics, the Tak Mountain Cube is worth exploring12.

Sources:

1. https://tripsitter.com/magic-mushrooms/strains/tak-mountain/
2. https://sporehunter.gwellamushrooms.com/home/product_detail/127
3. https://www.shroomery.org/forums/showflat.php/Number/6425240

Tapalpa

The **Tapalpa strain** is a fascinating variety of Psilocybe cubensis, a type of magic mushroom. Here are the key details about this strain:

Origin and Discovery:
The Tapalpa strain was discovered in Mexico near the town of Tapalpa in the Jalisco region. It has been circulating in the western spore market for several years and has gained popularity. The strain was acquired and developed by the team at SporeLab. The original wild spore prints were donated by an amateur mycologist based in Guadalajara. The name "Tapalpa" comes from its place of discovery, which is the town of Tapalpa in Mexico.

Characteristics:
Fruit Appearance: The mushrooms produced by the Tapalpa strain have bulbous golden-brown caps and white stems.
Unique Speckles: The caps also exhibit a unique speckle of white spots, similar to those found on the Mazatapec strain, another Mexican variety of P. cubensis.
Potency: Tapalpa is **above average** in potency compared to other cubensis strains.
Growth Patterns: Despite their small size, the fruits of Tapalpa are mighty. They tend to grow in dense clusters, allowing for large yields over several flushes.
Aggressive Colonizer: Tapalpa is known for being an aggressive colonizer, making it easy to cultivate.
Resistance: It is resistant to bacteria and mold growth.
Fluctuating Potency: While generally **stronger than the average** cubensis strain, the potencies of Tapalpa can fluctuate widely from one harvest to the next.

Cultivation:
Tapalpa is easy to grow even for beginners.
It can thrive in an unoptimized environment and colonizes quickly.
Cultivators can produce mushrooms quickly without requiring much equipment, knowledge, space, or time.
Substrate Recommendations: BRF & Vermiculite, Coco Coir & Vermiculite.

Where to Obtain:
Tapalpa spore samples are available from vendors such as Spores 101, Miracle Farms, Sporeslab, and The Magic Mushrooms Shop.

In **summary**, the Tapalpa strain offers a well-rounded experience for cultivators of all levels. Its small but potent mushrooms make it an intriguing choice for those interested in mushroom cultivation1.

Sources:
1. https://tripsitter.com/magic-mushrooms/strains/tapalpa/
2. https://ralphstersspores.com/product/tapalpa/
3. https://www.sporelab.com/tapalpa.htm
4. https://tripsitter.com/magic-mushrooms/strains/palenque/

Tasmanian

The **Tasmanian** strain is a unique variety of Psilocybe cubensis, a type of magic mushroom. Let's explore its characteristics and origins:

Origins and Discovery:
The Tasmanian strain gets its name from the location where the original sample was collected — Tasmania.
Tasmania is a large island off the southern tip of Australia, known for its rich flora and fauna.
The climate in Tasmania is perfect for fungal growth, and thousands of species of mushrooms, including some psychedelic ones, thrive there.
The Tasmanian strain was collected from somewhere on the island during the early 2000s, although the exact mycologist who collected it remains unknown.
Rumor has it that the first samples were obtained by an amateur mycologist known as "BIO" (his online pseudonym).

Characteristics:
Fruit Appearance: The Tasmanian strain produces medium to large-sized fruits that occasionally reach heights of over 20 centimeters (8 inches).
While tall, these mushrooms are relatively slender, and their caps don't reach enormous sizes.

Cultivation:
The Tasmanian strain is a fast colonizer and is incredibly resistant to contamination.
It prefers higher temperatures compared to some other strains and doesn't do as well in cooler environments.
Despite this, it remains an easy strain to grow, making it a good choice for beginners.

Potency:
The **potency of Tasmanian shrooms is low, producing around 0.40% psilocybin**.
This **mild potency** makes it suitable for beginners or those interested in microdosing with psilocybin.

Spore Production:
For those interested in producing spores for microscopy or reproduction, the Tasmanian strain is excellent.
These mushrooms are prolific sporulators, and collecting large samples of spores is easy.

In **summary**, the Tasmanian strain offers a mild psychedelic experience, ease of cultivation, and abundant spore production for microscopy enthusiasts1.

Sources:
1. https://tripsitter.com/magic-mushrooms/strains/tasmanian/
2. https://mushly.com/tasmanian-mushrooms
3. https://completemyco.com/blogs/complete-university/strain-highlight-tasmanian

Teonanacatl

The **Teonanacatl strain** is a fascinating variety of Psilocybe Mexicana, also known as **"god's flesh."**

History of Psilocybe Mexicana (Teonanacatl):
Name: The South American Aztec Indians called it "Teonanacatl", which translates to "god's flesh."
Sacred Use: Before the Spanish invasion, the Aztecs used this species in special, sacred ceremonies.
16th Century Reference: A historian and Franciscan friar from Spain, who lived in the 16th century, referred to Teonanacatl in his writings.
Modern Rediscovery: Ethnopharmacologists in the 20th century became intrigued by this historical reference and embarked on a search for the identity of Teonanacatl.
Active Principle: Scientists discovered the active principle in these mushrooms, which is psilocybin. Psilocybin-assisted psychotherapy is now being studied for treating depression, anxiety, and addictions.

Potency: Above Average

Growing Teonanacatl Shrooms:
Habitat: Teonanacatl shrooms grow in high elevations in Florida, Mexico, Costa Rica, and Guatemala.
Natural Environment: They grow in moist meadows, mossy deciduous forests, and manure-rich soils.
Indoor Cultivation: They can also be cultivated indoors.
Legal Considerations: Before attempting to grow psilocybin mushrooms, it's essential to check local and state laws. Psilocybin decriminalization efforts have been underway in various US cities and states.
Best Ways to Take Shrooms:
Empty Stomach: Users should take magic mushrooms on an empty stomach to prevent a prolonged onset.
Methods: Common methods include chewing, making tea, or using the Lemon Tek technique.

In **summary**, Teonanacatl (Psilocybe mexicana) has a rich history, sacred significance, and potential therapeutic applications. Its name, "god's flesh," reflects its revered status in ancient Aztec culture12.

Sources:
1.]https://flavorfix.com/mushrooms/psilocybe-mexicana-mushrooms/
2. https://tripsitter.com/magic-mushrooms/strains/teonancatl/
3. https://www.shroomery.org/forums/showflat.php/Number/18728671

Texas

The **Texas mushroom strain** is an intriguing variety of Psilocybe cubensis, a type of magic mushroom. Here are the key details about this strain:

Origins and Discovery:
The Texas strain's exact origin remains unclear, but it is associated with the state of Texas, USA.
Texas provides ideal growing conditions due to its cyclical humidity and temperatures, as well as abundant cow dung scattered across the state.
Several offshoots of the original Texas genetics exist, including Texas Penis Envy and Texas Redcaps.
However, there is no official "Texas Strain," and different vendors may offer variations.
The true Texas strain is characterized by the production of small but dense mushrooms.
These mushrooms have very little water content, resulting in rock-hard consistency when dried.
The strain is also noted for its higher-than-average potency, although specific potency testing has not been performed to confirm this.

Characteristics:
Fruit Appearance: Texas mushrooms are small but densely packed.
Their low water content makes them rock-hard when dried, with minimal size change.

Cultivation:
The Texas strain is intermediate in terms of cultivation difficulty.
It grows well on substrates such as rye grain or brown rice flour.
Resistant to contamination.

Potency: Above Average
While no reliable analytical reports cover the potency of the Texas strain, users claim it to be notoriously potent.
Increased density contributes to its strength, with individual mushrooms weighing up to 60% more than others of the same size.
Estimated tryptamine content (psilocybin and psilocin combined) falls between 0.9% and 1.8% based on qualitative effects.
Many users consider it among the strongest mushrooms they've tried.

In **summary**, the Texas mushroom strain offers a unique combination of small size, density, and potent effects, making it a favorite among experienced users1. ♠

Sources:

1. https://tripsitter.com/magic-mushrooms/strains/texas/
2. https://www.bing.com/search?q=Texas+mushroom+strain+synopsis&FORM=bngcht&toWww=1&redig=6EBF888B0CCB4EC98A693CE740F1F851
3. https://magic-mycology.com/the-ultimate-guide-to-psilocybin-mushroom-strains-varieties-origins-and-effects/
4. https://www.texasmonthly.com/travel/texas-star-state-mushroom/

Texas Goliad

The **Texas Goliad** mushroom strain is a unique variety of Psilocybe cubensis, a type of magic mushroom. Here are the key details about this strain:

Origins and Discovery:
The Texas Goliad strain's name comes from the location where the original sample was collected — Goliad County, Texas.
It is associated with the state of Texas, USA.
Texas provides ideal growing conditions due to its cyclical humidity and temperatures, as well as abundant cow dung scattered across the state. The Texas Goliad strain is characterized by the production of small but dense mushrooms. These mushrooms have very little water content, resulting in a rock-hard consistency when dried. While there is no official "Texas Strain," different vendors may offer variations, and the Texas Goliad strain is one of them.

Characteristics:
Fruit Appearance: Texas Goliad mushrooms are small but densely packed.
Their low water content makes them rock-hard when dried, with minimal size change.

Cultivation:
The Texas Goliad strain is intermediate in terms of cultivation difficulty.
It grows well on substrates such as rye grain, brown rice flour, and vermiculite.
It is resistant to contamination.

Potency: **Above Average**
While no reliable analytical reports cover the potency of the Texas Goliad strain, users claim it to be notoriously potent.
Increased density contributes to its strength, with individual mushrooms weighing up to 60% more than others of the same size.
Estimated tryptamine content (psilocybin and psilocin combined) falls between 0.9% and 1.8% based on qualitative effects.
Many users consider it among the strongest mushrooms they've tried.

In **summary**, the Texas Goliad mushroom strain offers a unique combination of small size, density, and potent effects, making it a favorite among experienced users12.

Sources:
1. https://ralphstersspores.com/product/texas-goliad/
2. https://bestspores.com/texas-goliad
3. https://www.shroomery.org/forums/showflat.php/Number/1928874
4. https://www.lilshopofspores.com/cgi/display.cgi?item_num=3755&title=-Psilocybe-cubensis-Texas-Goliad-Spores

Texas Orange

The **Texas Orange Cap** strain, also known as the **Texas Orange** Mushroom, is a captivating variety of Psilocybe cubensis. Let's explore some key details about this intriguing strain:

Origin and Appearance:
The Texas Orange Cap strain is a phenotype of Psilocybe cubensis.
It is known for its vibrant orange-colored caps, which give it its distinctive name.
The caps of these mushrooms are usually quite large, reaching up to 8 cm in diameter, and are often relatively smooth with a convex shape.
The cap center may be slightly depressed, and the gills are white with a light purplish-brown edge.
The stems are usually white and can be up to 8 cm long1.

Potency and Dosage:
Texas Orange Cap mushrooms are **moderately potent**.
An average dried dose ranges from 1 to 2.5 grams.
For those new to psychedelics, starting with a low amount (around 1 to 1.5 grams) and gradually increasing over time is recommended.
Always be mindful of your dosage and respect the power of psychedelics to ensure the best experience1.

Effects and Benefits:
Texas Orange Cap mushrooms produce intense euphoria, a sense of connectedness, and introspection.
Many users experience heightened senses, increased creativity, and improved mental clarity.
This strain also produces vivid visuals, such as fractal patterns and colorful shapes.
Compared to other strains, Texas Orange Cap has a relatively mild body load, making it well-suited for those seeking a gentle psychedelic experience with strong closed-eye visuals1.

Cultivation and Legal Considerations:
Cultivating Texas Orange Cap mushrooms is relatively easy.
The recommended substrate for cultivation is brown rice flour.
Always be aware of legal considerations regarding the cultivation and use of magic mushrooms in your area.

In **summary**, the Texas Orange Cap strain offers a unique combination of vibrant color, moderate potency, and a gentle psychedelic experience. Remember to approach psychedelics with respect and mindfulness for the best journey!1

Sources:
1. https://thickspores.com/mushrooms/texas-orange-cap/
2. https://completemyco.com/blogs/complete-university/strain-highlight-texas-orange-cap
3. https://speedgreens.co/product/texas-yellow-caps/

Texas Penis Envy

The Texas Penis Envy (TPE) is a potent magic mushroom strain that has gained popularity among psychonauts.

Origin and Genetics:
The Texas Penis Envy is the result of crossing a Texan Psilocybe cubensis with the very potent Penis Envy (PE) strain. The PE strain itself is a dense, phallic-shaped, psilocybin-packed cubensis mutant that emerged in the 1970s. Legend has it that it was found growing in the rich grounds of the Amazonian rainforest, where the renowned entheogenic botanist/mycologist Terence McKenna stumbled upon a gargantuan patch of these beastly-looking mushrooms. After cultivating the spores he had brought back, McKenna sent the newly harvested breed to his colleague Dr. Pollock, who is believed to be the designer of the unique, odd-looking species we know today as PE. The original specimen found in the Amazon is also suspected to be the ancestor of the Amazon strain (also known as PESA).

Appearance and Characteristics:
The Texas Penis Envy inherits the fierce potency of the PE strain and the prosperous nature of the Psilocybe cubensis, which is one of the most widespread species of magic mushrooms.
The caps of the Texas Penis Envy are typically dark brown and have a thick, bulbous shaft.
Despite its laborious and slow growth, the Texas Penis Envy is highly regarded for its effectiveness and trippiness.
It thrives in climates that range from cool to warm, making it well-suited for Texas, the second-largest state in the USA.

Psychedelic Properties:
Like other PE strains, the Texas Penis Envy is known for its potency.
It contains psilocybin, the psychoactive compound responsible for the profound changes in perception, mood, and thought associated with magic mushrooms.
The Texas PE is a fruitful candidate for micro-dosing, which can enhance performance and foster a sense of well-being.

Cultivation and Consumption:
Growers appreciate the Texas Penis Envy due to its combination of easy growth and **potent effects.**
From the Amazon rainforest to the rolling hills of Texas, this strain has adapted and is now cultivated and consumed worldwide.

In **summary**, the Texas Penis Envy is a remarkable example of the adaptability of these fascinating organisms, and its genetics trace back from the Amazonian rainforest to the labs of McKenna and Pollock, and finally to the fields of Texas1234.

Sources:
1.   https://microzoomers.co/strains/texas-penis-envy/
2.   https://magicmushroomiez.com/product/texas-penis-envy-mushrooms/
3.   https://budlyft.com/product/texas-penis-envy-magic-mushrooms/
4.   https://tripsitter.com/magic-mushrooms/strains/texas/

Thai

The **Thai mushroom** strain is a fascinating variety of Psilocybe cubensis, a type of magic mushroom. Let's explore its characteristics and origins:

Origins and Discovery:
The Thai strain was discovered by the renowned mycologist John Allen on the tropical island of Koh Samui, which is particularly rich in psychedelic mushrooms.
Allen found the Thai strain growing alongside several other popular strains on the island, all of which share similar growth characteristics.
Genetic Relatives: The Thai strain shares genetics with other strains discovered on Koh Samui, including the Koh Samui, Ban Hua Thanon, Lipa Yai, Ban Thurian, and Ban Phang Ka strains.

Distinct Growth Characteristics:
The Thai strain produces rounded caps that are golden-brown in color.
Its stems are creamy-white and relatively thick, although not as much as the Thai Koh Samui strain.
Unlike the Koh Samui strain, the Thai strain is far less likely to produce "Fatasses"—mushrooms that are short and fat in appearance.
As the caps mature, they gradually flatten out, and if left to sporulate, they become convex.
Confusion with Lipa Yai: Many people also confuse the Thai strain with another Thai variety called Lipa Yai, which seems to produce thinner and taller fruiting bodies.

Cultivation and Potency:
The Thai strain is ideal for beginner cultivators due to its several qualities:
Contamination resistant
Can grow in an unoptimized environment
Produces good yields through several healthy flushes
Mushrooms hold average to above average potency

Substrate Recommendations: Rye Grain, Bird Seed, BRF (Brown Rice Flour)
Where to Find Spore Samples: Available from vendors such as Spores 101, Miracle Farms, Sporeslab, and The Magic Mushrooms Shop.

In **summary**, the Thai mushroom strain offers a well-rounded experience for cultivators, combining ease of cultivation with intriguing growth patterns and moderate potency1.

Sources:

1.   https://tripsitter.com/magic-mushrooms/strains/thai/
2.   https://www.magic-mushrooms-shop.com/en/blog/thai-magic-mushroom-strain
3.   https://mushly.com/thai-mushrooms
4.   https://fungimaps.com/strains/thai/
5.   https://tripsitter.com/magic-mushrooms/strains/ban-hua-thanon/
6.   https://premiumspores.com/product/thai-lipa-yai-spores/

Thaitanic

The **Thaitanic** mushroom strain, also known as Thai Tanic, is a sought-after variation of the Psilocybe cubensis species. Let's explore some key details about this intriguing strain:

Origins and Discovery:
The Thaitanic strain was discovered growing in the tropical environment of Koh Samui, an island in Thailand.
Mycologist John Allen found this strain alongside several other popular strains during his explorations.
It shares genetics with other strains discovered on Koh Samui, including the Koh Samui, Ban Hua Thanon, Lipa Yai, Ban Thurian, and Ban Phang Ka strains1.

Distinctive Characteristics:
The Thaitanic strain produces rounded caps that are golden-brown in color.
Its stems are light, creamy-white, relatively thick, and less likely to produce "Fatasses" (short and fat mushrooms).
As the caps mature, they gradually flatten out and may become convex if left to sporulate.
People sometimes confuse this strain with another Thai variety called Lipa Yai, which produces thinner and taller fruiting bodies1.

Cultivation and Potency:
The Thaitanic strain is ideal for both beginner cultivators and experienced growers.
Its qualities include:
Contamination resistance: It grows well even in unoptimized environments.
Multiple healthy flushes: It can yield good harvests over several flushes.
Average to above-average potency: The mushrooms offer a satisfying psychedelic experience1.

In **summary**, the Thaitanic strain combines ease of cultivation with desirable characteristics, making it a favorite among both beginners and experienced mushroom researchers! 12

Sources:
1. https://tripsitter.com/magic-mushrooms/strains/thai/
2. https://sporeswaps.com/shop/actives-spores/cultures/thaitanic-research-plate-thai-lipa-yai-2/
3. https://sporesmd.com/product/thai-tanic-mushroom-spore-syringe-10ml/
4. https://theshroomzstore.com/product/thai-tanic-psilocybe-cubensis-spores-10ml/
5. https://strainly.io/en/listings/430444-thai-tanic

Tidal Wave

The **Tidal Wave** strain is a hybrid of the Psilocybe cubensis species of magic mushrooms. Let me provide you with a comprehensive overview of this intriguing strain:

Genetics and Origins:
Tidal Wave is a phenotype (or strain) of Psilocybe cubensis mushrooms.
It is a cross between two potent strains: Penis Envy and B+.
Both Penis Envy and B+ are well-known members of the Psilocybe cubensis family.
The combination of these genetics results in a unique strain with distinct characteristics.

Potency:
Tidal Wave is known for its **extreme potency**.
It inherits its strength from the Penis Envy strain, which is renowned for containing up to 100% more psilocybin than the average Psilocybe cubensis.
In fact, Tidal Wave currently holds the record for the highest psilocybin and psilocin content ever tested in the Psilocybin Cup.
While the average potency across multiple samples of Tidal Wave is slightly lower, it still remains significantly above average:
Psilocybin average: 0.87%
Psilocin average: 0.27%
Total tryptamine average: 1.17%
The peak achievement recorded for Tidal Wave was an astonishing 3.82% total tryptamines[1].

Appearance and Growth:
Tidal Wave is a fast-fruiting strain, meaning it produces mushrooms relatively quickly.
Its appearance may differ from standard Psilocybe cubensis mushrooms due to its unique genetics.
As a hybrid of Penis Envy and B+, it exhibits distinct color and size variations.

Cultivation and Availability:
Tidal Wave can be cultivated by experienced growers.
It is recommended to use rye grain as the substrate for growing this strain.
Spores of Tidal Wave are available from various sources, including Sporeslab, Spores 101, High Desert Spores, and Mushroom Prints.

In **summary**, Tidal Wave mushrooms offer a powerful psychedelic experience, thanks to their exceptional potency and unique genetic lineage. If you are seeking an intense trip, Tidal Wave might be the wave you are looking to ride! 1234.

Sources:

1.   https://tripsitter.com/magic-mushrooms/strains/tidal-wave/
2.   https://www.floweravedc.com/post/tidal-wave-shrooms-strain-profile
3.   https://healing-mushrooms.net/tidal-wave-shrooms
4.   https://thefunguys.co/product/tidal-wave-cubensis-dried-mushroom/

Tidal Wave 2

The Tidal Wave 2 mushroom strain is an enthralling fusion of two renowned Psilocybe cubensis strains, harmonizing the powerful attributes of the renowned Penis Envy and B+ strains, resulting in an extraordinary magic mushroom hybrid1. Let's dive deeper into the details:

Genetics and Origins:
Tidal Wave 2 is a hybrid strain created by crossing the well-known B+ and Penis Envy strains of Psilocybe cubensis.
Both B+ and Penis Envy are celebrated for their potency and unique characteristics.
The combination of these genetics results in a strain that offers a powerful psychedelic experience.

Potency and Effects:
Tidal Wave 2 inherits its strength from the Penis Envy strain, which is renowned for containing up to 100% more psilocybin than the average Psilocybe cubensis2.
While the exact potency of Tidal Wave 2 may vary, it is known for its **extreme potency**.
Users can expect effects such as intense visuals, euphoria, and deep introspection.
Due to its potency, it is recommended that users approach Tidal Wave 2 with caution and start with a low dosage.

Appearance and Growth:
Tidal Wave 2 mushrooms exhibit variations in color, size, and appearance due to their unique genetic lineage.
They typically have a classic psilocybin mushroom appearance, with a conical cap and a sturdy stem.
Cultivating Tidal Wave 2 requires intermediate-level experience, and it is often grown on rye grain substrate.

In **summary**, Tidal Wave 2 mushrooms offer a potent and mind-expanding journey for those seeking a profound psychedelic experience. Remember to approach them with respect and mindfulness, as their effects can be transformative!

Sources:
1. https://1upmaps.com/tidal-wave-mushroom-a-high-potency-award-winning-strain/
2. https://tripsitter.com/magic-mushrooms/strains/tidal-wave/
3. https://healing-mushrooms.net/tidal-wave-shrooms
4. https://thefunguys.co/product/tidal-wave-cubensis-dried-mushroom/

Trans Envy

The **Trans Envy** strain is a fascinating hybrid of two renowned Psilocybe cubensis strains, resulting from an unplanned combination of genetic material. Let's explore the intriguing qualities of this strain:

Genetics and Creation:
Origin: The Trans Envy strain emerged when two rye grain spawn bags—one containing the South African Transkei strain and the other containing the Penis Envy strain—were unknowingly combined on a fruiting tray by workers at Spores Lab.
Hybridization: The resulting hybrid mushrooms were carefully isolated, leading to the creation of a new genetic lineage.
Characteristics: Trans Envy exhibits characteristics from both parent strains, making it a unique blend of their potent attributes1.

Characteristics:
Appearance: While Trans Envy mushrooms don't retain the famous phallic shape of Penis Envy, they share the notoriously thick white stems. Additionally, they display larger fruiting bodies and wider caps influenced by the Transkei genetic side of the strain.
Effects: Trans Envy preserves the vibration and stimulating experience of Transkei and the vivid visuals and intense euphoria associated with Penis Envy.
Sporulation: Like Penis Envy, Trans Envy is a light sporulator, which makes collecting spores for future grows more challenging but results in less mess if shrooms aren't harvested promptly.
Potency: Trans Envy is **highly potent**, making it ideal for those seeking a stronger psychedelic experience than typical strains.
Cultivation: It is contamination-resistant, colonizes quickly, and can thrive in unoptimized growing environments. It produces several dense flushes before succumbing to mold growth1.

Cultivation:
Recommended Substrate: Trans Envy grows well on rye grain and wild bird seed substrates.

In **summary**, Trans Envy is an interesting and potent strain, perfect for both beginners and experienced cultivators. Its accidental creation resulted in a happy fusion of genetics, offering a transformative journey for those who seek it!1.

Sources:
1. https://tripsitter.com/magic-mushrooms/strains/trans-envy/
2. https://tripsitter.com/magic-mushrooms/strains/south-african-transkei/
3. https://www.leafly.com/strains/envy

Transskei

The **South African Transkei** magic mushroom strain, scientifically known as Psilocybe cubensis Transkei, has a fascinating origin story. Let me share some details about it:

Origin and Characteristics:
The South African Transkei shrooms are one of the only magical mushroom strains known to have originated from the Rainbow Nation. They come from the former Transkei province of South Africa (now part of the Eastern Cape province).
These shrooms have distinct pyramid-shaped caps and gnarled or twisted stems, making them easily distinguishable from other Psilocybe cubensis strains.
Unlike many other strains, the South African Transkei shroom doesn't resemble any other cubensis strains we know of.
It's interesting to note that this strain is the first psychedelic mushroom strain ever discovered and documented in modern history that is native to South Africa1.

Growing Conditions:
Magic mushrooms grow worldwide, but they prefer moist climates for at least part of the year.
South Africa's hot, arid deserts are typically unsuitable for psilocybin mushrooms, which is why there are so few Psilocybe cubensis strains originating from this part of the world.
The original sample of the South African Transkei strain was collected in the early 2000s, growing in a pile of cow dung in the shade of a tree near the Indian Ocean. The documentation surrounding this sample is stellar, and the spore collection site can be pinpointed on a map1.

Potency and Effects:
Most users report a more intense trip with South African Transkei shrooms than with most other strains.
Effects include open-eye visuals, fractals, and a sense of connection to the world.
Only one sample has been submitted for testing in the bi-annual Psilocybin Cup. This sample registered 0.83% psilocybin, 0.02% psilocin, and 0.92% total tryptamines.
While this classifies the Transkei strain as **average** (0.5% to 0.9% tryptamines), cultivation under optimal conditions may yield even higher potency.
The typical potency of this strain is estimated to be well above average, with tryptamine concentrations in the 0.8–1.6% range1.
So, if you're interested in exploring the world of magic mushrooms, the South African Transkei strain is definitely one to consider! 23

Sources:
1. https://tripsitter.com/magic-mushrooms/strains/south-african-transkei/
2. https://mushly.com/transkei-mushrooms
3. https://3amigos.co/all-about-african-transkei-magic-mushrooms/

Treasure Coast

The **Treasure Coast** magic mushroom strain, scientifically known as Psilocybe cubensis Treasure Coast, has its own intriguing story. Let's delve into the details:

Origin and Characteristics:
The Treasure Coast strain was originally collected from the eastern coast of Florida, which is often referred to as the Treasure Coast.
Unfortunately, there is no specific information about the mycologist or hobbyist who first discovered and isolated this strain.
These mushrooms exhibit medium-sized fruiting bodies with slender, fibrous stems and convex to plane or umbonate caps. The caps are usually a light caramel or golden color, sometimes featuring a slightly darker center[1,2].

Forms and Potency:
The Treasure Coast strain comes in two main forms:
Original TC: This is the standard version.
Albino (Leucistic) Version: This form produces lighter-colored fruits.
While many reports online suggest that the Treasure Coast strain is nearly twice as strong as common strains like Golden Teachers, quantitative testing shows that it's more likely on par with average strains.
Two separate samples submitted for testing in the Psilocybin Cup showed an average of 0.59% psilocybin and 0.08% psilocin, resulting in an average total tryptamine concentration of 0.67%.
This places the Treasure Coast strain right in the range of what we'd consider **average potency** (0.5% to 0.9%).
The strongest sample submitted contained 0.69% total tryptamines by dried weight, but very potent cubes can test as high as 3.8%[1].

Cultivation and Use:
Cultivating the Treasure Coast strain can be a challenge due to its unique characteristics.
For cultivation, it's recommended to use substrates like rye grain or brown rice flour.
The typical dose range for this mushroom is 2–3 grams, providing a potent yet manageable experience.
Expect introspective effects, mild visuals, and a relaxing trip when consuming the Treasure Coast strain[1,3].

In summary, the Treasure Coast strain offers a fascinating journey for those exploring the world of magic mushrooms! [1,2,3]

Sources:
1. https://tripsitter.com/magic-mushrooms/strains/treasure-coast/
2. https://completemyco.com/blogs/complete-university/strain-highlight-treasure-coast
3. https://fungimaps.com/strains/treasure-coast
4. https://mushly.com/treasure-coast-magic-mushrooms
5. https://healing-mushrooms.net/treasure-coast
6. https://tripsitter.com/magic-mushrooms/strains/albino-treasure-coast/

Trinity

The Trinity strain is a distinctive hybrid in the Psilocybe cubensis family, combining the genetics of three well-known strains.
These three strains are:
Penis Envy: Known for its potency and unique appearance, Penis Envy contributes to Trinity's exceptional characteristics.
Aztec God: Another parent strain, Aztec God, adds its own genetic influence to the mix.
Tidal Wave: Tidal Wave is a cross between the B+ strain and Penis Envy, further enhancing Trinity's genetic diversity12.

Appearance and Identification:
Trinity bears a more than passing resemblance to Penis Envy, with a narrow cap and a relatively thick stem. However, it's not as obviously phallic in appearance.
Unlike Penis Envy, which lacks a veil, Trinity sometimes has a veil, and its cap color is typically a light caramel brown with hints of blue bruising.
While it shares some visual similarities with Penis Envy, Trinity remains distinct and recognizable3.

Potency and Effects:
Trinity mushrooms are said to be **extremely potent**, although the exact tryptamine content compared to other strains isn't precisely tracked.
Users report an intense, very visual experience grounded in bodily sensations. Trinity has been favorably compared to the Z-Strain, although it's not as cerebral.
Keep in mind that individual experiences can vary significantly due to factors like mindset, biochemistry, setting, and dosage.
At higher doses, hallucinations may occur, but even at moderate levels, Trinity offers a profound journey3.

Medical and Spiritual Use:
Psilocybin mushrooms, including Trinity, have been used for personal and spiritual growth. While there's no definitive proof of medical efficacy, some people explore psilocybin for conditions like depression, anxiety, and epilepsy.
Regardless of medical claims, psilocybin can facilitate valuable personal experiences, leading to insights and altered thought patterns3.

In **summary**, Trinity offers a unique and potent adventure for those curious about magic mushrooms!12

Sources:
1. https://thinkmushrooms.ca/product/trinity-mushrooms/
2. https://fungushead.com/product/trinity-spore-swab/
3. https://healing-mushrooms.net/trinity-shrooms
4. https://cannablossom.co/product/trinity/
5. https://shroomsxpress.cc/product/trinity/
6. https://www.zoomiescanada.ca/buy-mushrooms-online/dried-shrooms/trinity/

True Albino Melmac

The **TAM mushroom** strain is an intriguing and relatively rare variety within the world of psilocybin mushrooms. Let's explore some key details about this strain:

Origin and Genetics:
The TAM strain is derived from the crossbreeding of two other strains: OG TAT and Melmac.
The genetic lineage of this strain is sometimes referred to as the True Albino Melmac or the TAM project1.

Appearance and Characteristics:
The TAM strain showcases the mesmerizing beauty of true albino mushrooms.
It is a pure albino Melmac TP isolate developed by a cultivator named Dave Wombat.
The most striking feature of the TAM strain is its white appearance, which sets it apart from other varieties.
When fully grown, these mushrooms exhibit a captivating and intense psychedelic effect2.

Psychedelic Effects:
Like other psilocybin mushrooms, the TAM strain contains the active compounds psilocybin, psilocin, and baeocystin.
Users of the TAM strain report a unique and visually stunning experience.
The intense psychedelic effects associated with this strain make it a sought-after choice for those seeking profound journeys2.

Sclerotia Formation:
Interestingly, the TAM strain is also related to another rare psychedelic mushroom called Psilocybe tampanensis.
Psilocybe tampanensis forms psychoactive truffle-like sclerotia, which are known and sold under the nickname "philosopher's stones"3.

In **summary**, the TAM mushroom strain offers a combination of rarity, visual appeal, and potent psychedelic effects. While it may not be as widely recognized as some other strains, its unique characteristics make it a fascinating choice for those exploring the world of psilocybin mushrooms2. If you ever encounter the TAM strain, consider yourself fortunate to experience its distinctive qualities!

Sources:
1. https://sonoranspores.com/product/mvp-spores-2/
2. https://magic-mycology.com/the-ultimate-guide-to-psilocybin-mushroom-strains-varieties-origins-and-effects/
3. https://en.m.wikipedia.org/wiki/Psilocybe_tampanensis
4. https://www.psychedelicpassage.com/psychedelic-mushroom-strains-by-potency-30-popular-varieties/

True Albino Teacher

The **True Albino Teacher** (TAT) is an albino variant of the famous Golden Teacher strain (Psilocybe cubensis).
It carries all the qualities of the original Golden Teacher but with albino traits, meaning it lacks pigmentation.
TAT produces pure white fruiting bodies that stand out due to their ghostly appearance.
The strain was developed by a Shroomery user named "Jik Fibs", who isolated the albino variation during Golden Teacher cultivation.
Through dedicated work and multiple generations, Jik Fibs successfully produced fully albino mushrooms12.

Potency and Psilocybin Content:
True Albino Teacher mushrooms are above average in potency, slightly stronger than the original Golden Teacher strain.
Samples submitted for testing at the Psilocybin Cup revealed the following **average content**:
Psilocybin: 0.81%
Psilocin: 0.06%
Total tryptamine concentration: 0.87%
While technically classified as "average," many users report slightly higher potency.
The strongest sample tested had 1.11% total tryptamines, and private tests have shown levels as high as 1.4%.
Notably, TAT spores lack pigmentation, just like true albinos1.

Cultivation:
Growing True Albino Teacher can be a bit more demanding than the Golden Teacher strain.
However, with proper knowledge of cultivation, several flushes of these white mushrooms can be produced without much trouble.
Reliable albino spore samples are available from select vendors across the United States and Canada1.

In summary, the True Albino Teacher strain offers a unique and visually stunning experience for those interested in exploring magic mushrooms! 12

Sources:
1. https://tripsitter.com/magic-mushrooms/strains/true-albino-teacher/
2. https://askmushroom.com/lander
3. https://magic-mycology.com/product/true-albino-teacher/

US Virgin Islands

The **U.S. Virgin Island Psilocybe cubensis** is a remarkable strain of magic mushrooms that captivates both researchers and enthusiasts. Let's explore its key **features**:

Origin and Rarity:
The U.S. Virgin Island strain is relatively rare and was initially available only through donations and trades. Its scarcity adds to its allure, making it a sought-after specimen among mycologists and cultivators.

Similarities to Asian Strains:
Interestingly, this strain shares similarities with the **Ban Nathon** strain, which has its roots in Asia. Perhaps the tropical vibes of the U.S. Virgin Islands contribute to its robust growth and unique characteristics.

Microscopic Beauty:
Under the microscope, the U.S. Virgin Island Psilocybe cubensis reveals intricate mycelial networks and spore-bearing structures. Its microscopic beauty hints at the transformative experiences it offers to those who partake in its consumption.

Psychoactive Properties:
Like all Psilocybe cubensis strains, the U.S. Virgin Island strain contains the psychoactive compounds **psilocybin** and **psilocin**. These compounds induce altered states of consciousness, vivid visuals, and introspective journeys.

Invitation to Exploration:
Whether you're a seasoned psychonaut or a curious soul, the U.S. Virgin Island strain invites you to explore inner landscapes. It whispers ancient wisdom from the mycelial network of existence, touching realms beyond mere chemistry.
In **summary**, the U.S. Virgin Island Psilocybe cubensis is a tiny emissary of wonder—a bridge between continents, cultures, and consciousness.
Sources:

1. https://tripsitter.com/magic-mushrooms/strains/
2. https://www.thebluntness.com/posts/different-psilocybin-strains-and-effects
3. https://www.spores101.co/virgin-island-mushroom-spores.html
4. https://www.shroomery.org/13859/Psilocybe-Cubensis-Strain-Information
5. https://healing-mushrooms.net/psilocybe-cubensis-strains

Venezuela

The **South American Shroom** Strain.
The South American shroom strain, also known as the "laid-back cubensis," holds the distinction of being the world's largest magic mushroom strain. It was originally collected in Venezuela and has some intriguing characteristics1. Here's what you need to know:

Origin and Collection:
The first sample of the South American shroom was taken by a magic mushroom spore vendor called Spore Chicks (which has since gone out of business).
Unlike other strains named after specific regions (like the Argentina strain or the Amazon strain), the South American strain is named more broadly.
It's possible that this strain is a direct descendant of mushrooms used in religious ceremonies by tribes inhabiting the area hundreds or even thousands of years ago.

Potency and Experience:
The South American shroom has an above-average concentration of psilocybin and psilocin.
Users typically report a well-balanced psychedelic experience, which isn't as overwhelming as some other potent strains.
Trip reports suggest that it's comparable in strength to strains like Tapalpa, True Albino Teacher, and Xapuri.

Record Holder:
A South American shroom grown by a user named P. Menace holds the record for the largest cubensis fruiting body ever harvested.
Previously, a sample of the Orissa India strain held this record.

Estimated Tryptamine Content:
The total tryptamine content in the South American shroom is estimated to be between 1.2% and 1.8% by dried weight.
For comparison, the average tryptamine content in Psilocybe cubensis strains ranges from 0.5% to 1%.

Cultivation:
If you're interested in cultivating this strain, it's recommended to use rye grain or brown rice flour as the substrate.

In **summary**, the South American shroom strain combines potency with a balanced psychedelic experience, making it a favorite among magic mushroom enthusiasts. If you are ever in Venezuela, keep an eye out for these remarkable fungi 2

Sources:
1. https://tripsitter.com/magic-mushrooms/strains/south-american/
2. https://tripsitter.com/magic-mushrooms/strains/
3. https://microzoomers.co/strains/south-american-cubensis/

Vietnamese Psilocybe Cubensis

Also known as the **Hanoi** cubensis, is a moderately potent magic mushroom strain indigenous to Vietnam. Let's explore its fascinating characteristics:

Origin and Discovery:
The Vietnamese Psilocybe cubensis was first discovered over a hundred years ago (in 1906).
The original specimen was found growing close to rice plantations near the city of Hanoi, the national capital of Vietnam1.

Growing Environment:
Like many tropical relatives, including Panaeolus Cambodginiensis, Psilocybe samuensis, Panaeolus cyanescens, and Panaeolus subbalteus, the Vietnamese Psilocybe cubensis can also be found growing in dung.
Its natural habitat benefits from the subtropical monsoon climate of Hanoi, characterized by intense rainfall—ideal conditions for Psilocybe cubensis species to proliferate1.

Appearance:
Vietnamese Psilocybe cubensis fruits into various sizes, with typically fleshy, sturdy stems and caps sometimes reaching up to 5 cm in diameter.
The coloration offers a variety of golden-brown hues that tend to end in straw yellow1.

Effects:
Consumers report that the Vietnamese Psilocybe cubensis magic mushroom offers **a balanced and memorable experience**: Smooth sensations of euphoria, Spiritual feelings, Subtle visual alterations. Some users compare its trip to that of other strains like Golden Teacher, B+, Conocybe smithii, or Inocybe Aeruginascens1.

Microdosing Potential:
Due to its **moderate potency**, the Vietnamese Psilocybe cubensis makes a great ally for those interested in microdosing.
It can offer a safe journey into microdosing, enhancing mood, creativity, and focus when used with intention1.

Cultural Context:
Hanoi, also known as the "Paris of the East," is not only rich in delectable cuisine, vibrant nightlife, silks, and handicrafts but also a place where the enlightening psilocybian powers of the Vietnamese Psilocybe cubensis grow1.
In summary, the Vietnamese Psilocybe cubensis is sought after by both growers and cultivators due to its moderate potency, smooth effects, and prolific growth tendencies. Whether for exploration or microdosing, this strain offers a fascinating journey into altered states of consciousness.

Sources:

1. https://microzoomers.co/strains/vietnamese-psilocybe-cubensis/
2. https://utopiamushrooms.co/product/hanoi-vietnamese-magic-mushrooms/
3. https://microcybin.io/product/vietnamese-cubenis/
4. https://starsfact.net/vietnamese-psilocybe-cubensis-a-beginner-friendly-magic-mushroom/

Wavy Cap

Let's explore the fascinating world of **Wavy Caps** (Psilocybe cyanescens), a potent and unique species of psychedelic mushrooms.

Appearance and Distinct Features:
Wavy Caps get their name from their distinct wavy cap shape. These mushrooms have large, flat brown caps that become even more wavy as they mature.
Creamy-colored gills and a white stem make them particularly attractive.

Psychedelic Properties:
Psilocybe cyanescens contains the psychoactive compounds psilocybin and psilocin.
While not as well-known as Psilocybe cubensis or Psilocybe semilanceata (Liberty Caps), Wavy Caps are gaining popularity due to their potency and unique appearance.
Their psilocybin levels are comparable to **potent** strains of Psilocybe cubensis.

Habitat and Colonization:
Wavy Caps flourish in the wild landscapes of Canada, Europe, and the United Kingdom.
They often grow in expansive colonies, making the harvest fruitful. If you find one cap, you'll likely find many more nearby.
These mushrooms are saprophytic, meaning they absorb dissolved organic matter from decaying wood.

Cultivation and Outdoor Thriving:
Psilocybe cyanescens can thrive on wood chips in simple garden vegetable beds.
Their excellent contamination resistance and ability to survive in various environments contribute to their popularity among mushroom enthusiasts.

Taxonomic History:
British mycologist Elsie Maud Wakefield first described Psilocybe cyanescens in 1838.
However, its true origins remain somewhat mysterious.

Remember, if you ever encounter Wavy Caps in the wild, exercise caution and ensure proper identification. Foraging for mushrooms is best left to the experts!123

Sources:
1. https://tripsitter.com/magic-mushrooms/species/psilocybe-cyanescens/
2. https://www.nxtlifescience.com/psychedelics/wavy-caps-mushroom-guide/
3. https://en.m.wikipedia.org/wiki/Psilocybe_cyanescens
4. https://mushies.co.uk/blogs/news/ultimate-guide-to-identifying-wavy-caps

White Rabbit

White Rabbit mushroom strain, a cultivated variant of Psilocybe cubensis, has an intriguing backstory. Let's dive into the details:

Origin and Genetics:
White Rabbit was deliberately bred by cultivators in Holland.
It resulted from hybridizing two popular strains:
Albino Penis Envy (APE): Known for its high potency.
Moby Dick: Recognized for its ease of cultivation.
The goal was to create a strain that combines APE's potency with Moby Dick's cultivation simplicity.
White Rabbit is leukistic, meaning it lacks significant pigmentation. Although not truly albino, it appears almost white when grown in darkness.
Its spores are dark purple-brown, and exposure to light can slightly color the rest of the mushroom[1,2].

Appearance and Characteristics:
White Rabbit does not resemble its parent, Penis Envy, in appearance.
It is shorter and thicker-stemmed than typical Psilocybe cubensis.
Depending on light levels during growth, it appears pale yellow to whitish.
Gray gills turn purple-black as spores mature, and the flesh bruises blue-green when damaged.
Veil remnants form spots on the cap, and a ring around the stem may turn black as spores land on it.
Since White Rabbit is a cultivated strain, the risk of confusing it with wild mushrooms is minimal[1].

Effects and Potency: Very Potent
While the debate continues about whether strains have unique effects, White Rabbit is sometimes described as particularly visual and introspective.
Its **potency is remarkable**, often testing at double the psilocybin concentration of the average cube.
Users should be cautious with dosing, as White Rabbit requires lower doses than expected due to its strength[1].

In **summary**, the White Rabbit strain offers a fascinating blend of genetics, potency, and visual effects. If you encounter this elusive mushroom, approach it with respect and curiosity! [1,2]

Sources:
1. https://healing-mushrooms.net/white-rabbit
2. https://tripsitter.com/magic-mushrooms/strains/white-rabbit/
3. https://www.magicmushroomsdispensary.ca/white-rabbit-mushroom-strain/

White Teacher

The **White Teacher** Mushroom strain, also known as the White Golden Teacher, is a hybrid variety that combines the characteristics of two well-known psilocybin mushroom strains: the Golden Teacher and the Albino Penis Envy (APE). Let's explore some key details about this intriguing strain:

Origins and Composition:
The White Teacher strain is a cross between the Golden Teacher and Albino Penis Envy strains.
It inherits qualities from both parent strains, resulting in a unique combination of ease of microscopy research (similar to the Golden Teacher) and the potency and distinctness of the APE.

Appearance:
The mushrooms produced by the White Teacher strain are characterized by their translucent or albino appearance.
They may resemble the classic Golden Teacher strain but with a lighter coloration due to the albino traits.

Cultivation and Research:
Researchers and enthusiasts use White Teacher spores for microscopy research to study their unique characteristics.
The strain's rarity and difficult-to-acquire spores make each sample valuable for scientific exploration.

Potency: Above Average

In **summary**, the White Teacher Mushroom strain offers a blend of rarity, unique appearance, and scientific interest. Remember that these spores are for research purposes only, and their cultivation is strictly prohibited.123

Sources:
1. https://tripsitter.com/magic-mushrooms/strains/true-albino-teacher/
2. https://qualityspores.store/shop/intermediate/white-teacher/
3. https://mushroom.cat/white-teacher-mushrooms/
4. https://westlandpsychedelics.net/product/white-teacher-mushroom-strain-cubensis-spores/

Wikidzon Cubensis

Also known as **Wiki** or **Wikid**, is a fascinating and relatively new or recently discovered variety of Psilocybe cubensis. However, the exact origin and story behind this strain remain unclear, leading to various rumors and speculations. Here are some details about the Wikidzon cubensis:

Origin and Unclear Story:
The origin of the Wikidzon cubensis strain is still shrouded in mystery.
There are several rumors circulating about its discovery:
Some suggest that Wikid is a strain of PES Amazonian.
Another rumor claims that it was found along the delta of the Amazon River in the rainforest.
Allegedly, these mushrooms were reaching over 17 inches out of clumps of Chima Lo (heavy blade grass).
The discoverer reportedly printed the specimen on the spot and shipped two prints to a friend.

Appearance and Characteristics:
While specific details about the appearance of Wikidzon cubensis may vary, it is generally considered a fascinating and unique strain.
Researchers and enthusiasts are intrigued by its potential potency and distinct features.

Spore Syringe and Microscopy Research:
Wikidzon cubensis spores are available in spore syringes for microscopy research purposes only.
Researchers use these spores to study their unique characteristics under a microscope.
The strain's rarity and difficult-to-acquire spores make each sample valuable for scientific exploration.

Disclaimer:
It's essential to emphasize that Wikidzon cubensis spores are not for cultivation or germination purposes.
Shipping of these spores may be restricted in certain states due to legal regulations.
Always approach the study of magic mushrooms responsibly and within the bounds of the law.
The effects of Wikidzon cubensis mushrooms are consistent with those of other Psilocybe cubensis strains, as they contain the psychoactive compound psilocybin. Here are some common effects reported by users:

Visual Alterations and Hallucinations:
Users often experience vivid visual changes, such as:
Color enhancement: Colors appear more vibrant and intense.
Patterns and shapes: Walls, surfaces, and objects may display intricate patterns, fractals, or geometric shapes.
Morphing and breathing: Objects may seem to shift, warp, or breathe.

Euphoria and Emotional Intensity:
Many users report a profound sense of joy, interconnectedness, and emotional openness.

The experience can be deeply introspective, leading to insights about one's life, relationships, and purpose.

Spiritual and Mystical States:
Some users describe encounters with a sense of unity with the universe, akin to spiritual or mystical experiences.
Themes of interconnectedness, divine presence, and cosmic understanding may emerge.

Time Distortion:
The perception of time can become altered. Minutes may feel like hours, and hours like minutes.

Body Sensations:
Users may feel a sense of lightness, warmth, or energy flowing through their bodies.
Some report physical sensations like tingling or waves of energy.
Enhanced Creativity and Insight:
The altered state of consciousness can lead to creative breakthroughs, new perspectives, and problem-solving abilities.

Ego Dissolution:
Some users experience a dissolution of the ego—the sense of self—leading to feelings of interconnectedness with all existence.

Intensity and Set and Setting:
The effects can be intense, so a supportive and safe environment (the "set and setting") is crucial.
The mindset and emotional state of the user significantly influence the experience.
Remember that individual responses vary, and some users may have challenging or difficult trips. Always approach psychedelics with respect, caution, and proper preparation. If you choose to explore Wikidzon cubensis, do so in a responsible and informed manner.

In **summary**, the Wikidzon cubensis strain remains an enigma, with its unclear origin and intriguing features. Researchers continue to explore its unique properties through microscopy research. Remember that these spores are strictly for research and educational purposes. 1

Sources:
1. https://pnwspore.com/product/wikidzon/
2. https://www.6mushrooms.com/blog/the-absolutely-ultimate-guide-to-the-amazonian-strain-magic-mushroom
3. https://pnwspore.com/product/wikidzon-spore-print/

Wollongong

The **Wollongong** Strain, a classic Australian magic mushroom that has intrigued cultivators and enthusiasts alike.

Wollongong Strain Overview
Name and Origin: The Wollongong strain (Psilocybe cubensis Wollongong) is native to Australia and takes its name from the coastal city of Wollongong, located just south of Sydney. While it has been popular among Australian cultivators for decades, it has only recently become available from spore vendors outside the country.

Appearance and Characteristics:
These mushrooms have light brown caps and white stems.
They are relatively large and grow in dense patches.
Despite their unremarkable appearance, other traits make them attractive to cultivators.

Cultivation and Traits:
The Wollongong strain is known for being an aggressive colonizer capable of producing good yields over several healthy flushes.
It's a popular choice for beginners, commercial growers, and those looking to quickly produce a large number of mushrooms.
Even inexperienced cultivators can achieve good results with little effort and minimal equipment.

Potency and Psilocybin Content:
We rate the Wollongong strain as having **average potency**, with an estimated total tryptamine content of 0.5%–0.9%1.

History and Availability:
Discovery: The Wollongong strain was initially found growing in South Eastern Australia, close to the city of Wollongong.
It was discovered at the bottom of an escarpment, thriving in the shade.

Popularity and Spread:
This strain has circulated within the Australian market for decades and has been favored by amateur cultivators. Outside Australia, it remained relatively unknown until recently. News of its contamination resistance and aggressive colonization qualities spread to the global mushroom community.

In **summary**, the Wollongong strain offers ease of cultivation, decent yields, and an average psychedelic experience. If you decide to explore this Aussie classic, happy growing!123

Sources:

1. https://tripsitter.com/magic-mushrooms/strains/wollongong/
2. https://frshminds.com/psilocybin-mushroom-species-guide/psilocybe-cubensis/wollongong-magic-mushrooms/
3. https://mushroomgenie.com/product/wollygong-mushrooms/

Xapuri

The **Xapuri Strain**, a massive and potent magic mushroom variety that hails from Mexico.

Xapuri Shroom Strain Overview
Origin and Size: The Xapuri strain was first collected in Brazil in 2009.
It takes its name from the side of BR317, a highway stretching from Boca de Acre to Senador Guiomard in the State of Acre.
These mushrooms are notoriously large, with fruiting bodies so massive that their stems often struggle to support them.
Imagine dinner-plate-sized caps atop thick, healthy stems – that's the Xapuri strain!

Cultivation Challenge:
Growing Xapuri mushrooms can be a challenge for novice growers due to their size.
If not careful, they can topple over and mold in the fruiting chamber.
However, for experienced cultivators, they are a great choice for producing photo-worthy fruiting bodies.

Potency and Psilocybin Content: **Above Average**
While there are no precise measurements for Xapuri's tryptamine content, users report that the experience is far more intense than most other strains.
Subjectively, we estimate the potency to be somewhere between 1% and 2% on average.
For context, the average Psilocybe cubensis strain contains 0.5% to 0.9% total tryptamine concentration (including psilocybin, psilocin, and other tryptamines).

In **summary**, the Xapuri strain combines impressive size with potent effects, making it a sought-after choice among magic mushroom enthusiasts.12

Sources:
1. https://tripsitter.com/magic-mushrooms/strains/xapuri/
2. https://driedmagicmushroomspores.com/product/by-xapuri-shroom-strain-online/
3. https://tripsitter.com/magic-mushrooms/strains/

Yeti

The **Yeti** Mushroom (Psilocybe cubensis Yeti), a rare and potent strain that has captured the curiosity of psychonauts.
Identification and Description
Origin and Legend:
According to legend, the first Yeti mushroom appeared as a spontaneous mutation grown by an anonymous mushroom enthusiast.
This enthusiast was initially attempting to develop an albino version of the Golden Teacher strain, which eventually led to what we now know as the True Albino Teacher.
Yeti, however, is not merely an albino version of its parent; it has distinct characteristics.
Physical Features:
Yeti mushrooms have a thick, meaty stem and a cap that never fully opens out—resembling the shape of Penis Envy mushrooms (though not to the same extent).
Both the stem and cap exhibit white or bluish hues. While the first flushes tend to produce smaller fruits, subsequent flushes often yield larger mushrooms.
Distinctiveness:
Although other albino or leucistic cube strains may appear somewhat similar, the Yeti's unique shape, midway between Penis Envy and typical cubes, sets it apart.
Notably, since Yeti mushrooms do not grow in the wild, the risk of misidentification is minimal.

Effects and Potency:
Debated Effects: While some argue that different cube strains may have slight variations in effects due to strain-specific biochemical differences, other factors (such as set, setting, personal biochemistry, and dosage) play a significant role in shaping the trip experience.
Yeti is sometimes described as a bit eerie, cooler, and more distant compared to most other cubensis strains.
Some users report that Yeti disagrees with them, while others love its unique qualities.
Potency and Dosage: **Above Average**
Yeti's potency consistently tests high, often twice that of the average cube strain.
However, potency alone does not necessarily translate to a more intense trip.
Proper dosage adjustment is crucial, as small variations in dose size can have extreme consequences.
Remember that safety and responsible use are paramount when exploring the world of magic mushrooms.

In **summary**, the elusive Yeti Mushroom combines rarity, potency, and an otherworldly experience. Whether you are a seasoned psychonaut or a curious explorer, approach it with respect and wonder!123

Sources:
1.   https://healing-mushrooms.net/yeti
2.   https://shroomsandedibles.net/product/yeti-mushrooms/
3.   https://www.mushlovegenetics.com/mushroom-spores/yeti-mushroom-spores/
4.   https://hiddenforestsporestore.com/product/yeti-mushroom-spores/

Yosterizii

Yosterizii, a name that sounds both intriguing and mysterious, has captured the attention of mushroom enthusiasts. However, let's explore what we know about this enigmatic strain:

Origins and Claims:
According to some sources, Yosterizii was developed by an anonymous cultivator who spent three years perfecting it.
The strain is often touted as having remarkable features, including **potency** and frequent flushes.

Description:
Unfortunately, detailed information about Yosterizii remains scarce.
Some claim that it produces potent mushrooms with a unique appearance.
The scarcity of verifiable data raises questions about its legitimacy.

Skepticism and Scams:
The mushroom community tends to approach new strains with skepticism.
Scammers sometimes create fictional strains to attract attention and sell expensive spore syringes.
Without concrete evidence or widespread cultivation experiences, it's challenging to validate Yosterizii's existence.

Recommendations:
While Yosterizii's allure is tempting, consider exploring well-established strains:
Equador: Known for its reliability and moderate potency.
Golden Teacher: A classic strain with balanced effects.
Puerto Rican: Resilient and suitable for beginners.
PESA (Psilocybe cubensis Penis Envy): Renowned for its potency and unique appearance.

In **summary**, Yosterizii remains shrouded in mystery, and its legitimacy is questionable. If you are seeking a reliable and proven strain, consider the classics.123

Sources:
1. https://www.shroomery.org/forums/showflat.php/Number/4043135
2. https://files.shroomery.org/cms/Psilocybe%20Cubensis%20Strains.pdf
3. https://www.psychedelicpassage.com/psychedelic-mushroom-strains-by-potency-30-popular-varieties/
4. https://www.shroomery.org/forums/showflat.php/Cat/0/Number/4040012/an/0/page/1

Z Strain

The **Z-Strain** (sometimes referred to as "Z-Cube"), a fascinating magic mushroom strain known for its unique growth characteristics and potential potency.

Z-Strain Overview:
Potency and Effects: Z-Strain is considered an **average potency** magic mushroom strain.
However, online trip reports often describe it as having especially strong physical effects. Users report intense tactile sensations, often described as a "gentle buzzing" of the skin.

Aggressive Growth:
What sets Z-Strain apart is its affinity for producing rhizomorphic mycelial growth. Rhizomorphic mycelium consists of thick "threads" that spread rapidly through the substrate.
This growth pattern is viewed as more resistant to disease, faster, and leads to dense flushes of potent mushrooms during the fruiting stage.

Origin and Controversy:
The exact origin of Z-Strain remains unclear and somewhat controversial.
Theories suggest it may be an isolation of the Golden Teacher strain, which originates from Mexico.
Some attribute it to the legendary mycologist Paul Stamets, while others mention a mysterious mycologist named "The Keeper".

Cultivation Difficulty:
Z-Strain is an excellent choice for hobby cultivators due to its vigorous growth.
It's relatively easy to cultivate, making it popular among those exploring the world of magic mushrooms.

In summary, Z-Strain combines average potency with unique growth patterns, making it an intriguing addition to the magical fungi family.123

Sources:

1. https://tripsitter.com/magic-mushrooms/strains/z-strain/
2. https://www.bing.com/search?q=z-+strain&FORM=bngcht&toWww=1&redig=E09D85E2172145BDA28122C2E99CC89D
3. https://medium.com/@iaskmushroom/z-strain-mushroom-the-most-potent-p-cubensis-strain-available-196d29e4e843
4. https://1upmaps.com/z-strain-mushroom-potency-effects-growing-tips/

www.ingramcontent.com/pod-product-compliance
Lightning Source LLC
Chambersburg PA
CBHW061037250726
48653CB00001B/142